Making Marriage
User Friendly
The Helping Solution

Russ Holloman, Ph. D.

WestBow
PRESS
A DIVISION OF THOMAS NELSON

Copyright © 2012 by Russ Holloman, Ph. D.

All rights reserved. No part of this book may be used or reproduced by any means, graphic, electronic, or mechanical, including photocopying, recording, taping or by any information storage retrieval system without the written permission of the publisher except in the case of brief quotations embodied in critical articles and reviews.

WestBow Press books may be ordered through booksellers or by contacting:

WestBow Press
A Division of Thomas Nelson
1663 Liberty Drive
Bloomington, IN 47403
www.westbowpress.com
1-(866) 928-1240

Because of the dynamic nature of the Internet, any web addresses or links contained in this book may have changed since publication and may no longer be valid. The views expressed in this work are solely those of the author and do not necessarily reflect the views of the publisher, and the publisher hereby disclaims any responsibility for them.

Any people depicted in stock imagery provided by Thinkstock are models, and such images are being used for illustrative purposes only.

Certain stock imagery © Thinkstock.

ISBN: 978-1-4497-4745-9 (sc)
ISBN: 978-1-4497-4746-6 (hc)
ISBN: 978-1-4497-4744-2 (e)

Library of Congress Control Number: 2012906483

Printed in the United States of America

WestBow Press rev. date: 5/11/2012

*After the verb "to love,"
"to help" is most beautiful.*
—Anonymous

In memory of my late wife,
Lenora Strebeck Holloman
23 January 1929 - 1 September 2008

Lenora made everything beautiful with her smile
And sunny disposition. Love, doing the right thing,
And serving others were guide posts on her journey
Through life as she walked humbly with God.

Contents

Preface	xi
Introduction	xiii
1. Courtship: Shall We Marry?	1
2. Marital Adjustment: What Kind of Marriage Do We Want?	19
3. Understanding the Helping Relationship	41
4. Readiness to Help: Eliminating the Negatives	61
5. Readiness to Help: Accentuating the Positives	85
6. Helping Through Listening and Information Sharing	121
7. Helping Through Acceptance and Attending	149
8. Helping in Decision Making and Problem Solving	181
9. Helping in Confrontation and Conflict Resolution	199
10. Maintaining the Helping Relationship	225
References	241

Preface

On Mother's Day 1949, at the height of our romantic love for each other, Lenora and I married. Our wedding was in her family Baptist Church, and was officiated by the priest of my family Methodist Church. Our honeymoon period, which we pledged to make last forever, was a continuation of the passion and excitement of our two-year courtship.

In the process of adjusting to the intimacies of married life and raising two children, we had a few challenging times. But we had a lot of really good times, and it was the good times we valued and remembered. As individuals we changed, each in our own way. Most importantly, our love changed from the glamorous, romantic kind to a more mature, conjugal love and continued to be the basis of our marriage.

Fast forward. After fifty-nine years of idyllic love, Lenora died on Labor Day 2008. I was at her bedside. After days in a coma, she opened her eyes. She was asking me to hold her. She was asking me to tell her again that I loved her. She was telling me that she did not want to go and leave me and the children alone. Still, she was asking, "Is it OK for me to go now?"

Through my tears and embrace, I nodded, "Yes." I waited for her next breath, the one that did not come.

I wept.

In time, I began the arduous, haunting process of terminating my psychotherapy practice and writing this book. Necessarily, some of it is written in the past tense.

Introduction

In 1973, I was licensed as a marriage and family therapist and my involvement in and concern for marriage relationships took on a new dimension. With a shingle on my door and my name in the yellow pages, couples experiencing difficulties in their marriage began coming to me for help. They invariably complained about some particular problem or dissatisfaction in their marriage. The similarities between what they were saying to me and what they most likely would say to their physician did not go unnoticed. "Our marriage is hurting, and we don't want to hurt," they seemed to say. "Remove the pain so we can be well again."

Typically, it was only after their perceived problems became intolerable that help was sought. However, as soon as the most distressing symptoms of their problems were dissipated, most of these couples felt they no longer needed help. As might be expected, many of them soon were back in therapy, often voicing their original complaints. The basic problems in their marriage relationship had not been solved, only the most painful and accessible symptoms had been relieved.

Practicing marriage and family therapy in terms of this remedial model was neither personally nor professionally satisfying to me. While I did take comfort in knowing that I was helping couples remove acute pain from their marriage, I was bothered by the fact that most of them left therapy without a vision of what their marriage could become. Their goal was to be normal again--normal in the sense that there was an absence of stress and psychological pain. Therapy was keeping them only from being unhappy; I was not succeeding in showing them the way to a higher-than-normal plane of marital happiness. For me that was not enough.

It was this realization that started me rethinking my philosophy and practice of marriage and family therapy. It also caused me to rethink my own marriage. I shared my concerns with colleagues and other professionals, and, surprisingly, I found a great deal of understanding and agreement. As I continued to wrestle with these concerns, the pieces of the puzzle began to fall into place. The answer, when I found it, seemed so simple, so logical, so available. It is a therapy based more on a growth or becoming model than upon a sickness or medical model. Finding that answer, first of all, made it possible for my own marriage to grow and become more actualized. And as I became more convinced of the goodness of my new approach, I began to incorporate it into my therapy practice.

It was this realization, too, that caused me to start planning the writing of this book. I wanted to share with people who already were married, and with those contemplating marriage, a vision of what a marriage could be. I wanted to engage them in some possibility thinking. This vision is of marriage as a helping relationship. Helping is viewed as an important aspect of a marriage relationship; it is a means of showing concern, interest, affection, and other positive feelings. It shows personal commitment to one's marriage--a commitment to making their marriage matter. Helping in a marital relationship has a meaning that is larger and more personal than simply assisting with household chores or other menial tasks. It also is different from the helping role of the professional therapist. It is based upon the idea that everything we do in our marriage relationship both affects and is affected by the behavior of our partner. Helping is feeling and behaving toward our partner in ways that produce desired, positive outcomes. Since what goes around in marriage tends to come around, the sought-for outcomes of the helping relationship are mutually beneficial.

This is not a how-to-do-it book in a few easy steps. Marriage relationships seldom permit such simplicity. It might more appropriately be called a "be-it-yourself" book in that it emphasizes attitudes and behaviors, more than rules and skills. It won't make you an overnight expert in helping, but your helping skills will increase as you become more sensitive to the need for and the benefits of loving in helping ways. These attitudes and behaviors will be described in simple behavioral terms. I have kept technical terms and clinical interpretations to a minimum in my quest for clarity and simplicity. For the same reason, I have kept documented references (which I could have provided in abundance) to a minimum.

As we explore together the idea of loving our partner in helping ways, I will from time to time share experiences from both my personal life and the lives of others with whom I have counseled. You deserve more than mere intellectual arguments for the differences that loving and helping can make in your marriage; you deserve the personal witness of people who have discovered that difference. You also need to know about the possible negative effects that non-helping attitudes and behavior can have on your marriage. When use is made of examples and dialogues excerpted from actual case histories, the details will be altered only for purposes of confidentiality. Otherwise, the examples are faithfully reproduced.

I am indebted to those of my clients who gave me the opportunity to know what was meaningful and helpful to them. I am similarly indebted to many of my professional colleagues who have helped me to look at things more clearly. Finally, I am grateful to my late wife, Lenora--lover, helper, and friend. She taught me much about loving (she was good at it), much about marriage (she had special insights), and much about helping (her attitude made the difference). When I consulted her about my work, she always was ready to listen, insightful in her questions, and helpful in her responses.

It must be clear by now that I have taken ideas and answers from many places. I cannot identify with precision when or from whom I obtained what I present here as my own. There's no doubt that there is much in these pages that almost everyone has thought or felt before. This book attempts to put it in some order and thereby make it more understandable and useful. This, I realize, is a very large order, one that cannot completely be filled. In any event, I alone take full responsibility for what is in this book.

Russ Holloman, Ph.D.
Evans, Georgia
2012

Chapter One

Courtship: Shall We Marry?

Many of our basic human needs can be satisfied only through relationships with other people. One of the most distinctive aspects of being fully alive and psychologically healthy is our potential for joy, caring, and personal fulfillment in relationships with others. Making new friends, deepening ongoing relationships, falling in love and getting married all depend upon our having the opportunity and ability to develop and maintain effective interpersonal relationships. The words we use to describe our attraction to other people and the quality of relationships with them--words such as like, love, affection, and sweetheart--are some of the most intimate words in our language.

Because we are social creatures, we seek the company of others, even while satisfying our more basic, physical needs. Eating is more enjoyable in the company of others; having a cup of coffee takes on added meaning with others. Inviting someone to join us for a movie is much preferred to going alone. Our need for sexual fulfillment, by definition, can be satisfied only in a relationship with another person. There is no way we can overemphasize the importance of interpersonal relationships in our lives. It is in relationships that we discover our being, realizing we can't be human alone. No wonder solitary confinement is often viewed as an inhumane punishment.

Why do we socialize with other people? "It's because 'people need people,'" we say. Why do we socialize with some people and avoid other people? The answer to this question also seems obvious. It is because we need or desire what certain people have to give, and avoid others because what they have to give is neither needed nor desired. This chapter discusses how we perceive and relate to other people. The question of what kind relationships we would like to have with other people and some of our typical behaviors in developing those relationships are also discussed. When the goal or outcome of this development process is marriage we have a special kind of relationship. It is this special relationship that is the subject of this book.

Development of a Relationship

Effective relationships don't just happen; no amount of wishful thinking can make them magically occur. Relationships are built, in a sense, and in addition to desire, relationship building also requires skill, hard work, and trust. Both people in a relationship add substance and shape to their relationship and their contributions determine its future direction and quality of the relationship. Whether the relationship will grow systematically and become a source of interpersonal reward or whether it will proceed randomly to become a source of tension and despair is determined by the couple's expectations of and commitment to the relationship.

Many people resist the idea of relationships being built; it runs counter to their belief that relationships just happen. Working to make a relationship happen, they argue, makes it less spontaneous, less exciting, and less romantic. In their view, work and relationships are unrelated. They admit that work--what they do from nine to five--requires effort, but believe that relationships just happen, propelled by some mystical force that wraps them and carries them forward. While we might relish the unplanned, exciting things that happen to us, can we realistically think of relationships--especially marriage--as being something not of our own doing? No. Every relationship is a unique creation of the persons in it.

There are four easily identifiable stages in this creating or building process (Thibet and Kelly, 1959). These stages begin with sampling and proceed through bargaining and commitment to the final stage of formalization. While it is easy to discuss each of these stages separately on these pages, in real-life, ongoing relationships, it usually is difficult to distinguish one stage from another. One reason is that these stages often overlap. Another difficulty is that each person in a relationship will not pass through the stages in the same order; nor will they spend the same amount of time in a particular stage.

Sampling (often labeled "dating") involves a variety of behaviors. In this stage we identify and seek opportunities to associate with other people who meet our minimum criteria of acceptance in terms of physical attractiveness, personality, education, family background, competencies, etc. Through the dating process this pool is gradually reduced. In fact, most relationships do not get past this stage.

After we have used the sampling process to identify someone with whom we would like to have a closer relationship, we move into a bargaining relationship with that person. In this stage we get to know each other better and determine whether we would like to have a more permanent relationship. It might be agreed, for example, that we will "go steady" (or whatever terminology is used these days for a "closed" relationship). Of the relationships that survive the sampling stage even fewer survive this second stage, since it depends upon the willingness of both people to make a commitment to one another. If this commitment, what we might call engagement, is genuine and there are no unforeseen barriers, the relationship may be formalized through marriage or other appropriate ceremony.

Let's now look at each of these stages in greater detail to better understand how our own marital relationship developed.

Sampling

One of the most basic things about this stage in the development of interpersonal relationships also is the most obvious: before any sampling can occur, we must meet other people. We seek certain situations, from church bazaars to coffee houses and singles bars, to increase our opportunities for meeting people. When we seek other people in these settings, we are implying by our behavior that these people are acceptable to us. It is from this pool of acceptables that we select the most promising. This selection process is called sampling and includes ritualistic behaviors, including dating, telephone calls, cards, e-mails, texting, and sharing leisure-time activities. The first (and safest) things two people in this initial stage of relationship development talk about is where they grew up, where they went to school, what they do for a living, etc. They are searching for common interests and background.

Can you remember when you first met your partner? For some people, recall is easy; it was love at first sight. Or maybe the circumstances under which you met made it special and easy to recall. For others, perhaps, the first meeting might not have been particularly important and can't be remembered. Whether or not you remember the specifics, it's safe to say that your relationship began with one of you making an inviting gesture to the other. Whatever it was, it was made to communicate an interest in knowing the other person better.

The first step we take in responding to someone who has made a gesture toward us is to form an impression of them by observing their actions: what they say and do in response to us and to other persons, objects, and events in our common environment. We notice their physical features, voice, dress, and other expressive movements. We also make assumptions about their values, attitudes, and what their intentions toward us might be. We then use this information to make judgments about how we should respond to their gesture.

We might respond with reserve or indifference, if we perceive that person's intentions as being incompatible with our needs and expectations. By the same token, we might respond with expressions of interest and liking for a person we perceive as liking us or sharing our feelings and values. In turn, the other person goes through the same process in making judgments about us. If our judgments and the judgments of the other person are acceptable to each other's expectations, the basis for further interaction is established. But if our judgments or the judgments of the other person are incompatible with our expectations, the relationship usually ends.

Bargaining

In this stage we turn from playing the field to exploring the possibility for a relationship with one person. The relationship that emerges is provisional since it depends upon receiving favorable answers to our questions and concerns. The most critical question to be answered in this stage is, "What would be the outcome of a relationship with this person in terms of satisfying my needs?" Or, to phrase it differently, "What's in it for me?" There are always costs involved in developing and maintaining a relationship. Costs can be measured in terms of effort, time, or dollars, and generally refer to what we have to do to attract and keep the other person interested in us. In short, whatever we do to satisfy the needs of the other person is a cost to us.

The other side of the cost coin is the rewards that come to us from the relationship. Rewards involve whatever the other person does or brings to the relationship those results in satisfaction for us. Using the two ideas of costs and rewards, we can determine the desirability of continuing a relationship. It involves a simple idea from mathematics: rewards we receive minus the costs we incur equal our benefit from the relationship. The greater the perceived rewards and the lesser the estimated costs, the greater will be the benefits from the relationship. In a provisional relationship, both people trade payoffs to determine whether it would be advantageous to enter into a deeper, more committed relationship. Each wants to determine whether the rewards outweigh the costs involved. During this period of giving and receiving rewards, the decision as to whether to continue the relationship usually is made.

When a tradeoff is determined for a particular relationship there remains the question of comparing the payoff with the payoff of another relationship. For example, one of the costs involved in becoming committed to person A is the loss of an opportunity for a relationship with person B. However, this comparison level can be made only for people with whom a relationship is possible. The process of determining and comparing payoffs continues until some best level of payoff is reached. "Does this person satisfy my needs to the greatest possible extent or must I look for another?" is the question that must be answered. If the answer is yes, the relationship usually progresses to a deeper level which we call commitment. If the answer to the question is no, the relationship is terminated and the search continues.

Commitment

Commitment occurs when we find the person that provides us the most favorable rewards-costs ratio. Commitment means we are willing to forego relationships with others to have a relationship with one person. The degree of commitment we are willing to make at this point tends to be equal to the commitment we perceive the other person to be making. A bargaining approach is used which one person implies to the other, "I will love you if you will love me." We are reluctant to express our love unless we are confident that the other person will reciprocate. At this point, the relationship does not have the trust and the genuineness that will be needed later. As the relationship continues, these attitudes hopefully will develop.

Commitment begins as a guarded relationship having a conditional nature. "I'll wait and see," is the attitude. Not all relationships that enter the commitment stage survive. Two people with common backgrounds--values, attitudes, and expectations--usually will find the cost of relating to be low. Since it is easier for them to behave in ways that are expected and accepted by the other, it is easier to reward each other. Since the rewards are high in proportion to the costs of rewarding the other person, the payoff of the relationship is high. As they see more of the other person and like what they see, the commitment becomes more binding.

Formalization

In our society, the most common and accepted method of formalizing a relationship is marriage. In marriage, two people go through a ceremony which has the effect of publicly acknowledging their relationship with each other. It also indicates their willingness to be bound by certain legal and religious constraints. Today, there is a lot of experimentation in which unmarried couples who are living together seek to formalize their relationship on the basis of commitment alone. "A marriage license is just a piece of paper," they argue. I am not suggesting that these relationships are less committed than married relationships. There might well be some other kind of symbolic ratification of the relationship and a mutual acknowledgment of the commitment these people have for one another. What is lost to them, however, is the recognition and legitimacy that society bestows when a commitment is formalized through marriage.

Our Needs and Our Relationships

The questions of why people marry and why they marry the people they do are difficult to answer. The debate over whether likes or opposites attract remains unresolved. One conclusion we can safely make, however, even in the face of these unresolved questions, is that we don't marry the person we choose by accident. Our choice of a marriage partner is determined, consciously or unconsciously, by our needs. Just as we eat to satisfy hunger, we marry a particular person because that person best satisfies some need we have. Both consciously and unconsciously we behave in ways that promise satisfaction of our needs.

Interpersonal relationships, what I often refer to as the path to marriage, cannot be understood in a vacuum. They have to be considered against a background of the needs of the people in the relationship. In this section I will discuss some of our basic human needs and how they influence our relationships with other people. It is helpful to take this brief inner journey so we can better direct our outward journey toward understanding and self-expression in our marriage. Our understanding of our marriage and how we embrace it can be deepened as we seek answers to fundamental questions about our values, needs, and expectations, and how they influenced our decision to marry the person we did.

One of the most useful ways to understand our needs and how they influence our behavior was developed by Dr. Abraham Maslow (1954). He sees our needs arranged in a hierarchy. The most basic needs--those lowest in the hierarchy--must be gratified before higher-level needs begin to emerge. This does not mean, however, that a lower-level need must be completely satisfied before a higher-level need can express itself. To the extent that a lower-level need is satisfied there is an opportunity for the next higher need to emerge. When we feel hunger we want to eat, but we would like to eat with another person, if possible. In this instance we are responding to two different needs on two different levels. In another situation, we observe two people having lunch together. One of them might not be hungry, lunching may be simply a way of satisfying a social need to be with the other person. In Maslow's view, these needs operate throughout our life span with the potency or strength of the needs changing as we and our circumstances change.

Physiological Needs

Our most basic needs are those related to the maintenance of our bodily functions. They include our need for oxygen, food, water, sleep, and elimination. Also included is our need for exercise, stimulation, shelter, clothing, and sex. These needs must be satisfied in order to maintain our bodies and perform necessary mental and physical activities. All these needs are prepotent in the sense that they must be satisfied before other higher-level needs are expressed. Persons who are starving usually do not concern themselves with the need for self-esteem until their hunger is satisfied.

How important are these needs in determining relationships? When they are being reasonably satisfied through our own efforts, they often seem unimportant. Although there are exceptions, our rising standards of living, levels of unemployment, and, in some cases, assistance programs provide most people a peace of mind about these needs and they are not motivated by them in pursuit of a relationship. Still, there are many relationships determined by the belief and expectation that the other person ". . . is able to support and take care of me."

Safety Needs

When the physiological needs are satisfied, the safety needs emerge. This group of needs takes many forms and, both consciously and unconsciously, influences our behavior in interpersonal relationships. They include the need for safety of our bodies, those we love, and our possessions. Important here is the need to know that the means of satisfying the physiological needs will not be lost or arbitrarily taken from us. Also included is the need for stability and continuity. Persons who live in unstable, threatening conditions predictably are greatly concerned about maintaining a sense of order and well-being. They want peace of mind about the future. They will relate to--even marry--another who can satisfy these needs for them.

Belonging and Love Needs

When our basic needs for things like food, drink, and safety have been satisfied, we then start responding to our needs for belonging, love, and affection. This is a need that can be satisfied only through relationships with other people. These relationships include participation in groups or contact with neighbors, friends, and colleagues. Another aspect of this need is for meaningful one-on-one relationships, including marriage.

Some writers have argued that belonging and love are more accurately described as wants rather than needs. In response to this argument we can notice that children who are deprived of satisfying, nurturing relationships fail to develop normally. Numerous psychological studies suggest that thwarting the need to both give and receive love is the most basic reason for personality maladjustments in our society. To love or to perish seems to be the choice we face, at least psychologically. Not being able to satisfy these needs might not be as critical as an unsatisfied need for food, but they drive and influence our behavior in ways similar to more basic needs. The physiological and the safety needs can, under certain conditions, be satisfied without assistance from other persons, but this is not possible with our social needs. It is only through relationships with others that we develop and maintain our humanness. To the extent that our relationships reflect friendship, love, and helping, we become more human. To the extent that these qualities are missing in our relationships with others, we become less human. I am not suggesting that we are less human when we are separated from others. I am suggesting quite the contrary. Our most valued relationships can be made more meaningful by short periods of separation. Moments of solitude--when we are alone, contemplating, discovering, and pondering our thoughts and feelings about others--can greatly enhance our relationships with them.

Esteem Needs

These needs are concerned with how we feel about ourselves and how others feel about us. First, we need to have a good opinion of ourselves, to have confidence that our mental, physical, and social skills are adequate to solve the problems and challenges which confront us. Secondly, we need to have the recognition, appreciation, and respect of others for our competencies. When we have these needs under control we can face problems with greater confidence. When we lack self-esteem and the respect of others we are crippled in our efforts to develop and maintain effective interpersonal relationships. Often we don't try.

Self-Actualization Needs

These high-level needs motivate us to know and become all that we are capable of becoming. Since it is near the top of the needs hierarchy, the need for self-actualization becomes important when we are reasonably content with the satisfaction of other lower-level needs. Contrary to popular opinion, however, this need is not peculiar to persons who have attained significant economic, psychological, and professional achievements. It will, however, vary widely from person to person and from time to time. My neighbor, Pete, sold his boat and started taking violin lesson. "Something I've always wanted to do," he explained. Further evidence of the strength and pervasiveness of this need is seen in people who are innately creative and seem to pursue self-actualizing activities in spite of the fact that their lower-level needs are not always fully satisfied (as in the starving artist syndrome).

An important aspect of the need for self-actualization is the fact that it expresses itself in different people in different behaviors. Pete wanted to develop his musical potential. Other persons may seek to develop their talent as a professor, an accountant, or a nurse. Whatever form it takes, self-actualization behavior is intrinsically rewarding. Although extrinsic rewards may result from self-actualizing behavior, it is not necessary for such behavior.

Desire to Know and Understand

Notice that the word desire is substituted here for the word need. While this change of words suggests a lower level of drive, in some people it is very strong and actually helps them in their efforts to satisfy some of their other more basic needs. Not to know or understand causes some people to feel helpless and dependent, thereby decreasing, for example, their self-esteem.

The Aesthetic Needs

This category of need is difficult to describe. There is, however, a lot of evidence that suggests that most people have a basic need for beauty--a concern about the order, harmony, and appearance of things. Consider the clothes we wear. In one sense we wear clothing to keep us warm, to protect our bodies from the elements. For some people, this appears to be their only concern. Clothing, for these people, satisfies a basic, physiological need. But for others, clothing--its style, color, decorations, etc.--serves many other purposes. The expression "Clothes make the man," is its own message in terms of a person's self-confidence in social and work-related activities.

How Needs Influence Relationships

My purpose in briefly discussing the hierarchy of our needs is to establish the idea that the way we relate to others is a function of our needs in that relationship. A person who is starving will relate to another in terms of that person's ability to furnish food. A person who is frightened and feels a need for security will relate to another person in terms of that person's ability to furnish protection. Since the way we relate to others is a function of our unsatisfied needs at the moment the behavior occurs, it follows that the nature of our relationship will change as our needs change.

Deficiency and Growth Needs

It is useful to distinguish between needs that are deficiency motivators versus needs that are growth motivators. Deficiency needs are represented by the basic needs for food, water, warmth, safety, etc. They are motivated by deficits. Maslow compared these needs to empty holes in one's existence that must be filled for the sake of good physical and mental health. Fulfillment of these needs is an end in itself. This fact sheds an important light on deficiency needs. When a deficiency need is satisfied--the empty hole in our existence is filled--additional inputs or acquisitions of the means of satisfaction do not result in a higher level of satisfaction of that need. Satisfying our deficiency needs does not contribute to our growth or actualization. To put it another way, satisfying our deficiency needs does not make us happy, it merely keeps us from being unhappy. Eating does not make us better; it only keeps us from being hungry.

For the greater part of human history the majority of people have struggled at the lower levels, attempting to meet the basic physiological and security needs. People who never have had what they consider *enough* material resources in their lives, likely will be occupied with overcoming their felt deficiency. Their basic needs are satisfied only by the acquisition of more things--they are victims of never having enough. The sense of security they seek in satisfying their needs is likely to remain beyond their reach since they are trying to forget a remembered pain--the pain of deprivation in their earlier lives. No amount of money or other possessions can completely satisfy their feelings of insecurity.

In the same way that the basic needs are satisfied by possessing material things, the upper-level needs are satisfied through valued social relationships and the development of personal skills and attributes. The former are concerned with "having"; the latter are concerned with "being." The means of satisfying the basic needs are always in short supply and we must always exercise a self-limiting discipline or else we deprive others of the means to satisfy their needs. As we are often reminded, "Live simply that others may simply live."

Our growth needs are aspects of our need for self-actualization, and they emerge when the deficiency needs are satisfied. When we seek to develop an artistic skill, for example, we are responding not on the basis of a deficiency but as an expression of our desire to do something new--to have a new experience. It is important to realize that growth-motivated needs never are satisfied in the same sense as deficiency-motivated needs.

Self-actualization, for example, is a process, not a goal that is reached. Self-actualization represents growth and becoming, and there is always room for more growth and always space for more becoming. Thus it is appropriate to speak of self-actualizing people, but not self-actualized people.

In developing interpersonal relationships, a deficiency-motivated person is far more dependent than a person who seeks a relationship for growth-related reasons. The deficiency-motivated person always sees other persons as a means of satisfying some unmet need. The growth-motivated person, on the other hand, seeks relationships for their own intrinsic worth. The relationship is an end in itself, not a means to an end. In one sense, partners who choose each other in marriage do so out of deficiency motivation rather than growth motivation. They meet each other's needs and these needs are a deficiency that seeks continuing satisfaction through their relationship. If, however, the needs the partners had when they initially were attracted to each other are satisfied, what then? It would follow that security in a relationship, achieved through continued satisfaction of their deficiency motivators, would permit a new level of needs to emerge. Predictably, this new level of needs is growth motivated, what Maslow calls self-actualization.

The being values associated with the upper-level needs are capable of limitless growth and development. There is, for example, no limit to the quality of a marriage except those limits put on it by the partners themselves. Since the upper-level needs are growth oriented, we can never "be" enough. After we eat, for example, we will refuse offers of more food. Self-actualizing people, on the other hand, are dedicated to finding something bigger and more encompassing than themselves. For most people, their religion and their family are the most satisfying and enduring responses to this search.

Harvey and Joanna married after graduation from college and both worked in the small business that Joanna inherited from her father. They worked long, hard hours to make the business a success and to make their dream of financial security come true. Working side by side in pursuit of these goals were happy years for both. At age 28, after five years of work, Joanna quit to have their first child. Both she and Harvey agreed that she should not return to work. The business was doing well and they considered it best for their child that she not work. Three years later, their second child was born. The business had succeeded to a point where they were financially able to move into a larger, more comfortable home. A maid was hired for two days each week to help with the household chores. As the business continued to prosper and demand more of Harvey's time, Joanna and the children saw less of him, even on weekends.

Harvey rationalized his time away from the family with the promise that as soon as the business and his career were better established he would make it up to them. "Everything I'm doing is for you and the kids. Can't you see that? Just be patient for a while longer, and I'll make it up to you. Honest." In time, Joanna's patience waned and she threatened divorce. When she was working in the business with Harvey, before the children were born, her needs for companionship were subordinated to their need for achieving financial security. Although she admitted that those five years were happy times for her, she argued that there was no longer a need to work so hard. She was confused and disappointed over the fact that Harvey could not understand and accept her feelings.

As each new goal in the growth of the company was reached, higher goals were set. "If you don't grow, you go backwards," Harvey now argued. "We can't stand still like your father did."

Joanna felt that their dream of financial security had come true and she wanted more time together to enjoy the good life which she felt they had earned. Her threat of divorce had ominous implications for Harvey since she was the majority stockholder of the business. (I'll share more about this case later.)

This idea of our changing needs and their influence on our behavior also can operate over a shorter period of time. A husband who arrives home from work tired and hungry is unlikely to be very interested in all the events that filled his wife's day, or even in her profession of love and admiration for him. Far more likely, he will respond to her in terms of the demands she spares him and the food she has prepared for dinner. Later in the evening, after he has eaten and rested, he will be in a different mood and express different interests, responding to different needs. This changed behavior is the cost of the reward he received earlier from his wife. This end-of-the-day scenario also works for his wife, but in reverse order. Feeding her family and letting her husband rest is a cost to her. It is the price she pays for the rewards of a more congenial, attentive husband later in the evening.

The case of Gerald and Letta also illustrates what can happen when one partner moves farther along the self-actualization path than the other. Gerald joined the Army after high school to escape an unhappy home life. Two years later, while he was stationed overseas, he met and married Letta.

Letta's parents were deceased and she was living in the home of an aunt. For one year after their marriage, Gerald and Letta lived near the army post in a one-room apartment before returning to the United States. Now stationed in a southeastern state, Letta began working to supplement Gerald's still meager income. She also started taking college courses at night. During this time, too, as she claimed and Gerald admitted, she "cleaned the house, cooked, washed clothes, and was a good wife to Gerald."

Several years passed during which they were again stationed overseas and later were reassigned to the same army post in the U.S. Also during this period, their first and only child was born. Letta temporarily stopped working, but was able to continue her college studies and finally graduated. When their child started school, Letta began working in real estate sales where she was very successful. As she earned more money and received increased recognition for her sales achievements, she became less dependent and more assertive. Her increasing unwillingness to play the role Gerald expected of her precipitated a crisis in their marriage.

"Why can't you just be satisfied with things the way they are? We're doing O.K.," Gerald demanded of Letta.

"Why can't you accept me the way I am; not the way you want me to be?" Letta insisted.

For Gerald, divorce was preferable to the fear and insecurity of changing his traditional values and role as head of the house. Not being able to financially provide for his family the things that Letta's earnings made possible was embarrassing to Gerald. "She wears the pants," he explained. For Letta, divorce was preferable to giving up her new-found sense of achievement and self-actualization. "If I can change, you can too. But you won't even try," she countered.

I purposefully have emphasized the focal issues in this case so you can more easily relate to what happened to Gerald and Letta. Gerald was driven to make up for a childhood in which he felt deprived of the home, food, clothing, and material things that other kids had. Erroneously, he thought that through hard work as an adult he could make up for the deprivations he experienced as a child. He could never get enough of these things as an adult, however, because he was being driven by a remembered pain. In terms of his own psychological growth and development, he was still responding to a need for security and safety from deprivation. In spite of an equally disadvantaged childhood, Letta was content with the satisfaction her marriage was providing until she became aware of the opportunities and benefits of further education and work involvement. She was driven by growth motivation to respond.

Unfortunately, the unmet needs that brought Gerald and Letta together were not enough to keep them together. The potential causes of the difficulties that emerged in their marriage were already present at the time they were married. Gerald and Letta lived the early years of their marriage in terms of the trade-offs they were willing to make. Surprisingly, there were few conflicts in their marriage until the "big one" came. Gerald behaved exactly the way he thought he should (and had a right to) behave. He earned the money, he made the decisions, and he provided for Letta and his child as best he could. Doing all these things, in his view, made him a good husband and father.

Letta complemented Gerald's needs. Where he needed to be dominant and controlling, she had learned to be quiet, submissive, and dependent. They were making mutually satisfying tradeoffs until the change in Letta's education changed the circumstances of her life. The process of adjustment which could have helped Gerald and Letta to continue responding to each other's needs did not occur as it should have. This process of adjustment is the subject of my next chapter.

Why People Marry

In my work with couples, whether in pre-marital counseling, marital therapy, or divorce counseling, I always ask questions about why people marry. Not unexpectedly, members of all three groups answer in terms of love and the expectation of happiness. Their answers are reassuring in that a sense of love should be a precondition of all marriages, and happiness is a laudable goal of marriage. Still, their answers are not specific enough to help me understand why a particular person or couple decided to marry. When I ask for more specific answers, some markedly different responses are offered. It is easy, for example, to note the differences between the reasons offered by women and those offered by men. Consider the following representative reasons, which I have heard many times in different forms.

Women
    a. I just wanted to be married; all my friends were.
    b. Working isn't all it's cracked up to be.
    c. Something was missing in my life.
    d. I got tired of playing the field.

Men
- a. I wanted to settle down.
- b. It seemed natural. Everybody gets married, don't they?
- c. I wanted to belong, have a family, a home.
- d. I knew I'd never get another chance to marry someone like Kate.

Note that women tend to express security-related reasons for marriage; men more often give reasons related to companionship. People differ greatly in the number of reasons they offer; they also differ in their awareness of their reasons for marrying.

Having unconscious motives or reasons for marriage can be so harmful to the success of a marriage that I want to comment on it briefly. The first and most important thing I can say is that consciousness and unconsciousness are not two separate mental states of knowing and behaving. Just as there is no hard and fast line or division between daylight and darkness, there is no hard and fast line between levels of consciousness. We often hear and make statements like, "Yes, I'm aware of that," or "I can't remember ever having that feeling." The difference between these two statements is a difference of degree in the levels of awareness. The difference is relative, not absolute.

Without venturing too deeply into the subject of consciousness, I want to pose a question. What is the content of the unconscious portion of our mental processes? Why is something in the unconscious portion rather than the conscious portion? A partial answer is that we repress into the unconscious mind any idea, feeling, or experience that we find psychologically uncomfortable. We banish it from our conscious mind. Included here are some of our reasons for wanting to marry, particularly any reason that does not have social acceptance or approval.

Couples in pre-marital counseling tend to be very idealistic in sharing their reasons for marriage, which typically center around love and happiness. To the extent that either of them might be aware of other questionable motives, the greater is the likelihood that they will not freely seek pre-marital counseling. Couples in therapy also claim love and happiness as reasons for having married, but they often will admit that there were other reasons of which they were not aware at the time of their marriage. Sometimes, too, these couples substitute reasons for staying married as reasons for getting married. Improvement of social or economic status, aid to a career, security, and the need to belong are examples.

Like most other human activities, there are good and bad reasons why people marry and why they marry the person they do. The good (socially acceptable) reasons are consciously and openly shared; the bad (socially suspect) reasons are shared less often. In therapy, I always question the single, simplistic, or isolated motive. This caution also applies in divorce counseling. Just as love may be the product of many small satisfactions, indifference or resentment can also result from a combination of many small annoyances. Some divorcing couples, for example, admit that they do not know why they can't get along with each other, and in their search for reasons why they are divorcing, they often concentrate on the symptoms rather than the causes of their failed marriage.

Are there wrong--not just bad, but wrong--reasons for marrying? Yes. People often marry because they feel obligated or sorry for the other. "We had sex while we were dating. When I tried to end the relationship, she claimed that I had used her." "He threatened suicide if I didn't marry him. I didn't want that on my conscience." Other people see marriage as a cure-all for sexual problems such as homosexuality, excessive masturbation, and voyeurism. Some believe that marriage will help them overcome a character defect such as gambling, shiftlessness, or alcoholism. Whenever marriage is seen as a remedy for personal problems or circumstances, selfishness emerges as the central motive. Selfishness is more invidious and malignant than self-interest. Everyone has a right to expect satisfaction of their needs in marriage. That's self-interest. Selfish people, however, want it all. Marriage cannot survive under these circumstances. In time, the loser will have nothing more to give and the winner will look elsewhere.

The reasons people give for marrying usually reflect their needs; marrying is their means for satisfying their needs. When their reasons for marrying are both numerous and diverse, the problem of finding needs-satisfaction in marriage is correspondingly complicated. When there are unconscious reasons for marrying or when there are conscious but not-verbalized reasons for marrying, finding needs-satisfaction in marriage is nearly impossible. In the latter situation, there are weddings but no marriages. The marriages are "still born."

People who marry today must contend with a multitude of new, onerous factors that work against a long-term commitment. Even with good reasons for marrying, including love, it is getting increasingly difficult for people to establish and maintain a satisfying and enduring marriage. All the social and economic rationales for marriage I studied in my college courses have come under scrutiny, if not direct attack. Whether a cause or an effect is debatable, but it is inarguable that tight-knit families and communities that serve as a support system for its members are becoming less common. Increasing emphasis on individualism in our society causes many partners to put individual needs before the needs of their marriage. When these feelings are strongly held, marriage finds it hard to compete. Another pervasive factor is the confusion about gender-related roles within the family. Right or wrong, the roles used to be clearly defined. Today, however, it seems that men are questioning the values and rewards of work at the same time women are attracted to it. Maintaining a favorable balance between family and career is complicated by shifting social and economic forces, often with serious consequences for a marriage.

Perhaps the most adequate response to the problems partners face today in maintaining a long-term relationship is more awareness, more realism, and more honesty about their expectations of and readiness for marriage. Contrary to what many people want to believe, even those marriages that were seemingly made in heaven require a lot of commitment and a lot of hard work. This caring, commitment, and hard work provide the energy and the means to make the process of marital adjustment work.

Chapter Two

Marital Adjustment: What Kind of Marriage Do We Want?

This chapter begins with a fantasy and you are invited to participate.

Let's pretend we can magically identify two engaged couples who are now getting married. As we begin our fantasy, let's be very selective and choose two couples that are as much alike as we can make them-- identical if we can imagine them that way. Let's choose two couples who have similar backgrounds in terms of family life, religion, education, and financial resources. Let's also match then in terms of age, personality, values, interests, and mental and physical characteristics and competencies. The two couples also should have had similar courtships in terms of length and intimacy. Now, let's give them the same wedding date. If you like, we will go to their weddings just so we can be sure that nothing happens at one wedding that doesn't happen at the other. Let's continue our fantasy and watch what happens. The couples return from their honeymoon and settle down into the routine of married life. As time passes, we notice that something we might have anticipated is beginning to happen. We all notice the same thing. What is it? One of the couples is enjoying a higher level of marital satisfaction than the other. In the more successful marriage, the partners have higher expectations of their marriage and are more committed to it. The process of adjustment, which all married partners encounter, is smoother for them. They are more open and honest in their communication; they take time to listen to and really try to understand each other. Decisions about sex, money, and social activities are made on a win-win basis. They show a sense of appreciation of and respect for each other. Marital spats or disagreements are quickly resolved without lingering feelings of resentment or animosity. The partners are more flexible in their behavior toward each other and demonstrate a greater sense of personal responsibility for nurturing their marital relationship. Their marriage is intrinsically valuable to them.

This differential outcome doesn't happen only in our fantasy; it also happens in real life. The most important question--the only question, in fact--we should ask about the differences between the two marriage is, "Why?" Why did these two couples, who were so much alike on their wedding day, experience such different outcomes in their marriage? The partners in both marriages were in love. They were confident that their marriage was blessed, they made similar promises and vows, and both had similar expectations. So, why was one marriage so much more successful and satisfying than the other?

The answer to this question, perhaps, is the most widely studied and best known part of our marriage and family therapy literature, though, arguably, it is the least understood and, certainly, the least followed in terms of avoiding the pitfalls that lead to unsuccessful marriages. What this chapter proposes as an answer to this question is the nearest thing we have to a manifesto for marriage and family living--it provides us with a clear description of what married life should be. No words or ideas sum up the intention of this manifesto better or indicate more clearly its challenge to contemporary marriages than the words "user-friendly marriage." These words are used to describe the goal of the never-ending process of adjustment that goes on between two people in a marriage.

Intentional Marriage

Throughout the ages we have searched: for Camelot, for the Golden Fleece, for Eldorado. No matter what name we gave the quest, it ultimately meant a search for meaning in our lives. Our search continues today with a new face and an enlarged sense of urgency. Encompassing both our personal and professional lives, it is a search for the blueprint of a happy, fulfilling marriage.

Everyone wants to be happy and successful in their marriage. Visions of that happy state are savored. However vague we may be about our dreams and hopes, there is a universal striving for happiness and fulfillment in marriage. Unfortunately, successful marriages don't just happen. It is worth repeating that wishful thinking and day-dreaming won't make them happen. Successful marriages are built and each partner enriches the marriage relationship and helps to determine its future quality by the contributions they make to it. Whether a marriage will become a source of interpersonal reward and satisfaction, or whether it will proceed randomly and unconsciously to become fraught with interpersonal tension is determined by the willingness and desire of the partners to accept responsibility for the kind of marriage that actually develops.

Too many couples do not accept this responsibility. It's not a case of simply refusing to accept responsibility; it's more a matter of not realizing they have a choice. What they do is drift along, being pushed, pulled, and molded by their own conflicting desires and unrealistic expectations on the one hand and subtle social pressures and prescriptions on the other. Not trusting their own feelings, not realizing they have a choice, they accept some culturally defined ideal type of marriage--a type that has worked for others--as the goal of their adjustment process. Their assumption is that only this generalized type of marriage will provide the closeness, the intimacy, and the happiness they seek. What they fail to recognize is that the more they search for closeness, intimacy, and happiness the less likely they are to find them. As traditional wisdom suggests, there is no way to closeness, intimacy, and happiness--these things are the way.

Just as no two marriages are alike, there is no one type of marriage that is best for everyone. Couples differ greatly in what they desire and what they believe is possible; an appropriate way of relating for one couple may be inappropriate for another. I have often been tempted to say to partners in therapy, "Whatever kind of marriage you have, you deserve it." While I do believe the judgment, I do not express it. Rather, I ask some alternative questions: "What kind of marriage would you like to have? How does your ideal marriage differ from your actual marriage? What kind of change will you have to make to achieve your ideal marriage?" In asking these questions, I am trying to get partners to become more intentional about their marriage. Let's take a more detailed look at the differences between what I'm calling an intentional marriage and its opposite, a default marriage.

In intentional marriages, partners realistically define their goals in terms of the opportunities and constraints in their lives. They experience the agony of having looked deeply into themselves to see things as they really are; they have also known the ecstasy of dreaming dreams that have not come true and asking, "Why not?" As a result, they become more aware of themselves and their potential for growth. They stop being critical of life and each other and become doers, making their dreams come true. They see themselves as a system in which each is mutually teaching and learning from the other. Each gives and receives; both are enriched.

In a default marriage, there are few dreams, even fewer questions, and little willingness to explore what marriage could be like outside the boundaries of what the partners have accepted as their comfort zone. Living always within this comfort zone causes the strength of their inner image and desires to weaken, while the various external pressures in their lives grow stronger. When this comfort zone is narrow and the partners' acceptance of it is high, they can know neither the agony nor the ecstasy of an intentional marriage.

Whatever kind of marriage partners have, they decided to have it. How did they decide? In therapy, I explore this question. "When you first married, what kind of marriage did you want?" I ask. It no longer shocks me to hear them reply, "I don't remember ever thinking about it that way. It was just a case of getting married. I didn't know I had to make all these decisions."

I once saw a sign in a novelty shop with the message, "Without a goal you may end up somewhere else." My first thought was that the sign was applicable to business, but it is equally important for marriages. Without a goal, the adjustment process becomes haphazard and random. Goals provide partners a sense of direction or purpose as they search for a mutually satisfying relationship; they pursue their vision of the kind of marriage they want to have. Partners in a default marriage, not having a conscious goal, spend their lives in a recurring pattern of failure, disappointment, and frustration. They work hard, but not always smart, to achieve something that is only vaguely understood and infrequently shared. The importance of having a goal to give direction and purpose to the adjustment process in marriage cannot be overstated.

What is Marital Adjustment?

As I write this chapter, I am struggling with an uneasy feeling about the word "adjustment." Were it not so awkward, I would prefer using the term "adjusting." For many reasons, it seems more appropriate and more helpful to write about "adjusting people" than of "adjusted people."

Adjustment often is taken to mean that there is an ideal pattern or norm of relating to which all people should be compared. This notion raises many questions. For example, what is the desired or ideal norm of adjustment? How is it determined? By whom? Must everyone be measured by it? Could a couple be considered well adjusted in the culture of rural Georgia and poorly adjusted in the shifting, heterogeneous culture of Atlanta? What if a couple exceeds the norm? Are these persons super adjusted or, rather, are they maladjusted since they deviate from the norm?

Another problem I have with the idea of being adjusted is that it suggests a fixed, unchanging state of existence. I often encounter partners who claim that their marriage presented no real problems (in adjustment). Consider the following:

> Helen: "Monty and I knew each other so long before we married that there was very little adjusting to do. I knew he was going to be a good husband. Once in a while we argue about in-laws, but no more than other couples we know."
>
> Monty: "Maybe unconsciously I've changed some, but I don't think too much. Some of our friends really have had a lot of problems, but Helen and I have had it pretty easy. I guess the fact that she and I have known each other since the fourth grade gave us a lot of time to get acquainted." The partners who shared these feelings with me thought of themselves as having done everything their unquestioned perceptions of traditional marital roles demanded of them. It was largely because of their feelings of being well adjusted that they let some unanticipated problems develop and fester before seeking help. "I'm embarrassed to come here," Helen said. "I'm confused," said Monty.

One of the issues we discussed early in their therapy was their belief that they had achieved a perfect adjustment. They shared a Pollyanna-like view that each had done all that a perfect wife or husband was expected to do. The basic difficulty in their marriage was that they had stopped growing; they were changing, but not growing. They were desperately trying to hold to a state or circumstance of adjustment they believed to be proper and socially desirable. Their marriage had lost its vitality and its ability to serve as a means of needs satisfaction for them. Because of their unrealistic, fair-weather view of their marriage, they were blinded to the problems that were hurting them. Change was resisted because it would require adjustments. In time they recognized that it's far easier for people who are adjusting to have a successful marriage than it is for people who have adjusted.

Marital Adjustment is a Continuous Process

Adjustment, in both a psychological and a physiological sense, is a process that begins at birth and ends only at death. So pervasive is this process that there is impressive evidence that it begins before birth and continues for a while after death, at least in the physiological sense. This continuous and unrelenting process can be understood best if we imagine a series of concentric circles. Within the inner, smallest circle let's imagine an infant. Of all living creatures, newborn children are the most helpless; they must depend upon others for their survival, their physical comforts, and their general welfare. Problems of adjustment are largely problems of eating, sleeping, and physical care. Their social adjustments develop only as they mature and learn. As they grow older, their adjustment to their physical environment begins.

In the next larger circle we see the infant growing into childhood with a new set of social and physical adjustment problems and skills. In the remaining circles we see the child growing into adolescence and, as time passes, into adulthood and, finally, old age. As the infant grows and matures into each of the successive stages of life, the required skills and patterns of adjustment undergo dramatic change. Each stage presents new demands, and successful adjustment requires new attitudes, skills, and behaviors. An adjustment pattern that was appropriate at one age under a given set of circumstances may be inappropriate at a later age under a different set of circumstances. Moreover, adjustment patterns that become rigid and fixed will restrict a person's flexibility to adjust as situations change. Successful adjustment necessarily depends upon a person's willingness and ability to give up old ways of adjusting when they are no longer appropriate. Making new adjustments without regrets, anxieties, or other defensive behavior is a basic requirement of growing up and living a productive, satisfying life in a constantly changing world.

What I want to emphasize by way of this discussion is the fact that people who do not adjust well to the demands of one stage of life are less able to meet the demands of the next successive stage. Unfortunately, many people reach adulthood and marry before they have attained an appropriate level of social and emotional maturity. Predictably, these people are handicapped in making the adjustments necessary for successful marriage. Their handicaps are especially harmful when they have not developed a self-concept that permits them to function effectively in the complex relationship of marriage.

Marital adjustment is more of a process than a condition or goal; it is a process in which partners, as individuals, always are in a state of change, growth, and actualization. We always are changing in our feelings, values, and needs, and these changes necessitate changes in our relationship with our partner. It also is necessary to recognize that a change in one partner requires some form of adjustment by the other. As I will discuss in the next chapter, marriage becomes a helping relationship when we are actively concerned about the possible effects of our behavior upon our partner. It is to this process that married couples commit themselves: to work together to nurture and enrich their marriage so that new levels of love, acceptance, and growth in psychological awareness and responsiveness can be achieved and enjoyed. I will, however, use the more conventional term "adjustment" in discussing this critical process, recognizing that it is both continuous and pervasive, touching almost every aspect of a couple's relationship. What I will advocate in this chapter is that through the adjusting process, partners can become more self-directing, deciding what kind of marriage they want, and working together to make it happen.

The idea of adjustment, as I have introduced it, has several possible meanings. I experienced one of them when I moved to Georgia and had to adjust to the climate, the weather, and the social and cultural norms. In this instance, adjustment suggests the idea of "becoming accustomed." In another instance, we might find ourselves in an undesirable circumstance which can't be changed and realize that we will have to adjust to it. Here, the idea of adjustment suggests "acceptance." Other ideas of adjustment are realized when we have to "conform" to some demand or expectation that society places upon us. Still another aspect of adjustment occurs when two people "compromise" their differences.

All of the above meanings of adjustment involve people responding to external situations, e.g., the demands made upon them by their physical and social environments. Another set of meanings focuses upon internal processes. One of these is the idea that people achieve harmony within by ridding themselves of external conflicts and self-condemnation and replacing these negative thoughts with positive thoughts which promote an overall sense of well-being. A second example of internal adjustment involves our growth in the direction of self-actualization. In this latter case, we always are becoming; we are driven by "what could be," rather than "what is" or "what ought to be."

Any concept of adjustment necessarily includes some dimensions of all the above interpretations. Successful adjustment involves recognition of and adaptive responses to the demands and expectations placed upon us in all areas of our life by our own internal nature and needs and by the external world of people and events. Thus, adjustment is viewed as a multidimensional, ongoing process that moves us in the direction of being able to respond to the demands and expectations of our social and physical environment without diminishing our well-being or limiting our potentials for growth and actualization. Obviously, the individual who has not adjusted to these personal demands to some optimal degree will be less able to adjust to the demands and expectations of a marital relationship.

Adjustment means change, and all living creatures constantly are in a process of change. But change does not always mean adjustment in the sense of improved functioning and relating. A lot of change is random and unplanned, often beyond our control, and often unwanted. Aging is an example of the latter.

The kind of change or adjustment I seek in my own life, and what I encourage partners in therapy to accept, is change that is planned-- change we seek because we believe it is good for us and for our marriage. Accepting the responsibility for directing this change process means we must stop letting things just happen to us. We must plan toward the things we want to happen. We must turn away from being merely reactive and become proactive. What I am suggesting here is that partners can have any kind of marriage they want. Whatever kind of marriage we presently have, we decided to have it. How did we decide? Openly? Or by default? Too many marriages simply evolve and persist without the partners giving any thought to or accepting responsibility for the kind of marriage that emerges. Change for these people, even when it is sought, can be difficult and scary. It is for this reason that partners responding to the need for change often seek therapy.

Marital Adjustment as a Merger

In our traditional ways of thinking about marriage, a man and a woman are said to become "one flesh" when they marry. According to the Biblical phrase used in many wedding ceremonies they are "no longer two but one." Does this mean that the two individuals who are merged in marriage no longer have separate identities? Can marriage be compared to the juncture of, say, the Allegheny and the Monongahela Rivers which lose their separate identities at Pittsburgh, Pennsylvania when they unite to become the Ohio River, which in turn loses its identity when it flows into the Mississippi River at Cairo, Illinois? The need for marital adjustment should not and need not confront a couple with the choice of becoming one only at the expense of rejecting the two. Why can't the one be two at the same time the two are one? Must the individual be totally submerged for the sake of marital solidarity?

> "To be united in our love,
> And yet independent in our thoughts.
> To be together in our hopes,
> Yet distinctive in our ways.
> To be one in our dreams,
> Yet two on our goals.
> This is the blessing of marriage."

The author of these words is unknown to me but I have always used them as though they were my own. When I thought it was appropriate, I have shared them with partners in therapy. Not unexpectedly, questions are provoked. A typical response is, "These words are contradictory. How can a married couple have it both ways?" That is a good question, but it also reveals a somewhat naive, parochial understanding of the difference between a devitalized, static marriage and a vital, growing, and adjusting marriage. If love, hope, and dreams are the glue that holds partners together, individuality and distinctiveness are the fuel that enriches and drives their marriage. Partners who slavishly surrender their individuality--their unique ways of thinking, feeling, and behaving--to foster a sense of oneness in marriage are denying their marriage their unique contributions. When both partners are contributing the same things--giving back only what is received--one plus one will always equal one. The synergistic effect of the marriage being greater than the sum of the partners' contributions can be realized only when each partner responds to the other in terms of his or her own commitment to and expectations of the marriage.

Lenora and I were diverse persons in some ways; we had a lot in common in other areas. Our differences and our similarities were reflected in our personalities, values, attitudes, needs, and behavioral propensities. I am more spontaneous, expressive, and open; Lenora was more deliberate, restrained, and private. She was more formal in relationships, entertaining, and dress. I like informality and do a lot of things she called crazy. Both our diversity and our alikeness contributed to the richness of our marriage.

I always encouraged Lenora to accept and nurture her individuality and discouraged all attempts on her part to conform to my expectations of her for the sake of harmony. She had dignity, meaning, and purpose because she was a person, an individual. This is true in or outside marriage. There is no reason that these qualities must be sacrificed at the price of a successful marriage. In our financial matters, for example, I insisted that she not feel the necessity of accounting to or seeking my approval for her spending. It would be demeaning for me to suggest that she should. Finally, we earnestly sought to avoid stereotyped and gender-based roles in our family. I felt good making the bed and washing dishes; performing these roles did not detract from my masculinity or my sense of who I am. Lenora freely and joyously joined me in washing the cars and did all the record keeping and check writing in paying our bills. Doing these things did not diminish her feminity.

Individuality and different marital interests presented no conflict to us. There was life for us, both as individuals and as partners, in an enduring and loving marriage. We had conflicts but we were not bickering types who took offense at every small transgression. We had a strong religious belief and followed the rule of love in resolving our conflicts. Our marriage was valued so greatly that we resolved not to let any conflict hurt it. And I would never serve my own needs or self-interest at her expense.

Marriage Adjustment as Culture Formation

The fantasy with which we began this chapter has been shared with numerous couples in both pre-marital and marital therapy. In these sessions, the fantasy is carried one step farther. Couples are asked to imagine that they are just now getting married. "Which of these two marriages would you like your marriage to be?" Predictably, the answer is the more successful marriage.

At this point I take leave of the fantasy by suggesting that it isn't simply a matter of identifying with or wishing for a particular kind of marriage. For pre-marital couples, it is a matter of modeling their marriage. Married partners, however, already have made a choice, already have joined in marriage with a particular person and, for better or worse, already have begun the process of building the kind of marriage they have. The problem they now face is making their marriage like the more successful marriage in our fantasy.

"Why was one of the marriages more successful than the other?" I asked. Since the marriage they were discussing was not their own, little prodding was needed for them to start sharing their opinions. They reasoned that since both marriages were nearly identical when they began, the explanation for the differences in their outcomes must be in the way the partners related after they were married. I, then, typically asked them to explain their conclusion or to give an example of what they had in mind. The discussion continued, alternately shifting its focus between the make-believe marriage in our fantasy and their own real-life marriages. Predictably, they began to realize that they had been projecting their own marital circumstances on the make-believe marriages. When this happened the door was opened to understanding the important role of culture in marital success.

Culture is the time dimension of a marriage. It incorporates and becomes a legacy of how the partners have done things in the past, are observed in the present, and will be guided in the future. Culture reflects the traditions of a marriage; it interprets how things have been done in the past which the partners can use to determine appropriate behavior in present situations. Marital culture, in this sense, serves as a control mechanism, providing partners a standard by which certain behaviors are approved or prohibited. Although partners inherit and act out the rules and norms of what they believe to be acceptable behavior, the essence of their marital culture cannot be directly observed--it must be inferred from other observable behavior.

In some marriages, for example, social get-togethers such as anniversaries, Thanksgiving, and Christmas are traditionally observed. But no matter how elaborate and controlling they might be, the rules, values, and assumptions which make up a marital culture are empty unless they are meaningful to partners who observe them. Marital culture is developed and sustained by partners because it provides a guide to what is proper and rewarding behavior. There is comfort in knowing that what is acceptable and expected will happen. Behaving according to the culturally prescribed norms of behavior provides partners a sense of psychological security in knowing that they have lived up to their part of the marital social contract.

When two people first marry, they have a strong desire to make the marriage work. Marriages are not created in a vacuum, however, and a new marriage is never a blank tablet. Each spouse brings to the marriage an accumulation of ideas, attitudes, beliefs, and assumptions about what a marriage should be like. Some of these ideas are good; others are not so good. The ideas of one partner might be in conflict with the ideas of the other. It is in the adjustment process that decisions are made about which ideas will prevail. In most marriages, decisions are consciously made about how things will be done. In too many marriages, however, ways of doing things simply emerge. They don't result from purposeful decision making; they emerge and persist by default (i.e., they are never questioned). Partners cannot exist in limbo. Decisions about what kind of marriage they will have must be made, either openly or by default.

Successful marital adjustment makes life simpler for partners. The rules and norms which emerge from the adjusting process make it unnecessary for partners to have to decide all over again what they will do in facing a recurring situation. Without norms a couple always would be solving the same problem over and over again. Ideally, norms are openly and intentionally developed over a period of time and agreed to by both partners.

Norms may develop to regulate almost any aspect of a relationship. Anytime there is observed regularity in the behavior of partners there is evidence of a norm. In our marriage, Lenora and I developed norms about such matters as on which side of the bed we slept, what time we (as guests) tried to arrive at a party, and what kind of gifts we gave to relatives on birthdays and anniversaries.

Sometimes the rules in a marriage are decided on the basis of ability or desire, such as who will water the household flowers. Other times norms are worked out on a trial-and-error basis. Lenora and I learned the "cold" way, not to start the washing machine or dishwasher while the other was taking a shower. Another way for norms to develop is through observation of other couples. Or, a couple might adopt as their own the norms of their parents.

The development of and compliance with norms in a marriage never should be such a rigid process that the marriage becomes rule-bound and loses its spontaneity and ability to adjust to changing situations. At issue is the right and responsibility of each partner to question the norms observed in the marriage. "Does it (a particular norm) still serve our needs? Is this the way we want to handle this matter in the future?"

A norm most often is challenged because one partner feels that it is unfair. For the complainant, the costs of complying with the norm are greater than the rewards received from it. Lenora and I experienced a particularly difficult problem of this type when I began playing golf. We had talked about our need for some recreational activity in which we could meet other people. She had a preference for bowling; I had always wanted to play golf. Little did I know how deeply the golf bug would bite me. As I took more lessons and played golf more regularly, our marriage began to feel the strain. When I started skipping church so I could play another round on Sunday mornings, Lenora questioned my intentions and my understanding of the decision we had made. In suggesting that I was violating our norm of recreation, she was appealing to my sense of fairness. She was comparing my behavior with the standard of right and wrong that we had always observed in our marriage. Let me point out that my behavior and the standard to which it was compared are different. The standard does not change; that is why we have it--so we can compare our behavior to it. A norm is fair only when our behavior under the norm is congruent with the goals of our relationship. In our case, Lenora was right. I had substituted a new goal for the one we originally had sought.

Another area of married life that easily can violate the standard of fairness is the idea of status or esteem. Do certain behaviors suggest a lowered sense of worth when performed consistently by one partner? We read and hear a lot of complaints today that wives experience such loss through the performance of household chores. It is not my purpose here to debate this matter although I have helped many couples in therapy to deal with their feelings about it and the problems it was causing in their marriage. In my own relationship, I always tried to be sensitive to Lenora's feelings about such matters. I found dignity and love in changing diapers and found rewards in performing household chores, including cleaning the bathroom. Secretly, I was driven by my belief that I could perform these chores better than either Lenora or our maid. Everything but cooking, that is. Cooking, for Lenora, was an art form. At my best I could only assist her and then later clean the kitchen.

Questions about esteem and status often evolve into questions about dominance and submission, questions about rights and duties. It is hard for me to imagine that loving and caring partners would agree to a marital norm that caused either of them to feel that they were being controlled or manipulated by the other. "Do I choose to do this? Does this norm serve the goals of our marriage?" These are pertinent questions that must be answered in the affirmative if the norm is to meet the test of fairness.

Partners do not ordinarily think of themselves as developers of or contributors to their marital culture. "I do what I am supposed to do," they say, implying their conformity to the norms of a proper marriage. This kind of behavior assures predictability and continuity in a single time frame, but over an extended period of time, any act of behavior, if repeated enough, becomes the embodiment of a marital culture. In some marriages, the manifestations of culture are adaptive, forward-looking, and oriented toward change and growth. Other marriages reflect a culture that is mired in the past, valuing tradition and stability. Some marital cultures are functional; others are dysfunctional. Some marital cultures pressure the partners to behave in ways that have worked well for their parents but offer no guarantee of working well in their own marriage. In other marriages, however, the partners are strengthened and motivated by the shared commitment to continue the traditions and rituals of their parents. The challenge to all marriages is to create and maintain a marital culture that encourages and supports their efforts to remain adaptive and responsive to the changing demands made upon their marriage.

At the time Lenora and I married, I was working for the U.S. Postal Service. As soon as I shared the news about my forthcoming marriage, I became the object of a lot of good-natured kidding and joke-telling by the "older hands" in the office. Much of it can't be repeated here but one story told repeatedly by Big Bad John (our nickname for him) has some relevance.

"On our wedding night, the little woman wanted me to pick her up and carry her across the threshold. Ha! I was glad to accommodate her, but as soon as I got her inside I took off my pants and told her to put them on. She acted like she didn't want to so I had to tell her again. 'OK,' she said, 'but they're too big for me.' Then I told her, 'Don't ever forget that.'"

In his own crude way John was telling us what was involved in his marital adjustment--an understanding and acceptance of a set of roles. John was seeking to establish, once and for all, a *modus vivendi*, a way of relating for him and his wife.

Surprisingly, there are cultures (and some individuals in all cultures) which rigidly prescribe roles for husbands and wives. Children are reared to anticipate their respective roles and one becomes a "good husband" or "a good wife" only by accepting these roles and behaving accordingly. To the extent that partners can accept these roles, role conflict is minimized and the adjustment process is simplified or, I should say, made unnecessary. Solutions to the problem of marital adjustment like the one Big Bad John attempted to force upon his wife are clear cut, efficient, and remarkably effective if both partners can accept them. If either partner cannot or will not accept his or her prescribed role, the problems of adjustment are made more difficult. Since the most visible and pervasive characteristic of this kind of relationship is one of dominance and submission, it is alien to the values underlying a helping relationship.

The culture of some marriages is very apparent and cohesive; in others it is fragmented and difficult to discern. However ill-defined a marital culture might be, it always reflects and is an outgrowth of the partners' values, expectations, and learned behaviors. Marital culture is a blueprint that partners can use to determine what is and is not appropriate and acceptable behavior. As a blueprint for appropriate behavior, marital culture functions as a guarantee against surprises, reinforcing, as it does, the traditional marital values of predictability and continuity. Culture is both the means and the end--the input and the output--of the adjusting process in marriage.

Adjustment Through Disclosure

"Dr. Holloman, I didn't come for marriage counseling. I have a special problem that I hope you can help me with. Maybe after I tell you my problem you'll think the whole family needs counseling."

The man sitting across the desk from me was 27 years old, college educated, married for five years, no children. He had called late the night before asking that I see him as soon as possible.

"You might have read about my father in the newspaper," he continued. "He was killed in the bank robbery last year. Actually, he was murdered. I just can't imagine him trying to stop the robber. It was so unlike him. I wish I could stay home and comfort my mother more, but I am on the road two or three days every week with my job. Well, let me get to the point. A while back Mom told me that I could have Dad's stereo system. It's a really good system. He liked classical music--played it all the time. Lots of CD's and tapes. There was a small box of blank tapes--the kind that you'd buy at Radio Shack. I hadn't even touched them until yesterday. I didn't know for sure whether they were blank or not, so I put one in the player. Now I wish I hadn't."

"Can you tell me what was on the tape, Philip?" I asked.

"Even if he felt that way, why didn't he just keep it to himself? I guess he knew that Mom would never play his stereo. I always thought my mother and father were happily married. Everybody else thought so, too. I never heard them argue; Dad never even raised his voice to Mom. That's why I don't know what to do. I can see Dad in my own behavior. It would break Mom's heart all over again to hear these tapes. But I don't want to destroy them either; I don't want Marianne (Philip's wife) and me to fall into the same trap."

Over the next several minutes, he became more connected and deliberate in his speech and was able to tell me what was on the tapes. Recorded over a period of several years, the tapes told a story of his father's dissatisfaction with his marriage, his dislike of his job at the bank, and how he despised himself for not having the "guts" to discuss his feelings with his wife.

As we continued our discussion, both Philip and I began to realize that his concern was greater than the question of what to do with the tapes. His good memories of his father had been crushed. "All my life I have tried to be like him; now I'm wondering. I feel bad about that. What was he afraid of? Why couldn't he tell Mom what he didn't like, the things he wanted to change?" After a few moments of silence and a sudden shift in composure and demeanor, he continued, "I'm afraid that Marianne and I are beginning to behave just like Mom and Dad. Every time I bring up a subject she doesn't want to talk about she says, 'Try to understand like your father; he was such a sweet person.' Well, I'm not sure I want to be like my father."

Philip invited Marianne to join him in therapy and she accepted. Progress in helping Philip to understand and accept the negative feelings he had about his father was made rather quickly--too quickly, perhaps. Paradoxically, as he began to think of his father in more positive terms, he began to picture his mother as the villain in his parents' marital difficulties. As he allied himself more with his deceased father, he started accusing Marianne of being like his mother. He said that Marianne wanted to treat him the same way his mother treated his father. At this point, Philip's mother was invited to join the sessions. It was painful for everyone as Philip shared his feelings about his parents and how these feelings were affecting his marriage. Philip destroyed the tapes without revealing their existence, and neither Marianne nor his mother ever suspected the real source or cause of his feelings. Philip and Marianne

Making Marriage User Friendly

remain happily married today in a lifestyle far different from that of his parents.

Why is it that two people who love each other find it so difficult to be open and communicative about the more intimate aspects of their relationship? Why do they contend themselves to talking about such things as the weather, neighbors, children, etc.? What kind of risk did Philip's father see in expressing his marital dissatisfaction to his wife? Was his fear real or imagined?

There is a common tendency to blame marital problems on the inability of partners to communicate. One of the more common admonitions is, "Why don't you two sit down and talk this thing out?" It would be illogical to argue against the idea that improved communications could lead to improved marital functioning, but poor communication too often is made the scapegoat for other more serious marital problems. When interpersonal relationships in a marriage are sound, communication problems tend not to occur. Rather than being the cause of poor interpersonal relationships, I view communication breakdowns as a result or consequence of unsatisfactory marital relationships. When good interpersonal relationships are developed through the adjustment process, partners become less suspicious of each other's motives and are able to communicate more openly. As partners exchange more intimate information the adjustment process is enhanced. Without self-disclosure, we can deal only with superficialities: roles, appearances, stereotypes, etc. Through self-disclosure we build trust and intimacy which, in turn, allow us to disclose more.

As you might suspect, there are many people who disagree with me on this subject. Self-disclosure is seen by them as being too risky. The advantages of disclosure must always be balanced against its attending risks and costs. To reveal personal feelings to another makes us vulnerable; to be known by another gives that person the power to hurt us. In rebuttal, I argue that however bad being vulnerable might be, not being vulnerable always is worse. Without taking risks--without being vulnerable--there can be no trust, and without trust there can be no intimacy, and without intimacy partners are not in a true marital relationship.

This subject of intimacy will be discussed in greater detail in a later chapter. At this point, I want only to emphasize the importance of an open relationship to self-disclosure, which both enhances and benefits from a successful adjustment.

Intermission

Before I continue with the last part of this chapter I want to share an unplanned but exciting experience I once had. Several couples had enrolled in a weekend marital enrichment workshop that I was conducting. On Saturday afternoon, after we had explored the question of how to develop win-win relationships in marriage, one of the participants surprised everyone by asking a rather innocent, but meaningful, question. "What is winning? How do I know when I am winning?" This question invited a variety of hasty responses, some expressed in a positive mode (e.g., having good sex); others expressed in negative terms (e.g., not labeling people). After a while, I suggested that we divide into two groups. One group was asked to give answers to the statement "We are winning when we ," and, in order to know when we are not winning, the other group was asked to respond to the statement, "We are losing when we ." After an hour or so the groups came back together and shared their responses.

Winning

We are winning when we have friends, take charge of our lives, know who we are, don't allow little things to get in the way, look for good in others, listen, express real feelings, have a sense of humor, fall in love, marry, accept others as they are, sleep late, don't argue, stop smoking, plan for the future, enjoy today, encourage others, stop and smell the roses, are young at heart, don't let others control or intimidate us, are congruent, etc.

Losing

We are losing when we bitch a lot, play destructive games, don't apologize, complain, never say "Thanks," cry a lot, make excuses, do not keep promises, are defensive, are self-centered, live alone, insist on our own way, smoke, cheat, don't flush the toilet, sulk, tell secrets of others, don't try new things, have to please others, don't say "I love you," look at the dark side, feel old, worry about the future, etc.

The responses of the groups were so personal and sincere that it was hard to overlook the emotional investment they had made in the task. Some of the partners had known a lot of trauma in their marriage and seemed to be sharing personal experiences. It was more than an academic exercise for them. One partner said that it was a winning experience for her to experience others being so open and honest in sharing their personal experiences. All the participants seemed to feel that they were winning by discussing this subject and did not want to move away from it.

After a short period of random discussion I asked, ""How can we make our marriage a winning situation? What kind of behavior sets us up to lose?" After several minutes of sharing feelings about my question, one participant responded, "I want my marriage to be like my computer: user-friendly."

"I'm with you," echoed another group member.

Soon we were discussing what a user-friendly marriage would be. Because having a user-friendly marriage can be viewed as an overall goal of the adjustment process, I want to share some of their thoughts with you.

I have always taken the word serendipity to mean finding something joyful not looked for, not expected. That's what happened to us that afternoon. Learning what people have to feel before they think of themselves as winners enabled me to help others to make winning decisions about their marriage. Likewise, knowing what constitutes losing for people helped me to help others to view their behavior more objectively in terms of its appropriateness. What I found was unexpected; it was joy without search. I wanted to share it with you.

Epilogue: Some Aftermaths of Faulty Adjustment

As a marriage and family therapist I was trained in a tradition which emphasized a helping or remedial model. As a consequence, I saw my role as being a helper to people who were experiencing difficulties in their marriage. As I worked with couples and families I began to view their problems in terms of a cause-and-effect relationship. Many of their problems, it seemed, could have been prevented or at least minimized had they had a better understanding of and preparation for marriage. Discussions with couples about their courtship have convinced me that more attention needs to be placed upon prevention of problems. Accepting pre-marital counseling as one answer to this dilemma, I extended my practice to include it, believing that it was better to prevent problems than to solve them later. In this effort I sought to familiarize engaged couples with the kinds of problems I typically worked with in couples therapy. As they gained a better understanding of the problems that could occur later they were more receptive to examining the circumstances of their marriage that might make them vulnerable to these problems. Subjectively, I felt that premarital counseling was helpful, but I had no way of knowing whether I actually did the good I intended.

During the next several years, I extended my practice in still another direction to include divorce counseling and divorce mediation. Before I briefly share my experience in this area with you, let me give you some background information. Georgia has a no-fault divorce law which provides that either one or both partners in a marriage can petition the courts for a divorce without having to allege a marital misconduct as the ground for divorce. They must state only that their marriage is irretrievably broken--that there is no chance or desire for reconciliation. With a mutually agreed-upon, equitable property settlement and custody agreement when there are children, divorces routinely are granted after a waiting period of thirty days. So simple is the process that no attorney is needed.

Against the background of this seemingly uncomplicated process, people came to me for help in one of two areas. First, there were those who want to divorce with a minimum of pain or trauma. Typically, these people were neither antagonistic toward nor resentful of each other. They most often were friendly, respectful, and even caring toward each other but they emphasized that it was divorce--not marriage– counseling they wanted. They would say, for example, "We don't hate each other; strangely, we still like each other. We just aren't able to get along. Maybe it is a case of our marriage ruining a good relationship. Anyway, we know that there will be some pain and misgivings as we divorce, and we want you to help us with it."

In the second situation couples request help in resolving some disputed questions prior to applying for divorce. The help they sought was in the form of divorce mediation-- and the disputes ran the gamut from financial and property settlements to child custody and visitation agreements. Their relationship was still sound enough to cause them to believe they could settle these questions outside the adversarial court system with its attending trauma and expenses. Helping them to find win-win solutions to their disagreements was the purpose of the requested service.

Although I continued to provide both divorce counseling and divorce mediation, it was not something I enjoyed. Even when divorcing partners expressed satisfaction with my service, I was left with a sense of loss. My success, I realized, was born of their failure. In every instance I tried to answer this question: "Why did this marriage fail?" In almost all instances, there was evidence of either a faulty courtship or an inability to make an effective adjustment after marriage. It always was a case of, "What might have been."

My purpose in this chapter was to show how critical the adjustment process is to a successful marriage.

Chapter Three

Understanding the Helping Relationship

Most interpersonal relationships involve both the need and the opportunity for helping. This especially is true of marriage. Compared to other relationships, marriage is more intimate, more shared, more permanent. These characteristics make marriage an interrelationship characterized by reciprocal expectations, rights, and responsibilities. Marriage also is an interdependent relationship--both partners must contribute to the relationship if it is to be mutually satisfying. In this contribution process, our values, attitudes, needs, and expectations guide our behavior and determine its effect on our partner.

This chapter will discuss the nature of and the basic requirements for an effective helping relationship in marriage. Helping, in this context, is different from that provided by professionals. As I view it, helping is a way of life for married people; loving and helping are opposite sides of the coin we call marriage.

We Are Always Helping

Hardly a day passes without our giving or receiving help in some way. All around us are opportunities for helping. Just recently, I loaned a book to a colleague; and invited a neighbor to winter a prized flower in my greenhouse. Help was received when a friend called to share information about the "turning of the leaves" in the north Georgia mountains.

Many married partners, consciously or unconsciously, adopt a division of labor in which the wife is responsible for, say, things inside the house and the husband is responsible for things outside the house. In this kind of situation, when one partner performs tasks normally done by the other, it is more an instance of assisting rather than helping. When I made the bed or washed the breakfast dishes, I was performing household chores--I was not helping my wife. Neither was she helping me when she typed an early draft of this manuscript or held the ladder while I changed a light bulb. Even though we may provide this assistance on a regular and continuing basis, each instance of assistance is completed when the task is finished. Each act is temporary and terminal; its goal or purpose is to complete a necessary task.

In the so-called helping professions--of which marriage and family therapy is one--the relationship between the therapist and the client also is temporary and terminal. Whether the therapist is a psychiatrist or a school counselor, the relationship between the person giving help and the person receiving help has a beginning and, necessarily, an end if it is to be deemed successful. The helping relationship in these instances is not undertaken to help people throughout their lives. It is problem-centered and there is no interest or desire to develop anything more than a problem-solving relationship. Professional helpers might receive great satisfaction from their helping, but it is a one-way helping. It does not have the mutuality of the helping relationship in marriage. The professional helping relationship ordinarily ends when a desired outcome is reached and the person receiving the help can say, "My problem is solved," or "My behavior has changed."

The helping relationship in marriage is not of the professional type. It is informal and there are no scheduled appointments. Neither does it have a determinable beginning or ending. It is continuous and exists alongside and in support of the love feelings partners have for each other. Helping behavior in our marriage involves everything we do to promote our partner's psychological and spiritual well-being. It is person-centered. Even though the helping is therapeutic, the helper is not a therapist in the professional sense.

It is not enough, however, that we want to promote the well-being of our partner--we must promote these outcomes in our partner for their sake, never as a means to some personal end. Helping behavior is distinguished by both its motives or intentions and its consequences. This is why it is important to know ourselves and our motives. What are our intentions toward our partner? Do we intend some valued consequence or are we simply trying to impress them in some way? Can we behave toward our partner in such a way to accomplish our intentions?

Helping is a Synonym for Loving

Sidney Jourard (1963) has come closer than anyone I know to grasping the meaning of my idea of marriage as a helping relationship. Let me share some of his thinking with you.

He argues that we generally like (love) another person because that person behaves in ways that satisfy some of our needs. In this sense, our marriage partner becomes a source of needs satisfaction for us. It is a widely accepted belief--I believe it--that our partner will behave in ways which satisfy us most when their needs are satisfied. Thus, it is to our advantage to promote their well-being. Our partner cannot be a source of satisfaction for our needs when his or her own needs are not being met; hence, we have a vested interest in helping our partner to grow, to become, and to actualize their potentials. Accordingly, we take active steps to promote their well-being. Doing this can be likened to insuring ourselves against the loss of satisfaction of our needs. Moreover, there is a synergistic effect produced by this mutual helping and the resulting needs satisfaction. By this I mean the total needs satisfaction in our marriage is greater than the sum of the efforts of two partners working independently.

Dr. Jourard hastens to warn us, however, that our concern for the well-being of our partner must never be an outgrowth of the calculated view that "If I take care of my partner, my partner will take care of me." When done for this reason, helping behavior becomes a means rather than an end; it becomes self-serving. Because it has strings attached, it is no longer freely given. We maintain a helping relationship with our partner because of our love, not because we expect something in return. The previous sentence is, at first glance, seemingly at odds with what I have argued above. But closer examination shows that it is not. If we love or help our partner only when they love or help us, we may never get around to loving them at all. No, we act in helping ways toward our partner because we love them, because it is our nature to love. When love or helping is not freely given it ceases to be love--it becomes devious and calculated. Rather than being concerned with the happiness and well-being of our partner, our concern is really for our self.

Russ Holloman, Ph. D.

Helping and Interpersonal Relating

The first step in developing an effective helping relationship in marriage is to remember that helping is an accompaniment to--a part of--interpersonal relating. Although interpersonal relating is a much larger concept than helping, it is possible to help another only within the context of a relationship. Thus, helping is an interactive process. In marriage, like all other two-person relationships, our behavior both affects and is affected by the behavior of our partner. Our approval or disapproval of some aspect of our partner's feelings or behavior, for example, affects them in predictable ways. We are, in turn, affected by our partner's approval or disapproval of us. When we behave in helping ways, we are expressing our desire to have a positive effect on our partner. We want our presence and our behavior to be beneficial to their well-being. Helping, in this sense, is more than contrived behavior done for our partner in a particular situation. Helping is actually interwoven into and becomes a part of our life with our partner, so much so that it becomes a way of life.

Intentions and Social Competence

A marriage relationship is healthy to the extent that both partners express an active concern for the overall well-being of the other. We are only passively concerned when we simply wish some special or valued outcome for them. We become actively concerned when we behave in ways most likely to produce that outcome. Our active concern begins only after we realize that wishful thinking or passive longing for a desired outcome is not enough.

Implied in the preceding paragraph are two important ideas. First, we can behave in a helping role only when we intend to help. Without the goal or purpose of helping we have nothing to guide us. Our behavior is random; it may or may not be helpful. Secondly, we can translate our intentions to help into actual helping behaviors only when we possess the prerequisite social and emotional competence. It is not enough to have good intentions, we must be able to turn our intentions into results. Recognizing the need for helping skills is not a suggestion that we must acquire or develop a wide range of professional skills before we can help. Nor is it necessary to identify ourselves with some particular theoretical orientation. More important than skills and theoretical orientations are our attitudes and feelings, which we communicate through our love. As our love is felt by our partner, our attitudes and feelings and our resulting behavior are perceived as being helpful. The most critical problem we face in the helping relationship is behaving in ways that are consistent with our attitudes and feelings of love.

Acting Out Our Feelings

It is my assumption that our feelings toward our partner are feelings of love. If this assumption cannot be made, why bother with either the writing or the reading of this book. Making this assumption, however, does not mean that love is the only feeling we ever have toward them. All of us, at times, have negative--even angry--feelings toward our partner. When we are conscious of these negative feelings, we suffer pangs of guilt and tend to avoid any sort of situation or encounter that might result in their inadvertent expression. It is often the case, however, that these feelings are held unconsciously. Because we feel guilty over having negative feelings, we avoid the pains of guilt by repressing them into our unconscious mind. Successful repression of these feelings means we are no longer bothered by them. But this repression doesn't mean we are actually rid of the feelings; it means only that they are submerged or hidden in our unconscious mind. The security we feel in these situations is tenuous, at best. It is tenuous because these negative feelings can surface at any time, whenever an appropriate provocation is faced. It is this real and always present possibility that presents us with a dilemma about all our feelings, including the positive feeling of love. This dilemma is the question of whether we will act out only our positive feelings, hoping any negative feelings we might have will remain hidden, or, as an alternative, confront our negative feelings and share them along with our love feelings.

Only the latter approach is consistent with the helping relationship. As humans we cannot escape responsibility for our actions, even when we claim "I don't know why I behaved that way." If I intended to behave in loving and helping ways toward Lenora, I had to be aware of and accept all of my thoughts and feelings about her, including the negative ones. Only when I am aware of and accept my negative feelings can I begin to control or change them. Being aware of and accepting negative feelings, whatever they might be, does not mean, however, that I am going to act on them. To do this would violate my grander feeling of love. This, I would not knowingly do.

Does being aware of and accepting negative feelings that I might have mean that I have to continue living with them, hoping they are never uncovered? No, there is a better way. Let me explain. Remember the father of the afflicted child who cried out to Jesus, "Lord, I believe, help thou my unbelief." (Mark 9:24 *Holy Bible*, KJV) This man professed his faith. It was only after this admission that Jesus made his son well. In a similar manner, whenever I experienced negative feelings toward Lenora I tried to say to her, "I love you, but I also am having some unloving feelings about you." If, for example, I was aware of having feelings of both love and anger toward her at the same time, honesty requires that I express both feelings. Expressing only one of them is being dishonest, and without honesty a loving, helping relationship is impossible. The fact that I did sometimes experience angry feelings toward her did not make me a bad or unloving person. Neither did the presence of feelings of anger mean the absence of feelings of love.

Admittedly, we help or hurt our partner more by what we say and do than by our thoughts and feelings. I can have angry feelings but keep them so well under control that there is no conscious danger of acting or speaking in hurting ways. But it takes psychological energy to keep threatening, unwanted feelings under control. It requires constant attention to prevent an "accident" or a "slip of the tongue." When I am preoccupied with the need to not let my negative feelings come out, I am less free to express my love feelings. All of my attention and my energy are directed toward controlling the threatening, negative feelings. If these feelings are not present, no energy expenditure is required to keep them under control. The energy that is saved can then be used in building and maintaining the helping relationship.

Rather than get caught up in the self-defeating process of buying psychological protection against inadvertent expressions of our negative thoughts and feelings, it is more economical (in terms of energy expenditure) and more loving to admit both feelings—both the feelings of love and the feelings of anger, or whatever. The greater our awareness and acceptance of our negative feelings, the more we are able to control and change them. The more open we are about the full range of our feelings, the more readily and honestly we can ask for our partner's help in examining and hopefully removing the cause of the negative feelings.

In therapy, I often use the example of squeezing an orange to help clients understand the need to get rid of negative, non-helping feelings. "What do you get when you squeeze an orange?" I ask. Being distrustful of any question with such a seemingly easy answer, clients will predictably ask, "What do you mean?" When I answer, "Orange juice." I always get an embarrassed laugh in return. You get orange juice because that is what is inside the orange--nothing else can come out. In marital relationships, we are squeezed when we are unjustly criticized, when our partner fails to do something we had requested, or when we don't get our way in something. When these things happen to us, how do we react--what kind of behavior comes out? Does anger come out? Do other critical, unloving feelings erupt? If they do, it's because that is what is inside us. We may try as hard as we can not to let these negative feelings come out, but in the heat of the moment, when we are being squeezed, the barriers come down and the feelings we wanted to keep inside come roaring out. The only way we can avoid the possible consequences of punishing, negative feelings is by not having them.

The extent to which we try to fool ourselves about possibly negative feelings will have a great influence upon our success in the helping relationship. When we cannot accept our own negative feelings or doubts, we cannot be fully effective in helping our partner deal with similar feelings and doubts they might have. It is only when we have our own needs reasonably satisfied that we can respond to their needs.

Helping the Relationship

We sometimes talk and write about marriage as though it had an existence separate and apart from the two partners. Expressions like "My marriage is a happy one" imply not only that our marriage has its own identity but also, that it is capable of having feelings--as though the marriage had a human-like existence. Marriage, as a special relationship between two people, is different from the wedding that initiated it. A wedding is an event; marriage is a process--a process that is reflected in the intentions and expectations of the partners. It was through my relationship with Lenora that my marriage is expressed. To be in contact with her--to react to and be influenced by her--establishes the relationship. And the kind of relationship that is established controls the amount, kinds, and quality of interaction with her. As soon as I express my love for Lenora and she responds positively, a relationship is established.

Before we can help another, we must establish a relationship of love, acceptance, and trust with that person. It is for this reason that I view marriage as a helping relationship. Partners can derive great satisfaction from their own as well as the other's self-actualization struggles and achievements. It does not mean that one partner is active in giving help and the other partner is passive in receiving it. It does mean that each partner is concurrently sensitive to and responsive to the needs and expectations of the other. Dr. Rubin (1983) uses the term "creative relating" to describe this kind of relationship. A mutuality of interests--rights, needs, and responsibilities--aids in creative relating, but the most important motivation in marriage is the desire to help our partner achieve a sense of overall well-being without any expectation of self-aggrandizement. In this sort of relating, there are no hidden motives, no keeping score, and no long-suffering martyrs.

The following seven questions are suggested as guidelines for determining our awareness of the various dimensions of the helping relationship. My purpose in discussing these questions is to bring into clearer focus the important characteristics of a healthy marriage--a relationship that satisfies both the maintenance and the growth needs of the partners. A critical aspect of the health of a marriage is the extent to which each partner functions in a caring and responsive manner toward the other. A marriage also is healthy to the extent that each partner contributes to the full extent of their capacities and finds satisfaction in their marriage without interfering with the other partner doing the same.

These seven questions are concerned with separate aspects of the helping relationship. One is not more important than another; each is important for different reasons. To concentrate on one to the exclusion of the other is to not look at the totality of the relationship. As each question is discussed, it must be considered against a background of the other six questions. To the extent that these questions can be answered in the affirmative, the marriage relationship becomes a helping relationship.

Can I be Sensitive to the Thinking, Feeling, and Behavior of my Partner?

In asking this question, I am in no way suggesting that we should try to get into the mind of our partner. Sensitivity, as I intend it here, is more related to awareness. Other words which could easily substitute for sensitivity are thoughtfulness and attentiveness. (The importance of these characteristics can be appreciated by looking at a relationship in which they are missing.) All these characteristics combine in a way to suggest that a helping relationship is one in which the overt behavior of our partner can be anticipated. Sensitivity to both the verbal and non-verbal messages of our partner enables us to respond more appropriately. As we increase our sensitivity to their thoughts, feelings, and actions we also get more in touch with our own. Egan (1975) refers to these two bits of knowledge as "social intelligence." This social intelligence includes two factors: sensitivity to our partner's feelings and needs and the flexibility to act appropriately in various encounters with them. Egan views sensitivity--the word he uses is "attending"--as a concomitant condition for maintaining the helping relationship and, as such, must always be present in the helping process.

Sensitivity to Lenora's feelings, needs, and behavior also made it possible for me to show respect for her. Her thoughts and feelings were a private part of her. Could I move about and enter into her private world and see things as she did? No. Could I show respect for her private world and not trample on meanings and values which were precious to her? Yes. To be sensitive to what was precious to her was to show understanding and respect when these things were shared with me. Sensitivity was not an invasion of her privacy, nor was it used as a means of gaining privileged information. When it was shown for any hidden, ulterior motive it ceased to be helpful.

It was through Lenora's overt behavior that her thoughts and feelings were revealed to me. It was also at this point that my sensitivity played its most critical role because her overt behavior could have both explicit and implicit messages. Too often, we respond only to the explicit message, overlooking the far more important and controlling implicit message. We qualify what we say by the tone of our voice, our facial expressions, our body movements, and the prevailing social context. For example, we can say "Yes" to a request in a variety of ways, expressing anything from eagerness to reluctance. In each instance, the explicit, spoken message (as behavior) is qualified by the implicit, unspoken intention. Sensitivity permits us to become more perceptive and respond more appropriately to the intentions, needs, and expectations of our partner. Sensitivity to their thoughts, feelings, and behavior is to be in their psychological presence. This presence will be discussed more fully in Chapter Seven.

Can I Communicate my Motives and Intentions in a Timely and Unambiguous Manner?

Without becoming overly involved in psychological theory, I want to define some terms I will be using. Conventionally, a motive is a psychological or physiological state that directs a person's behavior toward a goal or needs satisfaction. The goal is what the person is seeking or wants to make happen. When we see people go into a restaurant we can assume they are seeking food to satisfy their feelings of hunger. Motives of this sort are physiological in nature and are largely involuntary. They are what have been called primary motives. What I am concerned about at this point are motives that are more social in nature and that are largely learned. The people entering the restaurant could, possibly, be responding to both a hunger motive and social motive at the same time. This is especially likely if they sit together while eating.

Some social motives are learned through conditioning and we call them habits. Other social motives are the result of our thinking and willing processes. Because these latter motives are a result of decision-making processes, I use the term "intention" to describe them. My concern is with motives and intentions as guides for our behavior toward our partner.

As long as things are going smoothly in our marriage, we usually don't give much attention to our motives and intentions. But when we behave in some way that our partner did not expect, it can lead to the question "Why did you do that?" Or, to phrase their question another way, "What was your motive or intention?" Or, we can express our own concern about our behavior by asking, "Why did I do that? It's not like me to behave that way." We realize, of course, that we must have been motivated to behave as we did, but what was our motive and why? As you can easily see, motives are very complex and difficult to understand, especially when we are not aware of them.

Why should I want to let Lenora know my motives or intentions? First of all, I wanted and intended my motives to be consistent with my love feelings for her. The more consistently I behaved toward her, the more predictable and understandable my behavior was to her. Since she was more confident of my behavior she could consider it in her response to me. When she couldn't anticipate my reactions to her behavior, it contributed to a high degree of uncertainty on her part about our relationship.

What were my motives or intentions toward Lenora? Was I fully aware of them? Could I communicate my full awareness of them in a timely and unambiguous manner? Again, the assumption was made that my overall grand motive toward Lenora was love. Accordingly, my intention was to behave in ways that were at all times consistent with my motive or goal of love. Was I aware of any other motive that was incongruent with my love motive? Hopefully, "No." In answering "No," however, I also am hopeful that I had no unconscious, incongruent motives. Could I communicate all my conscious motives in clear, easily understood terms without any attempt to misrepresent them or mislead her. Obviously, the building and maintenance of a healthy, helping relationship depends upon a "Yes" answer.

Can I Project a Posture of Attitudinal and Behavioral Flexibility?

In many ways being married is like playing a role in an ongoing human drama. It is a role with a script determined by our mutual responsibilities, rights, and expectations. It is determined not only by our own internal strivings and motives, but also by those of our partner.

From time to time in therapy I encounter persons who accept certain things about themselves as fixed. "This is the way I am," they claim, implying not only an inability to change but also questioning whether anyone rightfully could ask them to change. These persons tend to approach all human situations as though they were identical. They also assume that their characteristic style of thinking, feeling, and acting is appropriate to all situations. Life is not that way--it is always changing. Situations change and problems seldom recur in exactly the same form as before. To expect life to be consistent and predictable and matched to our inflexible responses to it is to court a lot of disappointment and failure. Notice how some actors and actresses play the same role time and time again. John Wayne comes to mind. Even though he played it well, he played only one kind of role. Could he have played a comedy or musical role? Hardly. To that possibility he most likely would have responded, "That's not my kind of role."

If we are going to be responsive to our partner's needs, we first must be sensitive to their needs. But what if the satisfaction of these needs requires us to think, feel, or behave in ways which are not characteristic of us? Will we say, "I'm sorry. If your needs were different--something I'm comfortable with--I could help you. Maybe next time. O.K.?" No, sensitivity and awareness alone are not enough. If we are going to act in ways consistent with our love (motives and intentions) for our partner, we must be able to behave appropriately in terms of the present situation. Awareness of our partner's needs in a particular situation is of little use if we are limited in our response to it. We are not expressing love when we excuse ourselves by saying, "If things were different I could help." Nor do we show love when we try to change the situation so our fixed ways of responding will be appropriate. If we wait for the perfect match between the needs of the situation and our ability to respond, we will miss many opportunities for helping. We also will miss many opportunities for learning and growing.

As we become more flexible in our thinking, feeling, and behavior we are helped to better understand the benefits of the helping role in marriage. Being flexible does not mean being wishy-washy. Nor does it mean that we must become a puppet, manipulated by the strings of our partner's expectations. Rather, it means that we can be logical and rational (the mind0 when that is necessary, and we can be emotional and show feelings (the heart) when that is appropriate. It means, simply, that we have the freedom and the ability to be what the situation demands. Only then can we consistently and predictably be helpful.

Can I Behave in Ways That will Cause Me to be Perceived as being Open, Caring, and Trustworthy in Some Deep Sense?

Openness is virtually impossible without trust. In a like manner, caring requires openness. In turn, trust is meaningless without openness and caring. These characteristics of an effective helper are linked together in such a way that each both affects and is affected by the other two. To care for another is to be open to them and being open to them depends upon our trust in them. While it is theoretically easy to distinguish between these three qualities, in actual practice it is very difficult. It is possible, however, that in a particular relationship one of these qualities will be more evident than the others. But, if any one of the three is lacking to any great degree, the strength of the other two will be diminished accordingly.

Trust is both a condition and a result of full and honest communication between partners. When I knew that Lenora would let me know how she thought or felt about some aspect of my behavior I perceived her to be caring and honest, and I would accept what she said. There was nothing more uncomfortable and anxiety-provoking than not knowing what she really thought, felt, or wanted. Openness, in this sense, means sharing information that is germane to our relationship; it involves sharing information from the private, often guarded areas of our lives. To be open is to be vulnerable, but trust makes our vulnerability less threatening. Trust thus means that if I let Lenora know me she would not use the shared information to judge, criticize, or exploit me in any way.

Since openness without trust makes us vulnerable, it is ill-advised without some knowledge or belief of how the shared information will be treated. But as frightening as being vulnerable can be, it is even worse not to be vulnerable. This is where trust and caring enter. Trust is a result of months or years of courtship prior to marriage and grows from the basic satisfactions of experiencing affection and love. Trust emerges as the pillar of our faith in our own motives and intentions, our perceptions of how our partner will respond, and the quality of the helping relationship. Trust of this type can be, but need not be, hard to come by. But until we are willing to risk enough--or more appropriately, to care enough--to be open with our thoughts and feelings, we'll never know whether we can trust. As we learn to trust, more openness is made possible. And openness is evidence of our caring.

Sharing these three qualities must never be one-sided. If it is, there is a strong likelihood that the relationship is not valued by both partners. In their absence, the information that is shared is typically not germane to the relationship, and the risk in sharing is so low that neither openness or trust is evident. One other possibility is that a partner who behaves this way is either showing an exaggerated dependency or is attempting to manipulate the behavior of the other. Real openness, real caring, and real trust are always mutually felt, mutually expressed, and mutually enhanced. To the extent that I could cause Lenora to see me as open, caring, and trustworthy, I was helping to make it easier for her to respond in a like manner to me.

Can I be Patient and Wait for my Partner?

Anyone who has ever lived or visited my hometown most likely can recall an instance of having to wait for a train to pass at one of our many rail crossings. In one part of Augusta, a long-enough train can simultaneously block traffic at three different points as it follows its serpentine path through the city. My most memorable experience with the trains, and my longest wait, occurred one morning at the Greene Street crossing.

The barriers had fallen into place and several other cars had already stopped when I took my place in the line. Resigning myself to a long wait, I lowered the windows of my car and started reading a magazine I had with me. After what could not have been more than a couple minutes, I was distracted by the shouts and antics of a man three cars in front of me. He had gotten out of his car and was shouting all kinds of threats and obscenities at the train, which was slowly passing by. He alternated between kicking the wheels and pounding on the hood of his car and picking up stones from the edge of the road and throwing them at the train.

At first, I was passively amused at his antics. Then I became embarrassed because of the presence of other people. Finally, noting that the end of the train was nowhere in sight, I walked up to him and asked if I could be of help. His first response seemed to be annoyance and he directed some of his anger toward me. I realized that I had to somehow calm him.

"Have you ever seen any of those small, white crosses alongside our roads?" I asked.

"Yes, so what?" he retorted.

I explained that each of those crosses meant that someone had died at that spot. "They give them out for fatal heart attacks, too," I added.

After a few seconds of what appeared to be sincere confusion, he seemingly grasped the implication of my remark and started laughing--some of the most insightful, revealing laughter I have ever heard.

"So you think they might have to put one here for me?"

"Yes, especially if you continue behaving as you were until this train passes," I replied.

With a quick change in both his apparent feelings and demeanor, he began rubbing his hands together as though to remove any dirt on them and then extended his right hand to me as he introduced himself. After a few pleasantries were exchanged, he apologized for his untoward behavior and offered the observation that he really had lost control.

Without any explicit agreement with his self-indictment, I reached down and picked up a couple of small stones from the street. Handing one to him, I said, "OK, on three." As we threw the stones at the train in the spirit of our new-found comradeship, he turned to me and said, "You know something, that train doesn't give a damn how we feel. It is going to do its thing until the last car passes and then it'll move on to Fifteenth and ruin somebody else's day."

We continued to talk until we saw the end of the train approaching. As we parted he waved goodbye and called out, "Send me a bill for your help."

As I got into my car, my overall good feeling was suddenly replaced by some ugly memories of earlier times when I had behaved in inappropriate, self-defeating ways as I expressed my impatience at someone or something that had caused me to have to wait. I experienced private embarrassment as I recalled how I used to show my annoyance when I was kept from doing something that I wanted to do when I wanted to do it.

Making Marriage User Friendly

Lenora often said that since she first met me I had made an almost complete turn-around in my ability to handle the frustrations growing out of a denial of my personal needs and desires. If I have changed--and I want to believe that I have--most of the credit is hers. She always has been the patient one in our family. It was she who, without judging me, could and would be my mirror and help me to see my own behavior. I always apologized, but that didn't change my behavior. I was caught in a vicious cycle of annoyance, impatience, rudeness, anger, feedback, guilt, apology, forgiveness, etc. I wanted to break the cycle; I wanted to stop behaving in hurting ways every time I was squeezed. (Remember the analogy of the orange?) It took time, but with Lenora's understanding and support, I have achieved a large measure of success in changing that part of my life. I'm not claiming any self-righteous accomplishment but I do feel I have won an important victory. I like myself better the way I am today. When Lenora and our children say that they, too, like me better, the victory is all the sweeter.

Impatience and the negative behaviors which it brings to mind is one vice from which no one is free. We shudder when we see it in others, never imagining that we can be guilty ourselves. But if impatience can be thought of as a vice, its opposite--patience--has all the qualities of a virtue. As a virtue, patience is vastly different from the long-suffering endurance and tight-lipped resignation it is so often taken to be. Patience is also different from the martyr-like acceptance of something or someone not liked or wanted. These are all negative, passive images of patience; they typically flow from feelings of deprivation or lessened needs satisfaction resulting from some situation beyond our control. The patience I have in mind is neither negative nor passive; it is a positive, facilitating quality which enhances all our interpersonal relationships, especially our marriage. Successful marital adjustment is dependent upon the partners' values, attitudes, motivation, and their understanding of the dynamics of the relationship. This adjustment process is never without resistance, problems, and misunderstandings. Differences in age, education, socio-emotional maturity, and personal goals and expectations all complicate it. Still, patience is a necessary condition if the adjustment process is to be successful and mutually satisfying.

True patience has no room for being perturbed, discontented, or resentful, even when it means waiting. It flows from an inner strength that allows us to set aside our personal desires even when we are confident that they are justified, or that our answer or suggested course of action is more appropriate. It has a spiritual-like quality which projects serenity and a sense of acceptance of the fact that even when we set aside our personal desires it is because we choose to do it, not because we have to.

Can I Show a Sense of Humor in our Marriage?

I have known people who would admit to having a temper, drinking too much, or failing to spend adequate time with their family, but I have never met a person who would admit to not having a sense of humor. Is this because a sense of humor supposedly is so easily developed and so commonly found that anyone without a sense of humor is considered abnormal? Or is it because of the semantic confusion that exists about what a sense of humor is? Or, is it because the benefits of having a sense of humor are so widely recognized and appreciated that failing to have a sense of humor shows a disregard for one's overall psychological wellbeing? Let's look at some possible answers to these questions.

The first possibility easily can be dismissed. A sense of humor is an ability, a trait, or a characteristic that, for most people, can be acquired only through hard work and practice. A sense of humor is not something that a person inherits--there is no humor gene-- and not all persons who try to acquire one are successful. For people who do it well, however, it is an art. Admittedly, some individuals seem to instinctively use humor easily and effectively, much like Mozart was able to create immortal music without having piano lessons. A sense of humor for these people is both a cause and a result of their attitudes toward themselves and toward others. Defense-oriented people, for example, seldom see anything funny about themselves. Others, who are more oriented toward relationships, can share and enjoy a good joke on themselves in almost any situation.

The semantic difficulties we encounter in trying to define what we mean by the term "sense of humor" may make it easy for everyone to claim ownership of one. This same confusion also clouds its possible benefits. In the absence of an agreed-upon definition, everyone can claim to have a sense of humor without being disputed. Sometimes, however, what passes for a sense of humor is really an expression of hostility, e.g., when one person tries to be seen as superior by making another appear socially inept or inferior. This is the essence of so-called ethnic jokes. It also is evidenced in jokes about women, politicians, preachers, etc. Similarly, the intended humor of smutty or off-color jokes often represents an immature method of releasing sexual tensions by satisfying one's needs at the expense of another person in a more socially acceptable way. In mature adults, a sense of humor is well defined in terms of its use and its effects upon others. It is more subtle wit than traditional joke-telling, and it is void of any hostility or defense-oriented motivation.

The third suggestion is a more apt explanation of our desire for a sense of humor. It has the weight of both scientific evidence and personal experience to support it. On the scientific side, there is evidence that a good belly laugh has all the benefits of jogging around the block.

Aside from the psychological and physiological benefits claimed for laughter, it is, perhaps, the most effective, yet neglected, means of patching up misunderstandings in interpersonal relationships. It can be used to prevent small misunderstandings from evolving into damaging conflicts; it can be used as an apology when big misunderstandings do occur. A good sense of humor provides an atmosphere that facilitates handling both personal and professional problems.

What does all this mean in a marital relationship? First, laughter provides an antidote or release from the routine of the hum-drum aspects of marriage. Humor is not a substitute, however, for the need to deal with marital problems and concerns when they do arise. Rather, it provides a perspective, a way of looking at problems that does not overly emphasize their negative aspects. It indicates a propensity not to be always concerned with the serious side of life.

Second, most of us prefer being with persons who have a sense of humor. We also find it conducive to good marital relationships. In my pre-marital counseling workshops, I always ask the participants to list the qualities of an ideal marriage partner. With rare exceptions, a good sense of humor ranks near the top, along with honesty and integrity. This means that such qualities as good looks, money, and sexual attractiveness are viewed as being less critical than the good-natured disposition, healthy imagination, and spontaneous liveliness of a partner with a good sense of humor.

A sense of humor lets us laugh at the little things we do and the ones that happen to us; we can laugh with each other at the unexpected, fast-moving events in our lives. Humor can transform the simple and the routine happenings of our lives into occasions of special significance and remembrance.

Before I leave this part, I want to refine our understanding of what humor is by discarding some of the things it is not. It is not simply being always ready with a bag of jokes. People who always are pushing their jokes to center stage without any consideration of other people can cause them to feel that they have been pushed aside. Neither is a sense of humor the same as always having snappy one-liners. A clever retort and a sharp putdown may earn a person a reputation for smartness, but also may make enemies. Without a sense of propriety, people whose characteristic behavior is unbridled joking or storytelling often offends the sensitivities and feelings of others. Just as there are occasions when humor is beneficial, there are other times when it is inappropriate and counter-productive. Socially mature people are able to make this distinction.

A sense of humor that is mindful of and responsive to the demands of a helping relationship in marriage is reflected in both our view of ourselves and our feelings toward our partner. It is more a way of looking at a particular situation than a set of rules to be blindly followed in all situations. People who remain objective enough to be an observer of their own behavior are less likely to be controlled by it. As a positive emotion, a good sense of humor can create and nurture an effective helping relationship in marriage.

Can I be Responsive to without Feeling Responsible for my Partner?

Being in a helping relationship to Lenora means being aware of and responsive to her presence and behavior and her needs and desires; it does not mean feeling responsible for her. It involves making judgments, but it does not mean being judgmental. Nor does it involve any desire or effort to convert her into someone more to my liking. Helping, to be effective, must be unconditional, with no strings attached. Yet, the line between being responsive to without feeling responsible for is often very thin. Even when we do not intend it, even when we guard against it, our desire to help can cause us unwittingly to step over the line. Helping presents us a paradox, because the easiest way to avoid stepping over the line separating responsiveness and responsibility is to be less responsive or helpful than we otherwise would be if that danger were not present.

Have you ever noticed how some things that are very different always go together, e.g., peaches and cream? That's the way it is with stimulus and response. We can be subjected to various stimuli without our being aware of it. That is, there can be a stimulus without a response but there cannot be a response without a stimulus. For every response there is either an internal or an external, conscious or unconscious stimulus. We eat (response) when

Making Marriage User Friendly

we are hungry (stimulus). In a like manner we shudder when we hear a shrill noise. And because our partner is a stimulus to us we respond in helping ways to them. If we want to be effective in responding to our partner, we first must accept and be sensitive to them as persons who have meaning and value in their own right. But we can't have the kind of relationship I have in mind with everyone. We have neither the time nor the energy required. I used to think that because I valued and enjoyed this kind of relationship, I would seek more of them--if one was good, two would be better. But I found it consumed too much of me, both intellectually and emotionally. Now, I accept the fact that I can have this kind of relationship with only one or two people at the most. Because our marriage relationship is central in our lives it must come before all others.

What does it mean to accept our partner as a stimulus? It means that when they come into our presence, we acknowledge them. When they speak, we respond appropriately. When they are worried, we comfort them. When they are angry, we offer understanding. When they feel sad or lonely, we offer consolation.

In all aspects of our relationship, we must be supportive, patient, and appreciative. We listen when it is desired, and we speak when it is appropriate. However, helping isn't all sweetness and light--it can and should include confrontation when it is necessary. But, you might argue, "Doing all these things is simply being polite and considerate. I try to do that for everybody. What makes it so special when I do it for my partner?" It is special because the person to whom you are responding is special. Your understanding of your partner orients your response, making it more intimate and more purposive. Being polite to others is often nothing more than conformity to external societal standards and expectations. But when we respond to our partner in terms of a helping relationship, we are responding because of our feelings of love. We respond because we want to. The love, understanding, and honesty we invest in our marriage relationship is seldom required or experienced in any other relationship.

What happens when we step over the line? What are the possible consequences of our feeling responsible, being judgmental, and using persuasive, suggestive language to change or convert our partner? What happens to a helping relationship when we stop making it easier for our partner to do things and instead start doing things for them?

One major negative consequence of stepping over the line is the fact that we become over involved and protective, compromising our objectivity and our ability to help. Ironically, it is when we become over-involved that we become less able to recognize it. And when our involvement becomes overly emotional--as it usually does-- our judgment is impaired, with the result that our efforts to help often do more harm than good. It leaves our partner confused about their adequacy to function as a responsible, contributing marriage partner. As they question their ability to contribute to the relationship, they become more dependent. The message they receive is, "I can't make it by myself, I need your help."

Our understanding of what can happen in these situations can be helped by borrowing an idea from Dr. Eric Berne's book, *The Games People Play*. According to Dr. Berne, we have available three different patterns of relating to others. These are as a child, as an adult, and as a parent. We acquire the scripts for these patterned behaviors during our childhood and later life experiences. Our choice of a particular pattern in relating to our partner is dependent upon our perceptions of them and the relationship between us. Marriage always should be an adult-to-adult relationship. When we (in an adult role) relate to our partner (as an adult) we are, in essence, confirming them as our intellectual and social equal. It is our way of saying, "I'm O.K.; you're O.K." But when we start feeling responsible, our relationship to our partner takes on the characteristics of a parent relating to a child. Our message is, "I'm O.K.; you're not O.K." When this happens, spousal love (adult to adult) is replaced by familial love (parent to child). This crossed pattern of relating easily can harm our sexual relationship as we unconsciously observe the taboo against sex with children. While I theoretically can discuss the differences between behaving responsively and responsibly, in real life it often is difficult to determine where one stops and the other begins. It is hoped that by helping you to become more aware of their differences, it will be easier for you to avoid crossing the line.

Chapter Four

Readiness to Help: Eliminating the Negatives

Near the end of a group session in marital problem solving, I asked the members, "Suppose you were able to measure the overall quality of your marriage on a scale from zero to ten. Where would your marriage fall on the scale?" I then asked the group members to come to our next meeting ready to share with the group their estimate of the overall quality or level of satisfaction of their marriage. To encourage some discussion of the assignment at home, I asked each couple to agree to a single estimate--a consensus answer--between the two of them. I then told them that I would have additional instructions when we met again.

Marriage on a Scale of Zero to Ten

We often begin a question with the phrase, "On a scale of zero to ten..." to find out how strongly someone feels about a particular matter. We assume that the strength of the feeling about which we're asking actually can fall somewhere on the scale. A ten means that the feeling is very strong, that there is no room for compromise or change. A zero, on the other hand, indicates a total absence of feelings about the matter. Why people feel as they do about the matter is another question. At the next meeting, the members wanted to discuss some of the possible meanings of the word "quality." I had not anticipated their concern in this area, and several minutes of discussion was required to reach a definition of quality that all the partners could accept. One couple then requested a few minutes alone so they could arrive at a new consensual estimate of the quality of their marriage in terms of our accepted definition of the word. All the couples took advantage of the break. When we came back to the meeting room, each couple was ready to share with the group.

Gary and Paulette, the oldest partners in the group, agreed that the quality of their marriage was at the six level. Someone asked why they had chosen six instead of two, or eight. As they responded to this question it was apparent that they had given the matter a lot of consideration. They talked about their love for each other, their ability to communicate, sexual compatibility, etc. Then, almost apologetically, Paulette said, "The level would be a lot higher if we didn't have some troublesome problems we haven't been able to solve." The way Gary and Paulette explained it, their love and the other positive aspects of their marriage pushed the quality level up to six, but these positive aspects were not strong enough to push it higher. These aspects of their marriage can be described as driving forces because they push the quality level along the continuum away from zero toward ten.

If these driving forces operated in a vacuum, where there was nothing but driving forces, the quality level would be at ten. Unfortunately, marriage is not like that. In every marriage, even the best marriages, there are certain forces which prevent it from being as good as it might otherwise be. Gary and Paulette alluded to these forces in their marriage when Paulette talked about their unsolved problems. These forces can be called restraining forces since they block the quality level from moving toward ten. Some typical restraining forces might be finances, in-law relationships, questions about child rearing, etc.

Gary's and Paulette's quality estimate of a six represented an equilibrium state between the two sets of opposing forces in their marriage. That is, the quality level is at the point on the scale where the strength of the driving forces in their marriage is matched by the strength of the restraining forces. Improvement in the quality of their marriage can be made only by altering the relationship between the two sets of forces. Three different approaches can be used in trying to improve their marriage.

One way, perhaps the one most widely used, is to approach the problem from the driving-force side. On this side we look for new forces which can be added, i.e., things Gary and Paulette could do to improve the quality of their marriage that have not been done before or are not being done now. Another possibility is to search for ways the present driving forces can be strengthened. We have a sort of unquestioning faith in this approach. The football coach yells, "Hit 'em again, harder." The factory foreman demands, "Let's all put our shoulders to the wheel and make it work." And partners conclude, "We've got to try harder to make our marriage work." Use of this approach generates hope in the minds of people; it creates an air of expectation. As well-intentioned and encouraging as these efforts might seem, they don't always succeed. Unfortunately, when increased efforts are made to improve the quality of a marriage without weakening or removing the restraining forces, a lot of unintended and unanticipated stress can be introduced into the marriage. This stress causes the partners to lose faith in their efforts and to question the worth of what they are doing. At best, the positive change is going to be minimal, considering the amount of time, effort, etc., that is typically spent in making the improvement. To make improvement using this approach the restraining forces have to be overcome or pushed back, and they can be pushed back only so far before a new equilibrium is reached.

A second approach to improving the quality of marriage is to weaken or possibly remove the restraining forces. When partners have limited time, energy, or other resources to devote to the improvement effort, it is far more beneficial to use this approach. When these restraining forces are removed or weakened, the driving forces in the marriage naturally push the quality level upward to fill the vacuum created by the removal or weakening of the restraining forces.

A third approach--the one that I recommend--is to attack the problem from both sides simultaneously. As a couple works to strengthen the already existing driving forces and to add new ones, they also work to remove or weaken the restraining forces. This approach is complementary. It involves the partners in a total look at all the forces affecting the quality of their marriage. Use of this approach can produce quicker results with less effort, motivating partners to seek even more improvement.

Some Restraining Forces in Marriage

"Love is patient and kind; love is not jealous or boastful; it is not arrogant or rude. Love does not insist on its own way; it is not irritable or resentful; it does not rejoice at wrong, but rejoices in the right." (*Holy Bible*, 1 Cor. 13:4-6) If our love for our partner was like the love described by the Apostle Paul, there would be no restraining forces in our marriage.

Without restraining forces, the quality of our marriage would ascend unimpeded to the top of the quality scale.

Remember how God permitted Moses to look across the Jordan River at the Promised Land but forbade him to cross the river? Did the Apostle Paul describe for us a "Promised Land" of marital love that we are unable to actually achieve? I think not. Just as Paul was able to declare in Philippians 4:13, "I can do all things in Him (God) who strengthens me," I strongly believe that if we want to love the way Paul described, we can. Most of these negative, restraining forces are under our control--we can do something about them.

Let's think about these restraining forces from a different perspective. Because I behave in negative, damaging ways, my marriage is hurting. I don't want my marriage to hurt. I can stop the hurting because these negative behaviors are under my control. I can stop behaving in negative, damaging ways.

I have chosen to discuss eight restraining forces that have the greatest potential for hurting a marriage. They are potent forces, and their effect is immediate and far-reaching. There are many other restraining forces which might also seem appropriate for discussion, but the eight forces I have selected are basic--they tend to be the root cause of other restraining forces which sometimes do get a lot more attention. Also, these eight forces are made up of ways of thinking, feeling, and behaving which are under our control; we can remove or weaken these restraining forces if we want. In choosing to think of these particular forces as restraining forces, I recognize that the opposite side of the coin for each of them is a driving force. But the same force cannot be on both sides, i.e., it cannot be both a driving force and a restraining force. By labeling them as I have, I have chosen to discuss them in terms of their ability to cause us marital pain. When there is an absence of pain or distress in our marriage, we tend to be satisfied with it. In terms of a medical model, our marriage is healthy when there is no pain. But when there is pain and distress we are compelled to take remedial action. Let's now look at some of these restraining forces, what we can call ailments or sources of pain.

Judgmental, Punitive, and Rejecting Attitudes

Why, when we have an opportunity to help our partner feel accepted, adequate, and loved, do we instead become critical, hostile, and punishing? Some of the greatest harm we can do to our marriage is behaving in ways that raise doubts in the mind of our partner about their self-worth, their dignity, and their need to experience approval, acceptance, and love from us.

We tend to judge and criticize rather than understand and help. We display these negative attitudes toward our partner because we sometimes are too proud to admit that we have made a mistake. Even when we know that our mistake is known to our partner, we find it hard to apologize. To protect our image of ourselves, we attempt to place the blame for our behavior (mistake) on our partner. We find it difficult to accept that we behaved in unloving ways and punished our partner and that they still accept us and love us. As one client said of her marriage, "I didn't marry him because he was perfect, but because of his promise of love." Because we behave in ways contrary to our promise of love, we experience feelings of guilt and attack anyone who has knowledge of our failure. It is simply easier (not better) to do what makes us feel more comfortable than to do what is best for our marriage. Then we try to rationalize our behavior by claiming, "I was provoked; you made me do it. It wasn't something that I ordinarily would do."

Without attitudinal change, people who have behaved in punitive, judgmental, and rejecting ways in the past usually continue to behave in these ways. Their behavior is a reflection of their needs, their attitudes, and their values. They tend to view their world in black or white terms--there is no middle ground, no shades of gray. Other people are seen as being worthy or unworthy of their help. Thus, it often happens that in a marital crisis they reject or punish their partner at the very moment their help is needed most.

One of the facts of everyday living that we have the greatest difficulty accepting is human variability. This difficulty is especially great in marriage. Our ideas of oneness and mutuality of interests gained through the process of courtship and post-marital adjustment often blind us to our unwillingness to let our partner have a separate identity--an identity different and apart from ours. We tend to feel that our way is the "right" way--not only for us as an individual, but also for our partner. Hence, when they think, feel, or behave differently than we do, we are threatened. In an attempt to satisfy our need to be in control, we unconsciously attack our partner. We employ every tactic in our arsenal of punitive behavior--guilt, shame, threats, and criticism--to force them into thinking, feeling, and behaving in ways which conform to our expectations. For the most part, we engage in this behavior unconsciously. It happens, first of all, because our tone of voice, our gestures, and our mannerisms reveal more than our actual words and deeds about whether we are being judgmental, punishing, and rejecting. The tone of voice plus our acting out behavior give our words most of their meaning.

Lenora and I had a delightful pet--a miniature Pekingese dog named Miss Muffi. I could say loving words in a harsh threatening voice and she would show fear. She would lie on the floor in a way that signified hurt, rejection, and not being loved. Yet, I could say unloving words to her in a kind, soft voice and her tail would wag, her eyes would brighten, and she would move toward me for an affectionate touch. Let's learn from our pets. We respond not only to words *per se*, but to the total meaning of words, the speaker's tone of voice, their facial and hand gestures, as well as the social context in which the words are spoken.

Another consequence of our lack of awareness of the effect of our behavior on our partner is that while they are free to interpret our words and behavior in terms of their needs and expectations, we blind ourselves to how they actually perceive us. Whatever our intentions, if our words and behavior are perceived as being punitive, judgmental, and rejecting, the damage has been done. This realization points out the difference between a punitive attitude and a punishing act. A punishing attitude is, first of all, totally incompatible with our helping intentions. When our goal is to be loving and helping, punitive acts violate our relationship. The only way I know to determine whether we accurately and adequately have communicated our intentions to our partner is through the use of feedback. This technique will be discussed in Chapter Six.

How can we respond to our discovery that we do sometimes show punishing, judgmental, and rejecting attitudes? A full response to this question will be presented in Chapter Seven, but for the moment let me leave you with these thoughts. When we are open to feedback from our partner, we can discover the actual effect of our behavior. Then we can ask, "Is this the way I want to affect my partner?" If we learn from their feedback that the effect of our behavior is what we intended, we are encouraged to repeat that behavior. It is reinforced by our partner's feedback. But if the answer to our question is no, then it is necessary to say, "What I did to you is exactly the opposite of what I wanted to do. Help me to deal with these behaviors which hurt you and our marriage."

Defensiveness

"Doug promised he would come with me. But as you can see, he didn't. I hope you will see me alone."

Laura Kay was explaining her husband's failure to come with her for their first appointment with me. She had shared a few of her concerns when she called for the appointment, but I told her that I would need to meet with both of them together. I met with her that session but explained that if we were to work on her marital concerns, we would have to find a way to get Doug to join her. When she left she assured me that she somehow would find a way to get him to come. She called the day before her next appointment to tell me that Doug reluctantly had agreed to come with her. Following is an edited verbatim of what happened in the early part of that next meeting.

T: "Doug, I appreciate your coming today. Laura Kay wants to resolve some concerns she has about her marriage and we need your help."

Doug: "What's bothering her now?"

T: "Let's let Laura Kay tell us."

LK: "Doug, there are a lot of things that I want to talk over with you, but the thing we have to get some quick help with is our relationship. I know it's important to you and it's important to me. So, why can't we talk about it? It's blocking our efforts to look at other problems we have."

Doug: "I've told you a million times that I don't have a problem with our sex life. If there's a problem, it's yours."

T: "Doug, you seem rather adamant on that point. Would you explain?"

Doug: "Before we married I slept around a lot. She (pointing toward Laura Kay) knows all about it. There has been one time since we married. She knows about that one, too. But Laura Kay is the only one who has ever complained about my love making."

T: (I looked toward Laura Kay. She appeared to be angry. I waited for her reaction to Doug's remark.)

LK: "Well, you may think you're hot stuff but I can tell exactly when you turn the page in our marriage manual."

Doug (Now showing anger himself.): "Well, if you feel that way why haven't you said something about it?"

LK: "Me? Tell the great Don Juan--God's gift to women--that he is a lousy lover? You're kidding."

T: (As you can easily imagine, the fences were down; what Laura Kay called the big issue was on the table. And we had a lot to talk about.)

Laura Kay and Doug continued in therapy for over a year--first with weekly visits, then monthly. There was a lot of discovery, a lot of unlearning, and a lot of new learning and adjustment. The outcome was a happy one.

It is a peculiar human characteristic that people like Doug resist any challenge or threat to their self-concept. Included in a person's self-concept are the feelings and beliefs they hold about what kind of person they are. Another word that is often used for self-concept is the term self-image, which suggests the idea of a picture of the self. I prefer the term self-concept because it includes not only feelings and beliefs that might consciously be held, but also those feelings of which an individual might not be aware. Even though an individual might not be conscious of certain characteristics of their self-concept, they can and do reveal themselves in the person's behavior. It is our unconscious feelings and beliefs that cause the greatest difficulties in interpersonal relationships.

Ask someone to describe the kind of person they are and they might reply, "I have a positive outlook on life and don't let the small stuff upset me. I try to be honest and get along with everybody. I consider myself a successful person." This description is very complimentary; it is also introspective and seemingly honest. However, it describes only that part of their self-concept of which that person is aware. Is there another part of which the person is not aware--a part that might cause them to feel embarrassed or unworthy? For most people the answer is yes. Although one of the most enduring characteristics of a person's self-concept is its consistency over time, self-concept is not a static thing--it is always changing as people respond to both their internal needs and to changes in their external environment.

The feelings and beliefs which comprise a person's sense of worth are acquired from many different sources. Some are the result of self-examination or introspection; others come from opinions and feedback shared by family members, teachers, etc. Whatever feelings and beliefs people may hold about themselves, there is always a need to behave in ways that are consistent with their self-concept. People who view themselves as being socially and technically competent respond to problems differently than people who have feelings of inadequacy and question their competence to solve problems. The behavior of confident people tends to be more task oriented; the behavior of people who lack confidence as a result of a negative self-concept tends to be more defense-oriented. Defense-oriented people are more concerned with protecting themselves from embarrassment, blame, or rejection. To protect themselves, they behave in ways designed to divert others' attention away from their felt inadequacies. Blaming their inability to solve problems on circumstances beyond their control is a likely defense. Whatever their behavior, they are more interested in protecting their self-concept than in learning how to solve problems.

People who constantly need to defend their self-concept are like the aging matron who wears clothing appropriate for teenagers, in spite of her girth. Her girdle may be so tight that she becomes exhausted getting it on, but she will not admit that her clothing does not fit. With her well-mobilized defensive behavior, there exists a wide gap between the person she really is and the person she believes she is.

The various behaviors people use to protect their self-concept are referenced by the general term, defense mechanisms. By this term, I mean a behavior which we use to defend and, at times, to enhance our self-concept. Defense mechanisms have two characteristics worth noting. First, they are called defense mechanisms because that is exactly their purpose. Whenever the self-concept is threatened, not with physical injury, but with the possibility of being made to appear less admirable, less worthy, or less successful than we believe ourselves to be, then our defense mechanisms act to protect us. Like a machine, they operate in fixed and predictable ways. In the second place, defense mechanisms are used unconsciously--they are not willed. One does not decide, "I will now use a defense mechanism to protect my self-concept." They kick in automatically and we may or may not be aware of using them. Indeed, when we are confronted with an accusation of having behaved defensively, we often respond with more defensive behavior since it is embarrassing to be caught using defensive behavior.

Let's take a brief look at some defense mechanisms I often observed being used by married partners.

Rationalization

Substituting a socially acceptable reason or explanation for our behavior instead of the real one is the essence of this behavior. We consider ourselves to be honest but are caught with our hand in the cookie jar. What do we say? Often our response will be as transparent as, "I was just returning a cookie I found on the table." Our response is not a conscious lie; we actually believe our explanation is true and that it will adequately explain what we were doing. Our partner will begin to suspect that we are rationalizing when our behavior can be explained by other motives, or when the rationalization is blatantly transparent. Rationalization is triggered when our real motive violates our self-concept. Thus our real motive is replaced with a cover motive which makes it possible for us to maintain our self-concept.

Reaction-Formation

We may protect ourselves against unwelcome, threatening thoughts, feelings, and wishes by repressing them and, when repression doesn't work, by compulsively striving to feel and behave in opposite ways. A wife with unresolved, hostile feelings toward her traveling husband may say upon his return, "I always worry about you. I can't eat or sleep properly, imagining all the horrible things that could be happening to you." Reaction-formation reveals itself through compulsive and exaggerated behavior designed to convince others that the actor's real motives are socially acceptable. Unfortunately, the repressed motives and feelings have a tendency to leak out in unguarded moments.

Other defense mechanisms that easily can be recognized in marital relationships (in all relationships, in fact) are: (1) denial - our unwillingness to face the reality of the effect of our behavior upon another by refusing to recognize that there is a problem; (2) projection - accusing others of doing things or having feelings which we find unacceptable in our self-concept; and (3) scapegoating - blaming other innocent, defenseless people or circumstances for our alleged shortcomings. Whatever kind of behavior is involved, the role of all defense mechanisms is to serve as an emotional anesthetic or quick cure for anxiety. They dull the psychological pain that is being felt, but they seldom, if ever, contribute to solving the problem that was the stimulus for the anxiety.

Before I discuss how defensive behavior can impede our ability to relate to our partner in helping ways, I want to offer some additional notes of explanation about defense mechanisms. First, some use of defensive behavior can be observed in everyone. It can, in fact, be a valuable safety valve for helping us to maintain our self-confidence in ego-threatening situations. When used in moderation they can play a positive role in helping us to cope with the problems of living in social relationship with others. They are crutches, though, and like physical crutches, they should not be used when we can function without them. Over dependence on them mitigates against psychological growth and development. Defending our self-concept through use of defense mechanisms has the effect of keeping it constant. If the self-concept becomes fixated, it follows that our patterns of relating also will become less flexible, making adjustment and growth in marriage difficult, if not impossible. Secondly, people who make excessive, frequent use of defensive behavior most likely have deep underlying doubts about their self-worth. They tend to experience a compounding effect as they use one defensive behavior after another. Further, not all of their attempts to defend themselves will be successful. Some defensive behavior can be so elaborate and complex that it is actually counterproductive to the goal of psychological defense. Finally, certain behaviors can be used so frequently or in such exaggerated form that they become transparent as to their motive or purpose. The situation is even more complicated by the fact that defensive behavior fails simply because it does succeed. It is a failure of success.

What is the explanation for such a paradoxical statement? Rightly or wrongly, defensive behavior is able to reduce anxiety and preserve an individual's image over the short run; it may even provide a sense of accomplishment and satisfaction. But, in the long run, the vulnerability of the person to recurring anxiety and to further loss of image actually is increased. A person who continues to use defensive behavior as a means of escaping reality, will eventually lose contact with reality. It is a dangerous cycle that leads to reduced interpersonal effectiveness in its beginning stages; it can lead to marital breakdown if continued too long because of the loss of trust it generates.

How does this happen? People who are overly concerned with protecting their self-concept have little energy for or interest in being concerned about others. Use of defensive behavior is a case of buying psychological protection at a very high price. Initially, it is used to keep others out; eventually, it becomes a jail, making the user a prisoner.

In a psychologically unhealthy marriage, a lack of trust and acceptance can contribute to the need for defensive behavior. When defensive behavior is observed, attempts to bring it to the attention of the defensive partner are likely to induce further anger, guilt, anxiety, and other non-productive reactions. Use of defense mechanisms is an unhealthy response to threats because they prevent us from coming to grips with the cause or source of the threat. That unhealthy situation remains as a restraining force, keeping our marriage from maturing and becoming the psychologically healthy marriage it could be. The value of knowing about defense mechanisms is that such knowledge alerts us to their possible use and the resulting negative effects they can have on our marriage.

Unrealistic Expectations

"I've tried so hard to please Jenny, but everything I do comes up short. I don't make enough money, I don't socialize at parties, I don't even make love the way she wants me to."

Harry, a twenty-eight-year-old insurance adjuster, was venting his frustrations and disappointments in a private therapy session. "I'll never make enough money to belong to the country club; I'm not even sure I would want to. Why can't Jenny be satisfied? Why does she always have to compare me to the men she meets at the ad agency? You know, the thing that irritates me most of all is the sexual thing. Where does she get all those weird ideas? I sometimes suspect that she learns them at the office. I'd like to know but I'm afraid to ask."

"Mother was opposed to my marrying Harry. I don't want to admit it to her, but I can now see that she was right." It was a week later, and Jenny was having her individual session. "Even before Harry and I married, I could see what Mother was talking about, but I was confident I could change him. He was always trying to please me so I was sure that I could make him see things my way. Mother was right; I was wrong. God knows I've tried."

Jenny was unhappy in her marriage to Harry and had resurrected a long list of his shortcomings to justify her unhappiness. But what she saw as his shortcomings were often subjects of praise by others. As a little league coach, Harry was well liked by all the neighborhood children and their parents. As a neighbor, Harry had a reputation of doing anything for anybody, anytime. This reputation followed him to his Kiwanis Club, and to the small church he attended with their two children, often without Jenny. "Good old Harry" was a description often made of him--one that infuriated Jenny.

Jenny also tended to view everything that Harry did as good or bad, right or wrong. Because of her tendency to judge Harry, she confused giving advice with giving help. In response to the pressure Jenny was always putting on him, Harry decided that his best defense was to ignore her. For Jenny it became more a question of whether she should even try to help him than a question of how she could help.

Not only did Jenny show a lot of punitive behavior toward Harry, she also demonstrated a punitive attitude. She had given up on what she called, "Helping Harry drop his country ways," and now saw him as being undeserving of her help. She had always punished him for bad behavior and rewarded him for good behavior, now she was feeling that punishment would do more good than encouragement since it was more direct. But when Harry no longer feared her punishments or sought her rewards, she could no longer use these behaviors in her efforts to change him.

Jenny's persistence in changing Harry "for his own good" left him feeling rejected and alienated from her. He never questioned her sincerity but he did question her motive. He also resented her rationalization of her behavior whenever she would say, "But I was only doing what I thought was best for you." He emphasized that he had never asked for her help and, as far as he was concerned, she was talking to a stone wall.

To make matters worse for Jenny, her judgmental, punishing behaviors were revealed more by the tone of her voice and her facial expressions than by her actual words and deeds. What she was doing and how it was interpreted by Harry were largely unknown to her. When Harry failed to respond as she wanted him to, she considered her efforts a failure. Had she been more honest with herself as to her motives and to Harry's feelings, she could have been open to the feedback from Harry and used this information to change the way she related to him.

Dependency

Newborn infants are the most helpless of all living creatures. For sheer survival, infants need other people. Someone, usually parents, must provide them food and nurturing care in a physical and social environment that is compatible to their needs. As infants age and mature both physically and socially, gradually acquiring adaptive skills, they enter into a period of counter-dependency. In this stage there is a strong desire to rebel against the persons they have been dependent upon. This can be a difficult and sometimes conflicted time for both children and the people around them.

Gradually, children mature to the point of independence. This stage usually begins when they move away from their parent's home and become self-supporting, making decisions for themselves. Unfortunately, we have over-glamorized this state of being. Even the most independent people still need other people. Most of the satisfactions which make life worthwhile can be gratified only in relation to or with other people. Although healthy personality begins in the infancy period, characterized by almost complete dependency, it continues into adolescence and young adulthood with gradual acquisition of a more independent posture. The path of normal personality development, however, does not end with independence. The epitome of a healthy personality is not independence, but interdependency. There is no way we can ever acquire the skills and the means to satisfy all our needs and gratify all our wants.

Still, there is conflict in all of us between our desire to be independent and the necessity to be dependent upon others--to put ourselves in the hands of others for the satisfaction of our needs beyond our own resources. Everyone, at times, needs the help of others. At these times, dependency is both useful and legitimate. It becomes crippling, however, when we no longer seek to develop our own resources and to accept our dependency as the basis for all relationships. Ultimately, it destroys rather than builds relationships, and it cripples rather than builds people. The way each of us resolves this conflict will determine, to a large degree, how effectively we play our roles not only in marriage but also in life in general.

There are two dimensions or aspects of being dependent: the functional and the emotional. We are functionally dependent when we require or use the help of another person. For example, we are dependent upon our partner for satisfying various needs that we can't on our own satisfy. The fact that we are dependent upon them to satisfy our functional needs has both symbolic and emotional significance since the emotional aspect of dependency cannot be separated from the functional aspect. Most of the time, however, we take the functional relationship for granted, without recognizing its emotional importance to us. If our partner should, for some reason, not satisfy or threaten not to satisfy our functional needs, we would quickly feel a sense of lost status, a feeling of being rejected, a feeling of insecurity in our marriage.

Emotionally mature people--people who have moved from complete dependency as infants to interdependency as adults--accept the reality of their functional and emotional dependency on their partner as something that is natural, inescapable, and, hopefully, enriching. While our dependency as a child is a matter of necessity, the dependency we have on our partner in marriage is by choice. If our dependency needs are exaggerated, however, or if we become ashamed or afraid of even normal and unavoidable dependency relationships, then our dependency needs are unhealthy. On the other hand, when we accept marriage as an interdependent relationship, when we can accept our normal needs for a love relationship without feeling inferior, inadequate, or guilty, we have made real progress toward emotional maturity and removal of a restraining force that impedes a more growth-oriented and rewarding marriage.

Jealously

Bea, a forty-two-year-old mother of two college-age daughters, knows what it's like to live with a jealous husband.

Roger, her husband, is a forty-four-year-old industrial draftsman. He is jealous of anyone and anything that gets a share of Bea's attention: her job, her women friends, a book she is reading, anything. Three or four times each day he calls her at work. If she happens to be away from the phone when he calls, he inquires about her whereabouts when he next calls. He expects her to come directly home from work, and delays have to be explained. If she shops for food Roger wants to know if the bag-boy tried to talk to her. After her periodic visits to a male gynecologist Roger wants to know if anything "funny" happened. All this Roger does "Because I love her."

"I thought that after the kids grew up I could go back to my old job and sort of have a life of my own again. One thing I didn't count on was Roger's insane jealousy. He wasn't always this way; I don't know what has come over him. He seems to think he has a right to all my time and gets mad and sulks for days if he doesn't get it. As I said, he wasn't this way when we married. Why is he so suspicious of everything I do now? One thing I know is that something has to change."

Jealousy is a green-eyed monster that brings out the worst in us. It is an emotion that everybody experiences to some degree, but to which nobody likes to admit. Indeed, people don't like to admit it even to themselves. It smacks of deep-rooted dependencies and psychological insecurities, and the more dependent and insecure a person is, the more jealous they will be. Like a destructive cancer, jealousy breeds jealousy. It cannot be, as Roger argues, evidence of love, but evidence of insecurities and dependency. A jealous husband like Roger does not necessarily love his wife more than a non-jealous husband.

Jealousy is not a gentle emotion--the kind associated with love. It expresses itself in aggressive, sometimes violent ways. Although jealousy is focused on a love object (marriage partner), it is not justified by love of that object. The ugly side of jealousy is its goal of possessing the love object and removing all rivals. A jealous husband may truly love his wife but feelings of jealousy usually stem from feeling vulnerable in the relationship. Although it results from a fear of loss of love, paradoxically it can destroy the love it seeks to possess. It is detrimental to and a denial of the loved one's personal identity.

Theories about jealousy--what it is and what causes it--are as varied as there are writers on the subject. It has been variously defined as a cry of pain, a fear of loss, and the shadow of love. Almost certainly, it is not a single emotion but a mixture or composite of many different emotions. Definitions of jealousy typically include references to anger, anxiety, hatred, humiliation, shame, sorrow, and suspicion. Like love, jealousy can be whatever a person chooses to label it.

One distinction that must be made, however, is the difference between jealousy and envy. While both envy and jealousy are expressions of possessiveness, there are important differences. Envy is the feeling we have when we covet but have no right to what someone else has. Jealousy, on the other hand, is distinguished by our fear of losing something that we already have. To state this difference more succinctly, jealousy is a response to the fear of losing something we already possess or have a right to; envy develops when we desire something we don't have but would like to have. Roger, for example, may envy another man whose wife showers him with attention and is otherwise mindful of and responsive to him. He would experience jealousy if Bea showed similar attention to another man. He would be jealous because he feels that this attention belongs to him. Jealousy entails a threat to a person's self-esteem as well as to a valued relationship. The effect of jealousy upon the marriage relationship is the same, whether the threat is real or imaginary.

The experience of jealousy varies from person to person and within the same person from time to time. In spite of this variation, most flashes of jealousy come from the feeling of being ignored or being left out of some activity involving one's partner and other persons. Your boss wants to dance with your wife; a stranger learns your wife grows orchids and spends an hour in conversation with her. Such experiences trigger the jealous flash, but typically do not fan it into a flame. Feelings of jealousy usually subside after the event that caused it is over and the matter has been resolved.

If the jealous feelings we experience result from sharing our partner in ways normally considered appropriate among our circle of friends, what we feel may be a symptom of an underlying insecurity, a more serious type of jealousy. If we cannot tolerate letting our partner out of our sight or talk to another person, our jealousy perhaps is rooted in a persistent and recurring fear rather than in an isolated, temporary situation. This is more serious, but it need not be fatal to our self-esteem or to our marriage.

The more serious or painful form of jealousy is the fear of loss of our partner and the love, affection, and support they provide. This fear and the resulting jealousy can be terrifying and, not surprisingly, can cause us to become anxious and defensive. Believing that if we lose our partner, it will be to a particular person, we will tend to view that person with suspicion and distrust. Such behavior makes us less attractive, not only to our partner but also to others. Thus, our jealousy causes the very behavior (aloofness, for example) we expected from the other person and thereby deepens the basic fear of loss that leads to increased jealousy.

The process by which we learn to be jealous, how we express it, and how we react to it in others is life long and continuous. From infancy to adulthood, each of us learned about jealousy from what we heard and saw in others and from our own experiences. Most of this learning was unplanned, unstructured, and quite subtle. Most of it involved our relationships with our parents and our brothers and sisters. But if jealousy is learned, it can be unlearned, especially the more inflexible, harmful type.

The steps we can take to manage our jealousy depend upon the type of jealousy we usually experience and the events that typically cause it. To understand our jealousy is to know ourselves, and we cannot know ourselves apart from letting others know us. This, in turn, requires us to share with our partner how we feel when they behave a particular way, being careful to avoid saying, "When you do thus and so, you make me feel jealous." We must always take responsibility for our own feelings and with this responsibility comes the understanding that we can control our feelings. Honesty, openness, and trust are necessary ingredients in any effort to resist or control the feelings of jealousy.

Fear of Change

Change is not a neutral word; it produces emotional reactions in all of us. To many people, it is threatening, conjuring up visions of a loss of status or security, separation from a loved one, or having to adjust to a different life style. For other people, change is a welcome transition from a bad situation to a more favorable one, e.g., more leisure, improved health, or a new job. In marriage, the threat of change can produce reactions of insecurity, doubts about the relationship, and possible embarrassment that some aspect of the marriage has been unsatisfactory from the beginning. But for partners who welcome change, it can mean having children, spending more time together, and achieving a higher level of intimacy and love.

The case of Gerald and Letta, which was discussed in chapter one, illustrates the conflicts a marriage can face when the partners hold divergent views about the possible consequences of change. Gerald was frightened by the many changes which were affecting him, producing a situation that he could neither understand nor control. He resisted Letta's challenges to his traditional role as head of the family and the unquestioned authority he expected to go with that role. Letta, on the other hand, saw change as a way out of a life style she no longer found rewarding. She saw change not only as inevitable but as desirable and rewarding when it was understood and managed. She was motivated by higher-level needs (self-actualization); Gerald was controlled by his inordinately strong and persistent needs for safety, continuity, and stability.

Change has been described as something on which we always can count, as with death and taxes. In a sense, change is more pervasive than either death or taxes since negative changes in one's health lead inevitably to death. Death, in turn, leads to other far-reaching changes. And changes in our financial situation, for example, determine the impact of taxes upon us. Some change is voluntary; some is involuntary. Some change is planned; most of it is natural and random--unplanned. Some change is rapid and hardly noticeable, even while it is taking place; other change is slow and foreseeable. In either form, change is a relentless process that destroys some marriages but opens doors to growth and happiness for others.

As individuals, in or out of marriage, we are always changing. If you want evidence of this constant change process retrieve your high school yearbook from the attic and turn to that page you have perhaps been avoiding. Yes, it's you. "My, how I've changed," you silently say. The change to which you are reacting is of the unplanned type--it just happened. Growing older--a continuous process of change--also produces other related changes which contribute to a natural chronology of major family life events. Getting married, having children, acquiring a larger house, children leaving for college or marriage, retirement from work, and death of a family member are instances of change we all face. Because these changes are part of a predictable sequence of events, we are more conditioned to accept them. Ironically, there is a tendency to think of a marriage as being dysfunctional if some of these change events are not experienced.

Another type of change is planned: change which is conscious, deliberate, and desired. Planned change is made in a marriage because the partners decide that it is good for them. While unplanned change is often seen as a threat to the stability and continuity of a marriage, planned change can be undertaken to remove some obstacle or difficulty that threatens the marriage. Planned change also is undertaken to adjust to new demands that confront the marriage or to provide opportunities for growth and increased marital satisfaction.

All change, because it is concerned with the future and, therefore, is unpredictable as to its outcome, involves some risk; there is always the possibility of failure. New ways of behaving also upset the order and routine of a marriage. When Joan, who has always been passive becomes assertive, she faces a risk. When Tom, who is habitually a workaholic, becomes interested in relaxing and spending time with the family, he faces a risk. When one partner's behavior starts changing and becomes unpredictable, the other partner often becomes anxious and begins to question the intentions of the changing partner.

Norms and traditions that develop in a marriage over a period of time serve the same purpose as habits for an individual. They become the customary and expected ways of behaving. These norms make it possible for partners to anticipate and predict each other's behavior. Each knows what to expect from the other and can respond appropriately, confident that their behavior will be understood and accepted. Nonconformity to these norms and expectations is disruptive to the usual way "we get along." People who value this form of stability in their marriage are frightened by a suggestion to change, even when it offers the promise of improved marital quality and satisfaction. Why do people find this kind of change frightening? "The old ways are good enough," they reason. "Maybe things aren't as good as they could be, but I know where I stand. I know what I can count on." When marriage becomes difficult and frustrating for these people, they tend to become nostalgic about the happy days of the past. It is ironic that their avoidance behavior occurs at the same time that change could be most constructive and helpful.

This was the problem faced by Bryant and Laverne. Bryant said that it all started with Laverne's alcoholism. While denying she was an alcoholic, Laverne countered that she started drinking for company because Bryant didn't care for her anymore. Bryant rebutted that he didn't like to get close to her because she always reeked of gin. On and on, accusations and counter-accusations were exchanged. However it started, it all came to a head with Bryant's heart attack, which forced him to retire earlier than planned from his job as a department store manager. Referred to me by their pastor, I found them unwilling to face the reality of their new family circumstances. Instead of accepting their individual and marital predicament and adopting new ways of relating to each other, they had retreated even more desperately into their old and unproductive behavior patterns. Neither was willing to accept the responsibility for his or her own behavior, choosing to blame it on the other. They were dissatisfied with their present situation (evidenced by their reminiscing about the good old days) but the prospect of a changed life style aroused fear and anxiety that had to be overcome before their situation could be changed for the better.

While stability is a valued aspect of marriage, the willingness to accept and the ability to respond to needed change also is of critical importance. Not to risk change is to deny the marriage the opportunity to grow, to survive, and to become more satisfying. Partners who are able to accept this fact have taken a giant first step in taking charge of these aspects of their life together. Taking charge and making decisions about improving these concerns is risky, of course, because of their uncertain outcome. But not to risk is to avoid an essential part of being human--of becoming all you and your partner could be.

Marital Obligations

Imagine a childhood experience in which you are having a really good time playing outside with your friends. There is laughter, excitement, and unguarded spontaneity. You're totally involved in the play activity and you are devoting all you attention and energy to it. Suddenly, your play activity is interrupted by your mother's call to come inside and do your school homework. Your study is not very productive because you are thinking about your friends playing outside, about how much longer you have to study, and about how inconsiderate your mother is. In a matter of minutes you stopped something you really wanted to do and started doing something you had to do.

Or recall a recent experience in which you left the work place, rushed home for a quick dinner, and then hurried to the playground where you coached a little league baseball team. At the work place you were doing something you had to do. Because you had to do it, you probably did little more than you had to. Your maximum effort probably equated to your supervisor's minimum expectations. But in coaching the little leaguers, you're doing something you really want to do. In a similar manner, the head of the United Way Fund Drive in Augusta confessed to me, "Russ, I've never worked this hard in my business." He, too, was doing something he wanted to do--something in which he believed.

Let me share a related personal experience from still another area of life. Several years ago, before my mother died, she became ill one evening and I was called to drive her to the hospital emergency room. While she was being examined and treated by the doctors, I sat in the waiting room. The hours passed as I waited for some word about her condition. But the information was slow in coming. Soon it was three o'clock in the morning, and I was alone in the waiting room. In spite of my concern for my mother's well-being, I began to feel the need for sleep and rest. "Why am I sitting here by myself at this hour?" I silently asked. "There's nothing I can do to help." I answered my question by thinking, "I'm here because I'm supposed to be here. It's my duty. She is my mother and I'm her only relative."

As logical as these words were to me, they did not keep me from feeling tired and sleepy. Then, for some unknown reason, I started thinking in a different direction--away from the obligation of duty toward the choice of love. If I had no choice but to be there in the waiting room, would I be acting out of love? No. With these thoughts coming into my mind, I began to feel guilty for having used duty to justify my being there. As a son, a husband, a father, a professional person in a helping field, and as a Christian, I had failed the test of love. Silently, I prayed for God's forgiveness and I promised God that I would ask for my mother's forgiveness. As soon as I discarded the feelings of obligation and the resulting feelings of guilt I began to feel refreshed and alert. During the time before I was able to return my mother to her apartment, I experienced a real awakening to the difference between obligation of duty and the obligation to love.

"Do you love me?" Tevye asked his wife, Golde, in <u>Fiddler on the Roof</u>. "Do I love you?" Golde responds. "You're a fool.... For twenty-five years I've washed your clothes, cooked your meals, cleaned your house, given you children, milked your cow. After twenty-five years why talk about love right now?"

Tevye repeated his question and Golde says, "For twenty-five years I've lived with him, fought with him, starved with him. Twenty-five years my bed is his. If that's not love, what is?"

Twenty-five years earlier, according to tradition, their marriage had been arranged by the village matchmaker. They saw each other for the first time on the day of their wedding. For twenty-five years, up to the moment of Tevye's question, the word love had not been a part of their vocabulary, nor was it a conscious dimension of their relationship. Tradition had ruled their lives. But now, after two of their daughters had become engaged in non-traditional ways, Tevye and Golde talk of their love for each other. It was this newly found and expressed feeling of love--not tradition, not obligation--that helped them cope with other far-reaching changes which later confronted them.

Today, married partners still have expectations of each other which are understood and responded to as obligations. Jake is horrified at the idea that his wife wants to work and hire a housekeeper. "A woman's place is in the home," he protests. He can't understand how she could violate his expectations of her. But Barbara has expectations of Jake. "You don't do a thing around the house. This place could fall apart and you wouldn't even notice. I do the cooking, the cleaning, the shopping, and the chauffeuring. You name it. But I also have to do the fixing around the house. You're supposed to do that--it's a man's job."

When we become a slave to obligation we become a party to what Karen Horney (1950) called "the tyranny of the should." Our lives become outer or other directed, instead of inner or self directed. Much of our behavior is a response to a list of oughts, rather than expressions of our love or inner desire. We invite people into our home because they had us at their home the previous weekend. We agree to serve on a committee because we feel we ought to. We show expressions of sympathy, congratulations, etc., because we feel it is expected of us.

A quality marriage is obtained only through the free choice of love. "I will because I choose to; I choose to because I love you." This is the essence of unconditional love. Yet, for some partners, the words "I choose" are part of a strange, unused vocabulary--like the word love was to Tevye and Golde. Living by a list of oughts in marriage is a prelude to frequent and often painful feelings of guilt. When we fail to do something we feel we ought to have done, we are plagued by feelings of guilt and doubts about our partner's feelings toward us in return. When we have expectations of our partner which are communicated as duties, we are bound to feel hurt, unloved, and possibly angry, if our expectations are not met.

The Bible teaches us that love fulfills the law, not duty or responsibility or obligation. (Romans 3:2-3) When we recognize that we are free to act in love by choice, we are then free to do things because "I want to." As I discovered in the hospital waiting room, I can control my feelings, I can make choices. I am in charge of my own thinking, feeling, and behaving. It's a matter of obligation of duty versus the obligation to love--having to vis-a-vis wanting to.

Remember O'Henry's delightful Christmas story, *Gifts of the Magi*? Della sold her long, beautiful hair--one of the two prized possessions in the James Dillingham Young family--so she could buy a chain for Jim's watch, the other prized possession. At the same time, without telling Della, Jim had sold his watch so he could buy a set of combs for her hair. Jim and Della lovingly and freely sacrificed for each other the greatest treasures of their house. Like the wise men that brought gifts to Jesus in the manager, Jim and Della gave (and received) gifts that were more than mere presents. It was love that was given, and the greatest and most notable expressions of love are totally free choices, not acts of conformity.

A Concluding Thought about Restraining Forces

Restraining forces, by definition, block our path to the quality marriage we seek. Like a barrier in the road, they prevent us from moving in the direction we want to go. Too often, we accept these barriers as being immovable--something about which we can do nothing. Even though we know that beyond the barrier is our goal of a quality marriage, we resign ourselves to the fact that "This is the way the cookie crumbled." We feel frustrated, we feel sad, we engage in wishful thinking, all in vain. We are defeated by our negative attitudes, by our unwillingness to change them.

Remember my pet dog, Miss Muffi? Lenora and I used a cardboard barrier to keep her in the laundry room when we didn't want her in other parts of the house. Even though this barrier was only ten inches high, she never attempted to jump over it. She didn't realize that the hearth upon which she jumped easily was a couple inches higher than the cardboard barrier. Perhaps the effectiveness of the barrier lies in its symbolic message. It was a reminder to her that she was supposed to stay in the laundry room. Lenora and I realized, however, that if she ever attempted to jump over the barrier, she would have succeeded.

The barriers which prevent us from having the quality marriage we'd like to have are almost always under our control. Being under our control, we can remove them. Admittedly, there are some restraining forces over which we have little or no control. These barriers have to be accepted; we have to learn to live with them. But let's not automatically assume that all restraining forces are beyond our control. Let's accept them only after we have earnestly tried to remove them or to lessen their restraining influence on our marriage.

The eight restraining forces I have discussed in this chapter are under our control. We can, if we want, remove them. It's not always easy and sometimes their removal will be only temporary. Sometimes, too, we have to get professional help. But if we don't try, we'll never know the joy of the quality marriage that awaits us beyond the barriers.

Chapter Five

Readiness to Help: Accentuating the Positives

Lenora had asked me to accompany her to a local women's dress shop. The store was having a sale and she wanted my opinion on some items of clothing she had put on hold earlier. When she went into the dressing room, I sat in a chair that had been provided for "those who wait." On a table next to the chair were several "women's" magazines. One of them caught my eye. In bold letters on the cover was the title of an article, "How to Keep Love Alive Past Forty." With both interest and skepticism, I turned to the article and started reading. In summary, the article described eight steps a married couple could follow to invigorate or renew their love feelings toward each other as they got older. Another magazine featured an article titled, "Secrets of Happily Married Couples." It, too, offered some prescriptive rules for maintaining a marriage.

Later, over coffee, Lenora and I talked about the items of clothing she had purchased. She was pleased that she had found some pieces that both of us really liked. Then I changed the subject by telling her about the articles I had read between her visits to the fitting room. After sharing the content of the articles, I asked her opinion of them. "They really make it seem easy," I suggested. She explained that that kind of article appeared in almost every issue of those particular magazines. "Look at the titles. Everybody wants to keep love alive; everybody wants a happy marriage. For a couple dollars you get quick answers to your problems. What these articles offer can be helpful within limits. By that I mean certain other conditions must be present."

"I think I know what you have in mind, but what are these other conditions?" I asked.

Her response was insightful. It also provided a useful comparison between peoples' search for satisfying relationships through use of these generalized techniques and use of short-term therapy to help identify and resolve marital difficulties. Both are based on the medical model of therapy. When used in marriage and family therapy, this model guides the therapist to identify the critical problem(s) in a hurting marriage. Once the problem is recognized, a specific remedy or solution is suggested. No effort is made to examine the overall health of the marriage. The model uses a cosmetic approach; it focuses on immediate results. The conditions which caused or contributed to the problem remain, and, as might be expected, the problem often resurfaces later with the same attending symptoms. The fact that this kind of therapy does not always result in long-term improvement in a marriage is due to the absence of what Lenora called basic conditions--what I am going to refer to as pre-conditions. When these pre-conditions are incorporated into the sentiments and values of partners and practiced in their interpersonal relations, they empower partners not only to minimize the likelihood of problems in their marriage but also to quickly and easily resolve, on a more lasting basis, those problems they do experience.

In a like manner, popular approaches to marital happiness like the ones prescribed in the magazines are often misleading and misdirected. People who are attracted to them because of their promise of quick, favorable results often experience frustration when their efforts are misunderstood by their partner and are responded to with indifference or hostility. There are no simple techniques of which I know that can be applied effectively in the absence of a broad understanding and appreciation of the principles and attitudes underlying real interpersonal competence. What the magazine articles recommend is rules and techniques; what I am suggesting on these pages is an attitude. Use of rules and techniques alone leads people to attempt to manipulate and sometimes exploit their partners without regard for their partner's needs and desires. Attitudes germane to good marital relationships, on the other hand, help us to explore the structure, values, and functioning of our marriage while helping our partner to feel approved and adequate. Realizing that our behavior may have a profound effect on our partner, an attitude of love and responsibility would cause us to pause and ponder what kind of effect we desired to have on them. We would then try to behave in ways that were congruent with our intentions. It is important to remember that good marital relationships depend, in the long run, more upon attitudes rather than on rules and techniques.

In this chapter, I will discuss some basic pre-conditions for successful, satisfying marriages. I believe that the various techniques recommended in the magazine articles can be helpful only when these pre-conditions already are part of the fabric of a marriage. The situation is somewhat like the Biblical parable of "casting seeds upon fertile ground." The techniques suggested in the magazines can be viewed as the seeds; the pre-conditions I will discuss here constitute the fertile ground (attitudes) which makes it possible for the seeds to take root and work for a couple. In a similar manner, short-term marriage and family therapy can produce desired outcomes under favorable conditions. I make regular use of it, often requiring only two or three sessions to achieve gratifying results. Decisions about the duration of therapy always are related to a couple's understanding of their difficulty, their motivation to follow an agreed-upon plan of therapy, and the absence of any deep-seated pathology.

In chapter four I discussed how the overall quality of a marriage is determined by the relative strength of two sets of opposing forces. First, there are driving forces which have a positive effect on a marriage--they both support and help to improve the quality of a marriage. Second, there are restraining forces which block or get in the way of any desired improvement in the quality of a marriage. The actual level of quality in a marriage is represented by a state of equilibrium between these two sets of forces.

The restraining forces were discussed in chapter four. There it was argued that whenever we undertake to improve the way something works, we typically direct all our efforts to adding new driving forces and strengthening those already present. I suggested that, contrary to popular wisdom and practice, it would be both easier and more productive to remove or weaken the restraining forces. It was not my intent to imply, in any way, that the driving forces are not important. Quite the contrary. They are, in fact, absolutely necessary. If there were no restraining forces, the driving forces would be all that would be needed for a successful, fully satisfying marriage. The pre-conditions discussed below are driving forces which couples need to develop and nurture.

Marriage as a Hospitable Environment

I had completed a two-day personal-growth workshop at an island conference center off the coast of south Georgia. Participant involvement was high and their feedback complimentary. I was relishing good feelings about the workshop as I started my return trip to Augusta--a distance of approximately 200 miles. For some unknown reason I elected to take Georgia's well-known "Woodpecker Trail." It was mostly country, two-lane roads, but it would save me a few miles compared to the interstate highways. As I left the coastline and drove westward I could see threatening storm clouds ahead. I had a full tank of gas, my car was performing well, and I was feeling good. I thought, "Let it rain." And soon it did. It was raining like it can rain only in south Georgia. Necessarily, I slowed my speed and turned on the lights.

I found myself wishing I were already home. What a friendly place; what a good feeling just thinking about it gave me. Lenora would be waiting. We would have a glass of wine and talk and talk. Still over 150 miles away--maybe three hours driving time in the rain--was the one place I wanted to be. It was home, it was relationship, it was a haven from the rain and the other concerns my situation was presenting to me. Suddenly, after an indeterminate time, I saw a stopped vehicle ahead of me with the emergency lights blinking. I came to a stop immediately behind the vehicle and tried to determine what was wrong. The driver of the car hurried back to my car and explained why we had to stop.

"Two prisoners escaped this afternoon and the State Patrol has traced them to this area. They're presumed armed and dangerous. We can't pass through until we get the O.K. Pass the word then stay in your car with the doors locked and your lights on. Blow your horn if you see anything."

It was a long time before we were allowed to proceed and in the growing darkness and the rain, there was nothing to do except think, feel, and wait. I knew Lenora would be concerned, but there was nothing I could do to change my circumstances. (I didn't have a cellular phone at that time.) I arrived home much later than I had anticipated. Lenora was waiting and, although it was late, we took the time to talk and share. I told her about my ordeal and my many thoughts and feelings about my love for her. I told her that being with her made our home the most comforting place I knew of. "There's no place like home," I recall saying to her. I also remember her agreeing with me.

In chapter two I shared with you how a workshop participant wished his marriage to be user-friendly. His use of that term caught everyone by surprise. We were intrigued with the idea, however, and, almost intuitively, we started sharing ideas about what a user-friendly marriage would be like.

Making Marriage User Friendly

Agnes suggested the idea of equality. "A marriage is user-friendly when there is just one standard for both partners. Without equality there is no closeness, no intimacy. Early in our marriage I related to Gaines the way I always did to my father. I catered to his every grunt and groan. I thought it was natural. What really bothered me was that Gaines passively encouraged me to be that way. I learned to hate myself and him. There were a lot of fights, but we got through it. Today he and I are lovers, partners, friends, you name it. We don't keep score, we just try to see who can love the most."

Van offered a different perspective. "It's commitment and trust that makes a marriage user-friendly. Both Abby and I had a live-in experience before we married. No, not together. She was in Charlotte, I was in Atlanta. There was no trust, it was all a game--a lot of pretending. I got tired of it. Fortunately, Abby did too. That's when we met. Knowing that she trusts me makes me feel very special. I would never let her down."

Jay offered still another. "All these things are good but they don't get to the core of user-friendly marriage. Commitment and trust are important but it's the feeling of acceptance that makes the difference. Tami doesn't approve of everything I do, but she still accepts me, blemishes and all. When you're accepted everything else is O.K."

Mike offered a sentimental thought. "I travel a lot. Shirley's picture is always on the dash of my car. When I think of her she becomes so real I want to reach out and touch her. That's what user-friendly means to me. Sweet and easy, that's her way of coming on to me, even when I'm away from her. Often, when I get home she tells me she had the same feelings."

Sandy's response was, "When Buddy and I married we had some cockeyed notions of what it was all about. Both of us. Well, it hit the fan. We came close to chucking it. Got a legal separation because both of us thought we wanted to date other people. Guess we loved each other for reasons other than having someone to fight with because neither of us could date. It's really been great since we got back together."

I was listening and feeling so intently that I hadn't even thought of sharing my feelings with the group. Suddenly I was confronted by Abby's question. "What about you, Russ? What does a user-friendly marriage mean to you?"

"Well, when Jody surprised us with that term, I couldn't associate it with marriage. Computers, yes; marriage, no. But listening to you has really opened my eyes, and my heart. As you know, Lenora and I have been married over forty years, so I guess it has been friendly to us. What I like about marriage is that it provides me the comfort of acceptance and understanding and, at the same time, the freedom to be different-- like an actor I read about. He knew and followed his lines and expected everyone else to do so, but he could improvise nicely when someone forgot a line or missed a cue."

"I would expect definitions of a user-friendly marriage to differ for each of us. Look at the many ways we have already described it. This is not exactly computer talk but I would guess that a user-friendly marriage, for most people, is one that would cause then to say, 'This is good. Let it last.'"

"Let me share another thought that just came to me. Lenora is always talking about love as forgiving. For her, it's both one word, "forgiving," and two words, "for giving." Either way, it's something I can't get anywhere else, love and forgiveness. It does more than take the hassle out of marriage, it puts in something special."

I interrupted my response to tell the group about the scary experience I described earlier in this chapter. Then I continued my response to Abby's question.

After a few more sharings, I intervened with a question. "O. K., we've shared some really candid, beautiful ideas about what makes our marriage user-friendly. Let's take a look at the other side of the coin, "What makes a marriage user-unfriendly? What is it we would like to avoid? What is it that makes marriage a hassle? Do you understand what I'm getting at?"

Again, Loretta (wife of Gaines) was the first to respond. Apparently she was aware of it as she said, "See how impetuous I am. I don't like to waste time. Well, let's see now. Oh, yes, your question. My marriage was unfriendly for a long time when I didn't have control over the things that were happening to me. Remember, Russ, your telling us that we teach people how to behave toward us? Well, I knew I could never change my father but, damn it, getting married was supposed to be a fresh start. 'I'll teach Gaines differently,' I thought. Well, it didn't take me long to realize that I had bombed it. 'Why can't I relate to men?' I asked myself. The more I resisted and fought back, the more our marriage became a battleground. Definitely unfriendly."

"I thought I knew all about Fred before we married, except what he'd be like in bed, naturally. Well, I found that I had dated Jekyll but married Hyde." Turning toward Fred, Dale laughingly continued, "Honey, please understand this is all in the past." Fred nodded in a knowing way, showing a big grin that reflected a suggestion of embarrassment at what Dale was saying. His failure to object was taken by Dale as permission for her to continue. "Fred saw marriage as having won a wife rather than an opportunity to be a husband. He was Mr. Wonderful before we married; afterward, he started behaving by some different rules. He thought he was king of the roost. His way was the right way; my ideas didn't count. His needs came first; mine were not important. He even wanted me to quit my job so I'd be ready for sex all the time. Get the picture? He even quoted the Bible to me: the part about wives being submissive to their husband. Well, you can image how I felt, at least you girls can. Was my marriage user-friendly? No way."

Again, looking toward Fred, Dale said, "Honey, I don't know how we got through it, but we did. It was tough but it was worth it. I love you." Fred, who was sitting across the room from Dale left his chair and walked toward her. "Tommy, change chairs with me so I can sit by my wife," he asked. We noticed a lot of holding hands and exchanging glances of affection during the rest of the session.

We often talked about marriage as though it had its own existence, that it existed apart from the people in it. Maybe, legally, marriage is seen as an entity under the law, but it is made real only in terms of the relationship between the partners. Can we, then, accurately describe our marriage as being user-friendly? Maybe not. Maybe what we really have in mind are the feelings shared with and by our partner. Behind our feelings are our perceptions of and our thoughts about our partner. Also involved are our assumptions about our partner's motives and intentions toward us. We respond with love and affection when we feel love from our partner; we respond with understanding, acceptance, and forgiveness when they are shown to us. When our partner shows trust and commitment we want to give them back. When all these things are given, there is a synergistic effect--the total of love available to the partners is greater than the sum of their individual contributions. When this happens, our relationship with our partner--our marriage--is user-friendly.

The Non-Form Dimensions of Marriage

"Maybe I'm burning the candle at both ends. Maybe I should feel guilty. It bothers me that I don't."

It was early in Lara's first therapy session with me, and she was describing her feelings about the fact that she was involved in an extra-marital relationship. On a previous occasion, she had called for an appointment but failed to appear. When she cancelled a second time, I told her that if she would send me a prepayment I would give her another appointment. Her check was received a few days later, including payment for the missed appointments. With her check was a carefully worded, hand-written note on expensive, personalized stationary. She apologized for having failed to keep the earlier appointments and expressed appreciation for my patience and willingness to see her.

Lara was from a socially and politically prominent family and felt that her marriage was arranged in the sense that there were "eligibles" suggested by her parents. She was not bothered at the time by the arrangement because she saw it as an opportunity to continue the life style in which she had grown up. As she continued talking, I recalled some of the information I had earlier recorded on her chart. Her house address was in a "high-rent" part of town. Through my office window I could see her European automobile. Her dress, jewelry, etc., were all expensive and in good taste. Her speech, demeanor, and sense of presence all reflected the quality and values of her private-school education. Her resume of charitable memberships and activities was impressive. The mother of two children, she was, at age thirty-five, an attractive, warm and engaging woman.

"As far as everybody knows, Roland and I have the perfect marriage. What they don't know is that it is a facade. What others think of us has always been important to Roland. It seems that everything he does is done with that thought in mind. 'Got to think political,' he's always saying. We've never talked much about love, not even in the beginning. I didn't mind too much in the beginning, but now I realize what I'm missing. Still, I feel that Roland loves me in his own way and I guess I love him, too. I guess that's why I am here. But it's wearing thin and I'm tired of pretending. Our marriage is a farce. We both know it, but neither of us will do anything about it."

"Roland treats me as though I were a piece of menagerie--not as a person with feelings. I'm supposed to be at his side at the club, Hilton Head, wherever. It's like he wants to show me off, have me on display. And he's always telling me what is politically correct to say, like I don't have a mind of my own. He likes to choose my clothing. He once suggested a hair style for me. Well, what do I do when he is not home, which is most of the time. He doesn't care about what I feel--what is important to me. As long as I don't argue with him, as long as he gets what we wants and I don't make noises, he is super nice and will give me anything I want. But

Making Marriage User Friendly

that makes me feel like a prostitute. I'm tired of being a wimp and I'm tired of putting my needs down just to keep peace in the family. Maybe what we need is a good fight. On second thought maybe we don't care enough to fight."

I intervened with a question. "You haven't mentioned the children. What effect is the family life you've described having on them?"

"I'm a good mother and spend a lot of time with the children, especially Brad. He's older and notices more so I try to explain things to him. Even my mother-in-law thinks I'm a good mother. She is always scolding Roland for his failure to spend more time with the children. He'll go to a soccer game or two, then he's making excuses again. Church on Sunday? Always. The children are well-mannered and considerate. They're my world."

I listened attentively, feeling she was laying the groundwork for again talking about her affair. I was right.

"Can you have an affair without sex? I thought about it a lot before I met George. With him it seemed such a natural thing to do, and it was something I wanted to do. And I thought he would feel the same. He's so tender and kind, always thinking of me. He said that was the reason he couldn't make love with me. I've read about how some women felt put down when their sexual advances were rebuffed. I was confused, but I didn't feel put down. George puts me on a pedestal. Well, in his own way Roland does, too. But he leaves me feeling I'm being used. With George I feel loved. Can you understand? With Roland there's no feeling, no romance, no love. Isn't that what being married and having a family is all about?"

"What are George's expectation of you? What is he getting from this relationship?"

"Don't think badly of him, I made the first move. We were in a ceramics class. When the instructor told us to choose a partner to work with, I asked George if I could work with him. I don't know why I was so attracted to him. His circumstances are very different from mine. He's single, works for a modest salary, and attends night classes at Augusta State University. Not particularly good looking, but that's not what I'm looking for. I always try to pay the bills. What does that make me? I wish Roland had George's warmth, his sense of appreciation, his considerate manners. You won't believe this but George is a super good cook--belongs to a gourmet group. He has a girl friend who goes to the meetings with him, and I think he's been intimate with her. If he has, that's O.K. I know you're going to think badly of me but George really knows how to make me feel loved and important, even without sex. With a sample of only two men in my life, I'm sounding like an expert. Ha!"

I have shared a lot of Lara's story with you because it epitomizes a kind of relationship that is increasingly being experienced by couples in the age range of Lara and Roland with similar social and financial circumstances. These relationships evolve in various patterns, from the often conflicting, sometimes incompatible, demands of life and career--of love and work, if you will. During the past twenty years or so, generations of men and women have grown up believing they could have it all--that they could combine career and family, enjoying full and equal measures of both. This goal is difficult to achieve and even more difficult to maintain. Work-love strains inevitably occur, and when they do they are most frequently resolved in favor of work since the rewards of work are more immediate and direct than the rewards of love and family. Further, the rewards of work are particularly seductive for people who, because of benign neglect, are already finding home life more taxing but less rewarding. Love, obviously, finds it hard to compete.

Inevitably, people sooner or later begin to question whether they can really have it all--love and work--in life. They begin to question the values and assumptions that underlie their marriage. In words that Lara might use, the relationship that emerges places more emphasis on the form than on the substance of marriage. It is more concerned with presenting a good image of the marriage than nurturing the partners in the marriage. In this kind of marriage the label is more important than the contents. Marriages in which the partners hold these values are utilitarian in nature, i.e., the marriage is useful to the partners in ways not directly related to their emotional and sexual needs. Such marriages serve extrinsic rather than intrinsic needs.

This was the kind of marriage Lara and Roland had; it was the kind of marriage against which Lara was rebelling. It wasn't, however, a simple case of Roland being a guilty, uncaring culprit and Lara being a helpless, innocent victim. Neither is Lara's situation an isolated case; it is, in numerous ways, representative of all marriages which, for whatever reasons, loose the property of being valued and intrinsically satisfying. Marriages in which the partners become indifferent to sex, avoid even non-sexual intimacy, and assume a passive relationship with each other fall into the pattern of a utilitarian marriage.

Lara married Roland not because she loved him, but because she loved the life-style and the social and economic security the marriage promised her. In one session, she said, "I married a system. My parents and older sister were part of it before me, and their marriages are just like mine. Why did I ever think mine would somehow be different? If I had wanted to marry someone like George I would have been banished to Timbuktu. Looking back, I can see that my head was in the clouds. I never questioned the lifestyle, the values, or the trumped-up elitism of the system. When I did begin to question things, I was criticized and accused of being ungrateful. Daddy discretely arranged for both our family lawyer and my personal physician to talk to me. They must have thought I was going crazy. I hate the way they talked to me. The thing that hurt most of all was Roland talking to me like I was a child and he was my parent. 'Stop being childish and get over your school-girl idealism,' he said."

Lara adjusted to her situation by withdrawing from Roland and spending more time with the children. Unconsciously, she was trying to instill a different set of values in the children--to protect them from the system. Her efforts to do this led to numerous confrontations with Roland. She provided an example of how she and Roland fight by telling me the story of what had happened the previous Christmas. She and the children had made some very elaborate plans to decorate the house for Christmas. Together, they went to the stores and bought the needed decorations. She wanted the children to share in the joy and the excitement of decorating the house. It would be an opportunity for them to do something together. When Roland learned about their plans he objected, insisting that a well-known interior decorator be brought in to do the job. Roland didn't protest Lara's plans because he had not been consulted or because he had been excluded, but because he wanted the house to look its best for the Christmas party he and Lara traditionally held. Roland's wishes prevailed not because he screamed louder or threatened more, but because Lara didn't know how to stand up for her own rights and the needs of their children.

It was at this point that her adjustment to her situation took a bolder, more decisive step. She became an "affair" waiting to happen. She enrolled in the ceramics class because she wanted to do something for herself. It was, in her mind, an act of defiance of the system. There she met George and became infatuated with him, believing he could and would fill the void in her life. Psychologically ready for both an emotional and physical involvement with him, she experienced disappointment and confusion when George defined the boundaries of their relationship to exclude sex. Still thinking there must be more to a relationship than that, she pursued

George, unwilling to believe he could be so puritanical in refusing her sexual advances. In time, she became more understanding and appreciative of George's feelings toward her. But this only added to the conflict she was feeling. Realizing both the risks associated with her seeing George and the need to confront Roland with her feelings, she came to see me.

An enlightened philosopher once suggested that ninety-nine percent of what we are as humans cannot be seen, touched, smelled, measured, or weighed. This large part of us exists only in thought--it has no physical form. Only the remaining one percent has a physical dimension. It has also been suggested, and our own experiences testify to it, that we give ninety-nine percent of our concern and efforts to taking care of the one-percent. How the one-percent is dressed, fed, perfumed, entertained, and perceived by others is our primary concern. We pursue it to the neglect of the larger part.

I was helped to understand the truth of this sage observation when Lenora and I attended the forty-fifth reunion of my high school class. It was only the second reunion I had been able to attend, and I was excited about the prospect of seeing old friends again. During the early part of the festivities, note was made that seven members of our class were now deceased, and we appropriately remembered them. There were other members of the class that I had not seen since graduation and I had to be "introduced" to them. Later in the afternoon I was voted the person who had changed the least. Wow! I really liked that. However, the vote didn't mention the kind of change everyone had in mind. Was it physical? Was it personality? I assumed that I could interpret the selection anyway I chose to. Later still, I was voted the person who had lost the most hair. After the laughter subsided, I tried to reconcile the two votes. There was only one way to do it, I concluded. In the first vote, my classmates were referring to the non-form part of me: personality, values, goals, ways of relating, etc. In the second vote they were noting what had happened to the physical side of my being. In my own words they were saying, "Russ, there's more to you than the hair that you have lost."

It is perhaps symptomatic of our society that the basic unit of society--the family--shows such pervasive concern for *having* (big houses, fancy telephones and other gadgets, fashionable clothes) and *doing* (parties, vacations, work). For people who cannot balance these concerns in their marriage, the time devoted to having and doing takes time away from *being* (acceptance, love, togetherness). I'm not arguing that the needs of the physical dimension (the one-percent) are not important; no, more than important, they are necessary if we are to live productive, satisfying lives free of physical deprivation, hunger, and pain. But while they are necessary, they alone can never provide the sense of emotional and spiritual well-being we seek. The more we pursue the concerns of the one percent the more we show our insecurity. Neither is it a question of priority. Each area of concern is just as important as the other, but for different reasons. When a couple pursues the one percent to the detriment of the ninety-nine percent the internal dynamics of the marriage begin to erode.

This is what happened to Lara and Roland. When she tried to live more in the non-form dimension of her life and to define her marriage in these terms, she met resistance from her husband and her family of origin. She understood and freely admitted that her circumstances were largely of her own doing. "Where did I go wrong?" she asked. "Where is the good life I thought was just around the corner? I know I have made my own bed, but do I have to lie in it for the rest of my life?" She gradually realized that she didn't have to.

Maintaining a Win-Win Relationship

Must the relationship of marriage be lived as though it were a game of poker? Must every marital disagreement produce a winner and a loser? Is it possible for both partners to be winners at the same time? All the time?

These questions are not asked for their rhetorical effect. Nor are they intended as problematic questions. They are asked because they get to the core of the most pervasive difficulty partners have in developing and maintaining a mutually supportive and satisfying relationship. They touch almost every aspect of partners' lives together. Decisions about finances, social activities, in-laws, sex, and the raising of children provide fertile ground in which the germs of conflict can develop and flourish. Simply sharing time and space limits the freedom of partners to do what they want to do when they want to do it. Conflicts faced in marriage run the gambit from complex, deep-seated conflicts in which the partners pursue mutually exclusive goals to the more trivial tugs-of-war in which the partners attempt to assert their will over each other. Tragically, every conflict--important or petty--confronts a couple with a sense of emotional separation. How they approach the conflict and attempt to bridge the gulf of separation determines whether the conflict is short-lived or whether it will grow and polarize the partners into uncompromising positions. How well a marriage works can be seen as both a cause and effect of how well the partners learn to resolve their disagreements. If disagreements and differences of opinions are resolved according to the rules of right and wrong--of winning and losing--then there is no winner, there is only a loser and that is the marriage.

In a game of two-person poker, which is the equivalent of a win-lose relationship in marriage, only one strategy or way of playing the game is available: competition. In order for one player to win the other must lose, and what the winner wins is always equal to what the loser loses. The same constraints hold for athletic contests. Any attempt to cooperate would destroy the integrity of the game and deprive opponents of the opportunity to use and further develop their competitive playing skills. Fortunately, marriage doesn't have to be lived by the rules of poker. Partners can choose to cooperate to produce a win-win relationship. Both can win; neither has to lose.

Let me interject that I am not opposed to competition. When you bought the book you are now reading it was competing with other books for your interest and your dollars. This type of competition motivates me to work harder in my writing. Nor does my attitude deny the authors of competing books the opportunity to improve their efforts. When I started dating Lenora, I had to compete against other suitors who apparently felt toward her as I did. After marriage, I often competed against Lenora in a game of bridge as I did against my son in a game of chess. I like to compete and I like to win, but my well-being is not threatened when I don't win. If I have to win in order to feel good about myself, what am I when I don't win? Am I the same person? Yes. Am I less worthy as a person? No. Winning means I got the ball over the net one time more than my opponent did. Losing means my opponent got it over the net one time more than I did. That's all it means. Sometimes I win; sometimes I lose. No one is going to win all the time.

Winning and losing are sometimes viewed as opposites. In this view, you either win or lose; you can't both win and lose in a single contest. This is true of poker, and it's true of marriage when the partners view a conflict in terms of mutually incompatible interests. Either I get my way or I don't; either I win or I lose. However, in marriage the fact of not losing does not mean that I won. Similarly, not having won does not mean I lost. This is true because solutions to marital problems seldom fall into a simple win-or-lose category.

When her mother was ailing, Lenora tried to visit her as often as she could. I understood and supported her concern. I also sought to assure her that I would be able to take care of the house, our pet dog, and myself. On one trip to visit her mother she wanted me to accompany her. It was a particularly difficult time for me to get away and I begged off. Still, I felt that she really wanted me to accompany her and, without asking, I tried to understand her reasons. Was it because she had left me alone on previous occasions and didn't want to do it again? Or was it because she wanted me to go and visit with her mother? Or was it because the expense of flying alone be saved if we traveled by car?

Were these three motives or reasons incompatible? If one was satisfied, were the others denied? I suggested to Lenora that she plan on flying on the desired date and that she stay a few days longer than originally planned. I would then be free to follow her by car. After I visited a few days, we could then return together. She was agreeable and this is what we did. Our decision was a win-win outcome. There was never a conflict between us; our problem was learning how to manage our agreement.

People who have a need always to win express their need in a variety of ways. For them, every interaction is a contest. Unless they have an authoritative opinion about every question or problem they fear they will not be thought well of by others. They are highly competitive in relationships with others, always striving to prove their adequacy without realizing that they may, at the same time, be undermining the needs of others. They are driven to express their views in a dogmatic way that leaves no room for rebuttal or even further discussion. They are always moving against others rather than moving toward them; they talk at others rather than to them.

A person with this need was observed at a recent lawn party I attended. At parties, I like to move around, meet different people, and listen to what they have to say. In one small group of men, the conversation was focused on the question of how many miles per gallon of gasoline their autos were capable of delivering. Like escalating bids at an auction, each claim was topped by the next speaker. It was a game of one-upmanship, and it was being played with deadly seriousness--each person determined to have the most efficient automobile. I am convinced that if the game had continued to its inevitable conclusion, those men would have solved the energy crisis.

This competitive mentality also expresses itself in an individual's need to have the best quality of everything purchased at the lowest price, after the toughest bargaining. In whatever form, whatever the situation, this kind of behavior takes an exploitative approach in relating to others. Sometimes it is little more than the "big time operator" exaggerating every statement to the extent of boasting, showing off, or covertly competing with everyone. Other times, it evidences a debilitating personality maladjustment in which every perceived threat to one's self-esteem is countered by aggressive acts of anti-social behavior.

Problems occur when we transfer our competitive mentality from the playing field to the arena of marriage. This mentality causes us to see our marriage as an encounter and our partner as an opponent who is always trying to take advantage of us--someone who is seeking control over what we need to make us happy. Marriage then becomes a struggle in which one or both partners feel they are individually responsible for their own needs satisfaction. This view is unfortunately reinforced when we are unsure of our partner's intentions toward us. When this happens, we begin to see our partner as controlling us and our feelings of love become clouded by feelings of distrust and suspicion. Our goal of a win-win relationship becomes more difficult and elusive and we revert to the power-oriented, win-lose pattern of relating.

There are certain problems and decisions in marriage in which one partner might possess some demonstrated expertise. In these instances, that partner's competency might justifiably be recognized and deferred to by the other partner. All couples try to work out an agreement about who is to take charge in a particular situation and under what circumstances. If you are wondering why it is necessary for someone to take charge in every situation, I do not mean that the person who takes charge becomes bossy and the other partner remains submissive. If household tasks are to be accomplished and decisions made about all facets of married life, someone has to take the initiative. Seldom, however, does one partner's competency extend to all dimensions or aspects of a problem or decision situation. Thus, questions about a partner's competency and right to unilaterally make decisions that affect the other partner are always open to debate. The secret to an enduring, hassle-free solution to this problem is the development of rules that are fair and workable. Admittedly, this is not an easy task, as evidenced by the inability of so many couples to agree on the rules. The task is further jeopardized by the fact that many couples often make unclear or unfair rules which sow the seeds of long-term friction and other unanticipated, undesired consequences.

Most of the recognized approaches to conflict resolution are designed to produce a solution. This is especially true of the process of compromise. Even when partners accept a compromise solution, it is often a result of a power struggle in which the less powerful partner accepts a compromise solution as being better than losing or not reaching a decision at all. Because a compromise solution never gives the partners what they each want, they tend to engage in blue-sky bargaining in which unreasonably low offers and high demands are made. Partners ask for benefits or concessions which they know the other partner will not grant; they make offers or concessions knowing the other partner will not accept them. At its best, compromise involves an element of game playing; at its worst, it borders on deception.

A win-win or collaborative approach to conflict resolution, on the other hand, evolves from and contributes to the development of an attitude of love of the other partner and respect for their emotional and spiritual well-being. It is an attitude that says, "I don't want to win if it means you have to lose. I won't satisfy my needs at your expense." Is such an attitude practical? In spite of our nearly universal desire for a win-win relationship in marriage, there are many skeptics who argue against it. Practical realism causes them to dismiss the idea as blue-sky thinking. The instinct for survival through domination and control of the means of needs satisfaction, the distortions of subjective perceptions, the complexity of human motives, both consciously and unconsciously, are cited as obstacles to a win-win relationship.

Insights and understandings from my own psychoanalysis, plus those gained from twenty-six years as a practicing therapist, convinced me that a win-win relationship is possible. Note that I said it is possible. Even in the most supportive marriages valid constraints often make the approach inappropriate in certain situations. Beyond these constraints, however, I am persuaded that a win-win approach is both desired and possible, especially in marriages where the partners show concern for each other's needs for assurance and feelings of acceptance and importance. These partners realize they can help satisfy the needs of the other without jeopardizing their own needs satisfaction. This belief emanates not from adherence to a set of rules but from an attitude of respect for the worth and dignity of each other. Unlike many situations in which winners and losers are determined by counting ballots, a win-lose attitude in marriage necessarily assumes the winner prevails and the loser despairs. The winner emerges by virtue of having imposed power on the loser. The despair of losers is more severe when they have to suffer in silence. To be and feel like a loser in relation to a partner who is loved is not healthy for a marriage. Moreover, a win-lose attitude in a marriage typically fosters a pattern of destructive relationships. A win-win attitude, on the other hand, rejects both domination and submissiveness. It is an approach that affirms the integrity and dignity of the partners, and partners who commit themselves to using it find the rewards immeasurable.

Giving and Getting Helpful Feedback

Early in my marriage I decided that I would make it a rule for me to always get up first in the mornings. I steadfastly followed that rule, thinking of it as an act of love. But my reasons might differ from what you're assuming. Simply, it's because I didn't want Lenora to have to see what I see when I look into the mirror the first time. I even tried to spare our pet dog, Miss Muffi, the shock of seeing me. Looking into the mirror was without a doubt the most painful thing that I did all day. It was, with equal certainly, the most necessary thing that I did, for without the feedback the mirror gave me I could not change what little I was able to change. It's only after I shaved, combed my hair, and make the coffee that I awakened Lenora. Then, hopefully, she would be more pleased with what she saw.

In this situation, I depended upon the feedback from the mirror about how I looked. I used this feedback to make decisions about what I needed to change. Mirrors are honest and impersonal; they call a spade a spade. And, as painful as it was, I had to look into the mirror--there was no substitute for it. I cared about how I appeared to Lenora, but it is was only after I accepted things the way they were that I could do something about changing them. There is another mirror that all married persons must stand before. It is a social mirror; it is our partner. This mirror, too, must call a spade a spade, but in a caring, helpful manner. If it matters to us how our behavior affects our partner then we must invite and be open to feedback from our social mirror. So, feedback is communication between us and our partner that helps us to determine how we affect each other. As in a guided missile system, feedback helps us to keep our behavior on target and thus better achieve the effect we intend. In this sense, feedback becomes a corrective mechanism for us in determining how well our behavior matches our intentions. Otherwise, all we can do is to keep on muddling through, hoping we're doing the right things in the right way.

A marriage can be viewed as a social system in which the partners are dependent upon each other for pertinent feedback about the effects of their behavior. Consciously or unconsciously, we always intend a certain effect on our partner. What is imperative is knowing whether the effect we intend is congruent with the actual effect. Here we are faced with the question, "How am I doing?" and the only way I know to answer that question honestly and adequately is with feedback from our partner.

The case of Marcia and Felton provides insight to the difficulties that can compound in a marriage when the partners fail to request or share relevant information. Theirs was a case of faulty marital adjustment, impaired by the continued interference of Marcia's divorced mother to "protect her daughter" from men like Marcia's father. After several sessions of conjoint therapy in which I attempted to deal with Marcia's acting out the trauma of her parents' troubled marriage and eventual divorce, we still were confronted with incompatible perceptions of what each of them considered to be the primary problems in their marriage. I asked them to meet with me for an hour of individual therapy. Marcia asked if she could be first.

"I know what Felton will harp on, and I wanted to let you know my feelings first. I wouldn't mind having sex more often if he would do it differently. He doesn't do what I want him to do."

"Are you talking about the form of your lovemaking or what your husband does while you're having sex. Whatever, you're implying that he doesn't do the things that bring you pleasure. What does he say when you ask him?"

"I've never asked. No, I wouldn't feel right doing that. What I mean is I don't have a right. Do I? Wouldn't it look like criticism? Wouldn't it make him feel bad?"

"If Felton doesn't know what brings you pleasure how can you expect him to help you?"

"If he really loved me he would know what to do. Why should I have to tell him?"

Before reading further, please think for a moment about Marcia's question "Why should I have to tell him?" and then decide how you might respond to her. Also try to think through her implied value system and her assumption that Felton's feelings would be hurt if she did mention her sexual preferences to him. Perhaps your feelings are similar to what mine were. I felt a tinge of sadness because they were two people who loved each other and were struggling to save their marriage but could not share their feelings about the most intimate part of their marriage.

I asked for Marcia's permission to discuss her feelings when I met with Felton. Only after I assured her that I could broach the subject in a non-accusative, non-judgmental manner did she agree. Not surprisingly, I found Felton equally uncomfortable in talking about their sexual relationship. He explained that certain subjects had always been taboo. High on the list of these no-no subjects were sex and Marcia's mother. He recalled, with a touch of both shame and laughter, how he once tricked Marcia into going to see an X-rated movie. From that point on sex was simply something they did once, sometimes twice each month.

"Talking about sex has always been difficult for us. Marcia feels that if we talk about it we are just like the people in that movie."

As they continued in therapy, they began to understand the consequences of the limits they had unknowingly placed not only on their sexual relationship but also on other critical aspects of their marriage. With these breakthroughs, the light at the end of the tunnel began to get larger and closer. One more short story is appropriate to let you know how their therapy ended. It was in their next-to-last session.

Felton: "One more thing, Marcia, please don't make that spinach casserole anymore."

Marcia: "I thought you liked it. I saw you eat it at our rehearsal dinner. Remember? The one my sister brought."

Felton: "I was just trying to be nice."

Marcia: "You mean you've been eating that casserole for four years and you don't like it. I don't like it either. (Laughter) No more casserole."

Felton and I joined in her laughter.

When we interact with persons we leave an image of ourselves with them. Our behavior always causes some kind of impact or effect; it triggers feelings, impressions, and judgments about us. Others, in turn, use their judgments to determine how they will respond to us. Whether our behavior is effective (achieves the ends we desire) depends in large measure on the feedback we receive from others. This feedback is not limited to the verbal feedback we receive about our behavior. We must also be sensitive to their nonverbal cues as they respond to us. Such cues can actually tell us more than verbal feedback, particularly in situations where social moves dictate politeness or when a lack of psychological safety mediates against verbal feedback.

In marriage, this phenomenon assumes added significance because of the non-temporary nature of the relationship and the feelings and commitment the partners have for each other. Getting feedback from our partner provides us the opportunity to (1) increase our awareness of our motivations and intentions; (2) determine the consequences of our behavior upon our partner; and, (3) change our behavior to make it more congruent with our intentions. We can't avoid having an impact or effect on our partner, but we do have a choice as to the kind of effect we intend. Even though marriage is, ideally, a loving, trusting relationship it does not always provide enough psychological safety for partners to give and request feedback. One constraint relates to a lack of social competence of the partners; another constraint is their ambivalence about getting and giving feedback. Ambivalence refers to our mixed feelings of both wanting yet not wanting feedback. Our mixed feelings are caused by our fear that the feedback may not be what we want to hear. Regardless of whether we want to receive it, the data are still in the relationship and influence the partner's behavior toward each other. This confronts us with the question whether we love enough to face the consequences of our behavior or play a game of hiding from ourselves those aspects of our behavior that influence how our partner responds to us. When we choose to hide our feelings we are fooling no one but ourselves.

Partners can help each other to improve their intended behavior by giving feedback in a timely, supportive, and loving manner. If feedback is not given in this manner, the receiving partner often becomes defensive, counterattacks, or takes flight by withdrawing. Some couples tell me they have tried to provide each other feedback about various aspects of their marriage and that the results were not rewarding. This raises the question of whether there is a skill element in providing feedback. There is a skill element, and it can be learned. Over the years I have observed that feedback can be made more welcome and helpful if a few simple rules are followed. I will discuss some suggested rules below but, first, a reminder: do everything in the spirit of love with a desire to help your partner.

Focus Feedback on Behavior Rather Than the Person

It is important that we refer to what our partner has done rather than comment on what our partner is. This focus on behavior suggests that we use adverbs (which relate to actions) rather than adjectives (which relate to qualities).

Focus on Description Rather Than Judgment

The need to describe dictates a process for reporting what occurred, while judgment involves an evaluation of it in terms of good or bad, right or wrong, nice or not nice. Judgments arise from a personal frame of reference or value system; description represents neutral reporting. By avoiding judgmental, evaluative language, the tendency for our partner to become defensive is reduced. This kind of feedback provides even greater benefit when we tell our partner the effect their behavior has on us. Both the description of the behavior and the effect can be included in a sample statement: When we were planning our vacation you insisted on making all the decisions, and I felt forced to accept your ideas or face an attack from you.

Focus on the Benefit of the Feedback to the Receiver, Not the Giver

Feedback can have a counterproductive outcome when it is given to serve the needs of the giver. It always must be given and received as an offer, not an imposition. When a partner is truly ready to deal with the question "How am I doing?", there will be a greater likelihood of it being seriously considered and acted upon. Finally, to be effective, feedback must be directed toward behavior the receiver can change. Frustration and resentment often result when partners are reminded of some shortcoming or behavior over which they have no control.

Focus Feedback on Behavior Related to a Specific Situation Rather Than the Abstract

What you and your partner do is always specific to a time and place and you can increase your understanding of your behavior by considering it in terms of the forces acting on you at the time the behavior occurred. To be told "You never help me around the house" is not as helpful as "I was counting on you to help me take down the Christmas decorations."

Focus Feedback on the Sharing of Ideas and Information, Rather Than Giving Advice in the Form of Answers and Solutions

By sharing ideas and information we leave our partner free to decide how to use the feedback, or whether it will be used at all. When we give advice, we are restricting our partner's freedom to determine their most appropriate course of action. It might well be said that we are providing our partner answers and solutions for which there are no problems.

Focus on Sharing Feedback at an Appropriate Time and Place

In general, feedback is most helpful at the earliest moment after the behavior in question has occurred. Naturally, there are constraints which often make such timely sharing difficult. Helpful, well-intentioned feedback presented at an inappropriate time may do more harm than good.

Before leaving the subject of feedback, I want to suggest that our goal or purpose always should be considered before giving feedback. Always ask, "Are my intentions loving and supportive or do they reflect a need to punish and get even?" The latter motive is completely out of order in a helping relationship, but, unfortunately, it can dominate our thinking when we let ourselves become angry over something our partner has done. I'm not suggesting that a feeling of anger should be denied or covered. Doing this would violate the value of honesty which I also esteem. Rather, it should be shared in a context similar to: "When you reneged on our plans to attend the ballet, I felt angry toward you. But I don't like feeling angry and separated from you. Can we talk about it?"

When presented this way, the giver is not only being honest about the feeling of anger, but also about feeling guilty over feeling angry and separated. In my view, the giver is accepting full responsibility for both feelings: anger and guilt. The giver is honest and caring; there is no intent or desire to hurt or punish.

Feedback can also be given when we desire to support or encourage our partner. When Lenora shared her desire to be able to speak more comfortably before groups, I always tried to be on hand and observe her. I also tried to be helpful, and I found that my feedback not only helped her to improve her performance but also enhanced our relationship. On one occasion, she said, "Russ, I really appreciate your standing by me. It's been hard for me to get up before groups, but knowing you're on my side has made it easier. Thanks." Her words made me want to help her even more.

The ultimate goal of all feedback in marriage must be to help the partners achieve a higher level of satisfaction and fulfillment in their marriage. However, if feedback is given for self-serving reasons, or if the partners do not stay in the situation and deal with the consequences of the feedback, their marriage can be harmed rather than helped.

Loving With Head and Heart

During a couples therapy session, I gave part of the group a brief description of an imaginary person that included the following traits: Intelligent, skillful, industrious, warm, determined, practical, cautious

To the other portion of the group I gave the following description:

Intelligent, skillful, industrious, cold, determined, practical, cautious

I then gave everyone a list of fourteen pairs of contrasting traits such as polite-blunt, social-reserved, and imaginative-realistic. They were asked to choose individually one trait from each pair of traits that was consistent with the brief description I had earlier given to them. Members whose descriptions included the word "warm" tended to choose positive, complimentary traits such as generous, sociable, popular, and sensitive. People whose descriptions included the word "cold" consistently chose ,negative uncomplimentary traits such as ungenerous, formal, reserved, unpopular, and calloused.

I asked why some members tended to choose positive traits while others members chose negative traits. After a while they discovered the one-word difference in the two descriptions. They reacted with both embarrassment and anger. Embarrassment was experienced, especially by men, when they recognized how the words "warm" and "cold" caused them to choose different traits from the list of paired traits. What they did violated their perceptions of themselves as logical, rational thinkers. They were angry because they felt I had deceived them. "How did I deceive you?" I asked. "I gave each of you a description. Albeit, I did substitute one little, four-letter word. But look at the difference that one word made in the traits you chose."

When we encounter words like intelligent or skillful we depend upon the dictionary to tell us what they mean. When we read or hear words like warm or cold, however, we don't bother with the dictionary--our reaction is intuitive. The former words call for an intellectual understanding; the latter words involve an emotional or feeling response. It is the difference between head (rational, analytical, logical) and heart (emotional, intuitive, judgmental). It is also the difference between what today is being referenced as left-brain (logical, etc.) and right-brain (emotional, etc.) functioning.

When I asked clients which was more important "What you feel?" or "What you know?" they invariably answered in favor of their feelings. This discovery does not negate, however, the fact that our society puts a big premium on knowing. Have you ever been admonished to keep your personal feelings out of your work behavior? Or, more directly, were you ever scolded with the words, "What do you mean, you feel? You're supposed to know." Both classroom and work experiences condition people for this dependency on rational, non-emotional thinking and they respond that way, believing it will improve their chances for promotions, raises, etc. Then when these behaviors are rewarded, people behave this way more strongly. But when they behave this way almost exclusively at the work place they tend to take it home; they can't or don't leave that way of behaving behind when the workday ends.

Wade, a thirty-four-year-old engineer, took the thoughts home with him and it became a matter of great concern to Angela. In an individual therapy session, Angela was describing her feelings about Wade's habit of criticizing her whenever she could not explain to his satisfaction why she did a certain thing as she did. "Do I always have to give Wade a reason for everything I do? I don't know why I like chocolate, I just do."

"Whether I answer "Yes" or "No" to your question is not the real issue, Angela. What does seem to be important is how you can get Wade to stop giving you the third degree every time you say 'I feel....'"

"Yes, that's what I want. Why does he always want me to think like a computer? One Mr. Spock in the family is enough."

I was slow that day and had to ask who Mr. Spock was. "Aren't you a Trekkie?" she countered. My memory returned just in time to save me from asking another embarrassing question. "Oh! *Star Trek*. Yes, of course. Captain Kirk, Mr. Spock. I see what you mean."

Angela's concern is widespread. Although it is described in different terms, with different intensities and different consequences, it is found to some degree in almost all marriages. What are we talking about? Let's bring the problem into clearer focus by looking at the main characters in the TV program, *Star Trek*. First there is James T. Kirk, Captain of the United Star Ship Enterprise. In each show he is confronted with a problem, usually centering around people and things and two possible ways of solving the problem. One kind of solution is dependably represented by Science Officer Spock, half Vulcan and half Earthling. Mr. Spock is characteristically unemotional, logical, cold, precise, and thinks like a computer. An alternate solution is represented by Lt. Commander McCoy, the warm and caring ship's surgeon. Compared to Mr. Spock, Dr. McCoy is emotional, intuitive and human-relations oriented, and always is admonishing Mr. Spock to give a damn about people. With his two assistants giving him conflicting advice, the question always is "What will Captain Kirk do? Will he listen with his head (Mr. Spock) or his heart (Dr. McCoy)? Or will he try to balance the two?"

The essence of a vital, loving marriage relationship is emotional rather than intellectual; it is more Mr. McCoy than it is Mr. Spock. Over time, it is the give and take of feelings and sentiments that builds a relationship and provides a language for sharing with our partners our awareness of relevant experiences--for example, love, passion, loneliness, and fear. We always describe these experiences in terms of "I feel...." Thus, our feelings tell us whether what we are experiencing is pleasurable, threatening or painful. Because they serve this useful function, feelings are often described as our sixth sense--the sense that monitors, interprets, and directs the other five. Although we don't fully understand the physiology of feelings, there is nothing mysterious or mystical about their influence on both our thinking and our behavior. When feelings speak, we listen and act accordingly, even though we can't understand why in the intellectual sense.

Imagine that you have tasted a particular food for the first time and that you are trying to decide whether you like it. How do you decide? Is it through some complex intellectual process in which such features of the food as density, color, and nutrition are analyzed? Or is it an extemporaneous sensation of liking or not liking. We don't analyze; we respond. And we respond in the language of feelings.

Over the years I counseled numerous people, both men and women, who tried to rationalize an extramarital affair by claiming that it was just a physical thing--that there was no emotional involvement. My response was always somewhat the same. "In saying that there was no emotional involvement, do you mean that you had no feeling of love or liking for the other person, that you made no expressions of endearment or pleasure in the relationship, and that you looked upon the other person as an "it" rather than as a "thou"?"

"I'm telling you it was just physical. No feelings at all. It didn't mean a thing, so don't try to make me feel guilty."

Sex with an unfeeling partner has been the brunt of many off-color jokes and cartoons, most of them pointed at women. But when I talk to women about the unfavorable light in which these jokes place them, I get a very different story. "I have many feelings; they're just not the ones (her partner) wants me to have." There is no way for a woman or a man not to have feelings during sex unless they are brain dead, which would make sex impossible. Not to have feelings is not to be alive. From the viewpoint of a man, he cannot perform sexually in the absence of feelings of passion and desire. This observation is also true of nocturnal erections. The only difference is that they occur in a different level of consciousness. Feelings are present there, also.

Earlier, I described feelings as a special language through which experiences are shared and decisions are made. When experiences are pleasant and decisions easily are made, use of this language becomes an end in itself. It is valued because it meets the couple's emotional needs. Because this kind of communication is concerned with sharing our state of mind, it actually can enhance the intensity of our feelings, opening the door to real intimacy. The more open we are to the experience of feelings, particularly new feelings, the more comfortable we become with them. We learn to trust our feelings. We don't block out new, unrecognized feelings nor do we retreat from feelings which threaten pain or anxiety.

Like many other dichotomies in life, our feelings are generally of two kinds. One kind, positive feelings, is recognized and accepted openly within the limits imposed by society and our cultural conditioning. Laughter, for example, often is constrained by volume, exuberance, and duration; sexual feelings and intimate displays of affection are constrained to private places. The other kind, negative feelings, has an adverse effect since they interfere with or displace the experience of positive feelings. Although we easily can distinguish these two kinds of feelings in a theoretical sense, the line between them often becomes clouded when we put them into action. For example, one common response to feelings of anxiety and fear is laughter. Thus, we can observe a single response that can be motivated by two difference kinds of feelings. Because of our inability always to clearly distinguish our feelings and moderate even appropriate responses, we become suspicious and fearful of all our feelings. Clearly, this is a dysfunctional circumstance.

People who do resist or deny their feelings gradually lose touch with them. They also tend to develop a fear of their feelings. Feelings become something that is mistrusted--something to be avoided. When this happens there always are negative consequences for the relationship. When we are unable to share painful or threatening feelings we distance ourselves from our partner, fearing that discovery would lead to embarrassment, ridicule, or even rejection. Likewise, rejection of our positive feelings is a denial of opportunities for growth and renewal of feelings of love, kindness, and forgiveness. Accepting and working through negative feelings can have positive outcomes, especially when the goal is to remove hindrances to higher levels of interpersonal relating.

Remember Marcia? She felt victimized by her sexual feelings. She enjoyed sex with Felton and was secretly desirous of improvising their lovemaking in ways that would heighten her sexual pleasure. However, she felt she had to hide her sexual feelings because she had no right to them--that they, in fact, were wrong. Unable to accept the responsibility for her sexual feelings on the one hand, and being unable to express them to Felton on the other, she felt trapped. The pleasure she so much desired was actually placed off-limits by her. Still, she rationalized that if Felton, without her asking, did things that enhanced her pleasure she was not responsible, even though she would be pleased that he did. Gradually, as she was able to resolve her relationship with her mother, she was able to accept the legitimacy of her sexual feelings and claimed her right to satisfaction of these feelings in her relationship with Felton.

Given the importance of feelings in almost every area of our lives, it is difficult to understand our resistance to accepting them as a vital part of our psychological makeup. Have we become so scientific and logical in our high-tech world that any admission of feelings diminishes our sense of well-being. Do societal emphases on the objective dimensions of living blind us to the central role our feelings play in directing the performance of our lives?

To have feelings is not to be out of control. Rather, feelings reflect our acceptance of all aspects of our being, whether positive or negative. It is through our feelings that we recognize and respond to such emotions as guilt, anxiety, and anger. In a similar manner we use feelings to express love, caring, and forgiveness. Without feelings, our survival instinct would become less tenable. It's not a question of being emotional or rational. It is doubtful whether any of us ever will be as specialized as Mr. Spock or Dr. McCoy. Neither is it likely that we ever would have the freedom to choose between living wholly in one domain to the exclusion of the other. The holistic, well-integrated, highly-functioning person always will use an appropriate mix of the two. It is simply a matter of being able to function in the rational domain when, say, preparing income tax returns and having the courage to share feelings when expressing the sentiments and values of love, romance, and relationships. In another sense, it is having the freedom to use our intellect when it is appropriate and to express our feelings when use of intellect is neither feasible nor desirable. As Fulton Ousler once said, "...we must use the brains that God has given to us. But we must also use our hearts which he also gave us."

Enthusiasm

"A week ago I didn't even know what a marriage and family therapist was. Now I am one."

There are numerous versions of the above one-liner, each casting a disparaging light upon some particular profession or human circumstance. The reason is vague, but I was reminded of the above when I first read *Entropy* (Bantam, 1981) by Jeremy Rifkin. It was a description on the front cover that caught my eye: "Entropy is the supreme law of nature and governs everything we do." As I read the opening pages about the Law of Entropy, I began to reflect, "An hour ago I didn't even know what entropy was. Now I understand how everything in the physical world is influenced, if not governed, by it."

What is entropy? It is found in many forms and can be described or defined in many ways. In the mechanical world it is friction, which causes inefficiency and the eventual wearing out of a system or machine. In the world of communications, it is static which distorts the legibility of a signal or message. The field of electronics is always confronted with resistance, which impedes the free flow of electrical energy through a wire. In the world of nature, entropy is a measure of the disorder, chaos, or waste in a system. In essence, the Law of Entropy suggests that everything in the universe began with structure and value, but moves irrevocably in one direction: from being usable to being unusable, from being available to being unavailable, from being identifiable to being unidentifiable. To put it in other words, all systems, physical and social, tend to run down, wear out, or dissipate unless some means are found to thwart or combat the Law of Entropy.

Consider the family automobile. Even though quality again is becoming a goal of manufacturers and there is less programmed obsolescence, an automobile, from the moment it is built, follows its own path to an inevitable "automobile death." Of course this death march can be delayed by careful driving and disciplined maintenance, but it cannot be avoided. Replacement of worn-out parts can only delay the inevitable. Even a complete overhaul and new paint does little more than add a small measure of new life.

Does the Law of Entropy also apply to marriage? I think so. And only an understanding of what it is and how it affects a marriage can help us to combat it.

Marriage, as a form of social organization, shares with all creatures in the natural world, a predictable life cycle or pattern. Sequentially, marriages have a supple, ripening youth, an adolescence characterized by flourishing strength and change; a middle-age of striving and maturity; and, finally, a period of gnarled old age characterized by dysfunction and loss of meaning and purpose. While this life cycle is predictable, there is no fixed pattern that every marriage must follow. Nor is there a fixed length to each phase of the cycle. Further, there is no relationship between the phases of the cycle and the years of marriage or the ages of the partners in the marriage. I know of marriages which, after many years, are still experiencing the ecstasy of youth. Other marriages come to mind which, though young in years, already are showing the rigidities and stagnation of old age. I have described this cycle of marriage as predictable, but it is not an absolute. Marriages don't have to follow this pattern in an inescapable, inflexible manner. They often do, to be sure, but it is something that can be delayed. It also is possible for a marriage to go into a period of decline and to be renewed. Whether a marriage follows a path of decline in a lock-step pattern or instead follows a pattern of renewal and growth is a result of the choices the partners make.

Karl and Aretha chose the latter path. A part of their story follows.

Typically, I began an initial therapy session with a new couple by asking some routine questions. These questions, asked in a fixed interview pattern, were designed to secure relevant information about the couple as individuals and about their marriage. After this process is concluded, I then ask something like "How can I help you?" or "What changes would you like to make in your marriage?" After learning that Karl was a pathologist on the medical staff of a local hospital and that Aretha was a department head in a biomedical laboratory, I asked, "What's wrong? Where are you hurting?" In view of what I subsequently learned about Karl and Aretha I was glad that I phrased the question the way I did, although, in retrospect, I felt that I was a bit unprofessional since I was prejudging them.

"There's nothing wrong with our marriage. That's not why we are here," explained Aretha.

"There's nothing wrong? Your marriage is not hurting? Why have you come to see me?"

"Maybe I should have explained things a bit more when I called," Aretha countered. "Perhaps we haven't been fair with you."

Taking a cue from Aretha, Karl began to explain what they wanted. "My dentist schedules me for a checkup each six months. Same with Aretha. The Orkin man comes around every three months or so. I have to have our cars inspected each year. And both Aretha and I get a physical exam each year around our birthday. Everything gets inspected except our marriage. That's why we are here. Can you help us? As far as we know, there's nothing that needs fixing. We just want our marriage to be as good as it can be. Will you help us?"

My reaction to Karl's explanation and his unusual request ranged from intrigue to fascination. "Let's talk a bit more before I decide whether I can help you," I suggested. As I explored more fully with them what they wanted to do I became hooked with the idea. "Why didn't I think of that?" I silently asked. "Yes, I'd like to work with you," I decided. Eight years later, we were still in a therapist-client relationship. At six-month intervals, Karl calls for an appointment. "When the dentist calls me, I call you," he said.

For Karl and Aretha, their marriage was the most central thing in their lives. With three children and two grandchildren, they were, at ages sixty-one and fifty-nine, respectively, enjoying the privileges and opportunities of the empty nest. They remained committed to their marriage and to each other. During the eight years I knew and worked with them, Karl and Aretha taught me much about love and devotion. They also have helped me to understand that a marriage does not have to be hurting in order to get better.

At the end of that first session, I asked them to individually prepare a written history of their marriage, beginning with their first meeting and continuing on to include why and how they decided to get their semi-annual marital checkup. After I explained my purpose in making this request, I suggested that each time we meet we would be able to add a new chapter to their history. When I received their histories, I read them carefully, making notes of those things that I considered important in helping them accomplish what they wanted to happen in their marriage. When I compared their histories I was astounded by their similarity. There were some small difference about such things as dates, places, and events. But in their expressions of their feelings about their love, their marriage, their goals and dreams, and the psychological and spiritual forces in their lives there was an amazing amount of agreement. It was like they had been holding hands and talking ever since they first met. Before writing these pages, I retrieved their histories. I want to share some of the things I learned from them.

Arteriosclerosis and cholesterol are twin afflictions of the human heart and its system of arteries. The first disease is characterized by a thickening and hardening of the arterial wall with loss of elasticity and flexibility, thereby impeding normal healthy blood flow in the body. Cholesterol, often called the painless killer, is a yellowish, fatty substance that floats in the blood. Although it performs a useful function and we need some of it to survive, an excessive amount of cholesterol can be life threatening. It forms plaque on the artery walls, restricting the flow of oxygen-carrying blood to the body's vital organs.

Both of these diseases, according to Karl and Aretha (remember their professional training), provided a metaphor for marriage. A marriage's arteries are the channels through which the partners share feelings, experiences, ideas, and other pertinent information. How well these channels of communication serve their intended purpose also is affected by the partner's attitudes and predispositions, which may either facilitate or impede a two-way flow of communication. If these communication arteries harden or become blocked, partners lose most of their potential capacity to respond to each other in a caring, understanding way about new information and changed circumstances. On an almost daily basis new evidence is furnished that hardening and blockage of a body's arteries can be fatal. Unfortunately, the metaphorical effect holds for marriage. Although this disease process is comparatively easier to remedy in marriage than in our bodies, it must be realized that what a couple loses because of the disease can never be regained. Far better is the idea of prevention.

The idea of the twin maladies of arteriosclerosis and cholesterol, when applied to marriage, has the effect of reducing the flow of psychological energy needed to "fuel" the relationship. When this happens, the Law of Entropy takes over and the marriage begins to run down--losing its vitality and energy. Still, the marriage has maintenance needs that must be met or else it will deteriorate even further. The energy required for maintaining the marriage at some minimal level of satisfaction is often greater than the energy available to the partners. When the available energy is not used effectively, the marriage, figuratively runs out of gas. This condition is more serious and far-reaching than the state of boredom which often develops when the newness of marriage wears off. It is, however, often presaged by boredom since boredom can a predisposing factor of marital entropy. This is especially true when the underlying causes of boredom are not recognized and removed.

I discussed this concern with Karl and Aretha. After we clarified the matter somewhat they seemed eager to respond. As we talked, I made a mental note of the number of times they used the word "enthusiasm." This word, more than any other, explained the sources of psychological energy in their lives. In one instance Aretha referred to it as "life force." I had expected them to talk about their love, their commitment, or, maybe, their concern for each other. These things were important to them, but it was enthusiasm that made the difference between love with a small "l" and love with a large "L." Enthusiasm made the difference between cold-hearted loving and warm-hearted loving.

Their enthusiasm also gave an extra measure of value to their commitment. To them, enthusiasm was an attitude, one that was unconditionally accepted, carefully nurtured, and acted out in a spirit of love. It's more than eagerness, different from passion, and more powerful than simply wanting or desiring. To be less than enthusiastic in a relationship is to demean the integrity of the partners and their marriage. Enthusiasm, according to Karl and Aretha, is something partners owe to each other. Every shared moment and every happening in their lives is a miracle for them, and they always respond with an attitude of joyous anticipation and appreciation.

"Do you ever tire?" I asked. "Living on such a high plane obviously requires a lot of energy."

"Do you mean tired like being fatigued? Yes, of course, but we don't think of it as being something to avoid, like a cost. Rather, we find it exhilarating since it means we have used energy in doing something meaningful. We might get tired more often than a lot of other people because we try to stay active while they sometimes fall into the trap of thinking there's nothing to do. They get bored, even depressed. Well, you can't be active and depressed at the same time. No, being tired and needing rest is not a problem for us; it's a natural accompaniment of being active, of being alive. I feel tired after we have sex, but the feeling is overshadowed by my feelings of joy and contentment. Knowing that energy was used in doing something that was exciting and rewarding makes resting more enjoyable. Resting is a creative activity. It is not, as often described, a lack of activity. It is a means to an end, not an end in itself. Rest is renewal; it is transformation."

"Both of you seem to be saying that the self is a valuable, unlimited source of psychological energy. Is it available to all people? Is it something that's there for the taking, or does it have to be generated?"

"It might be easier to answer your question in medical terms but I don't think that's what you want. Yes, it's there for everyone. It has nothing to do with genes, age, education, or status in life. All people, for example, are capable of responding to external and internal stimulation. This requires energy. They also are capable of self-direction, which also requires energy. What I mean is that people can modify their behavior and their resultant feelings to meet varied situations. When they respond with a sense of enthusiasm--what some people call positive thinking--they generate more energy than is required for a particular response. Aretha and I choose always to be positive; we try to see the good in everything we do. Our time is too valuable to waste it in complaining, finding fault, criticizing, and blaming others. The real difference is in the way we use that extra energy. When I work in the garden I think of it as fun, not work. That's the difference I'm talking about."

"During the session with your children I got the feeling that they look on life much as you do. You said it was not genetic. How did they learn to be like they are--to have an attitude toward life that is much like yours? Aretha, as a mother, how do you explain it?"

"I never thought about what we are referring to as an attitude until Karl and I started dating. My family of origin didn't have it; Karl's family did. Anyway, he and I talked a lot about the meaning of life and what kind of marriage we wanted to have. We made choices which were consistent with our dreams and the pieces just came together. We helped our children to see that they, too, could make choices. We also helped them to see the possibilities in their own lives. Finally, we try to model our enthusiasm and sense of expectation to them, all in a sense of love and acceptance."

"One more question. Karl, you earlier said something about other sources of energy--sources outside of the self. Would you comment on that?"

"This time I'm going to the Bible (John 21:16-17) for my answer. Do you remember how Jesus asked Peter to "...Feed my sheep?" Aretha and I feel strongly that we are constantly being fed by others--our family, our friends, especially those in our church. We're part of a Christian community and we feed each other. Whatever we give always seems to come back to us in double measure, like the saying that what goes around comes around. Giving and receiving always has a synergistic effect: two plus two is always more than four.

Chapter Six

Helping Through Listening and Information Sharing

A brief article in the May 17, 1990 issue of our local newspaper caught my attention. It described the plight of Robert Polhill, who recently had been released after thirty-nine months of captivity in Lebanon. Because of a malignant throat cancer, the medical doctors at Walter Reed Hospital decided to remove his larynx. With the surgery, he would lose his ability to speak normally forever.

The article had a sobering effect on me. As I tried to deal with my feelings, I uttered a prayer to God to be with this man, his family, and the doctors who would perform the surgery. Then, naturally I suppose, I began to relate to Mr. Polhill's circumstances in a more personal way. "What if it were me?" I thought. "If I were losing my ability to speak, what would be my last words? With whom would I share them?"

Later in the summer, I posed these questions to the members of a marriage therapy group. Their responses reflected the full range of human emotions, from expressions of love to evasive, avoidance behaviors.

"I'd tell my wife and children that I loved them."

"I'd want everyone that I loved to be there. I couldn't leave anyone out."

"Maybe I'm looking at things differently. My last words would be a prayer."

"I'd let out a big yell, as loud as I could. Like in the movie, *Good Morning, Viet Nam*."

"I'd want to remember music; yes, I'd sing a song."

"Yeah, that's a great idea. I could always write Henry a love note."

"Gosh, this is just too awful to think about. But whatever I said, I'd make a recording of it."

As I listened to their answers and to their reactions to what others said, I reflected on our tendency to get serious and sentimental when confronted with the possible loss of something we have always taken for granted. Although we were discussing the loss of our voices in a hypothetical sense, the participants were responding as though they had suddenly discovered how precious the gift of speech really is. Why should we have to be confronted with the prospect of losing that ability to learn a great lesson about life? As my thoughts about what was happening began to take form, I shared them with the group. There was a long silence. No one said a word; there was absolute silence. After what appeared to be an eternity, we responded with nervous, muffled laughter as Janice's stomach made a thundering, rolling noise.

"Lamar, please do us a favor," I quickly asked. "Would you stand in the middle of the group and give us a sample of the big yell that you mentioned?"

As he finished we gave him a hearty applause. First, for his exuberant, spontaneous performance and, second, because what he did helped remove the pall that had settled over us. We seemingly applauded more for the second reason than we did for the first. Whatever, it brought us back to the here and now of the group process. And that was good.

The most frequent complaint I hear as I work with families--and with organizations--has to do with breakdowns in communication. Consider the following examples.

"Jeannette and I just can't talk anymore."

"Communication between us has broken down; Roy and I can't resolve anything."

"If only Saritha and I could talk without arguing...."

"What's the use of talking? Ted doesn't listen anymore.

In therapy these complaints become more specific.

Wife: "He argues, talks past me, and puts me down."

Husband: "She nags, won't say what she means, and misleads me."

Wife: "He ignores me, talks too loudly, and never offers praise for anything I do."

Husband: "She talks out of both sides of her mouth, talks too softly, and is unrealistic."
Wife: Etc.
Husband: Etc.

In all these complaints is the idea that couples have problems because they are unable or unwilling to communicate in a meaningful way. Poor communication is seen as the villain--it causes the problem couples are having. I would never argue against the idea that by improving our interpersonal communication skills we might be better able to solve our relationship problems. But I take issue with the conclusion people often make about the cause-and-effect relationship between poor communication and marital problems. In my experience, just the opposite is true. Rather than being the cause of marital problems, poor communication is made the scapegoat for other problems in the marriage. In marriages where relationships are sound, problems of communication tend not to occur. I'm not claiming that partners with good interpersonal relationships do not experience misunderstandings and conflict. They do. But when problems do occur, they are able to resolve them quickly in a win-win manner without any malingering feelings of rancor. In this chapter I will discuss communication in terms of the relationship between partners. Two aspects of communication not often mentioned in discussions of marital communication will be emphasized. These are perception, how we make sense of our world, and motivation, the question of whether we want to communicate.

Reality: Fact or Perception

Fact: At his company's Christmas party Ben looks across the room and sees his wife, Audrey, talking to his boss. She is laughing, smiling, and seems much more expressive and animated than usual. Ben's boss is articulate, handsome, and, because he has never married, is considered very eligible.

Ben's negative perception: Audrey is flirting with his boss.

Likely consequences: When Ben and Audrey get back together, he is cold and distant toward her. Sensing a show of jealousy on his part, Audrey responds with annoyance and a gentle admonition not to act ugly in public. Ben interprets her response as being insensitive to his feelings and that she would rather be with his boss than with him. A stony, cold silence dominates their relationship during the rest of the evening. Things really get hot, however, after they get home.

Ben's positive perception: Audrey is innocently lapping up his boss's jokes and stories about his overseas adventures. Ben knows Audrey understands office politics and that her behavior is designed to make a good impression upon his boss and thereby help him career-wise.

Likely consequences: When Ben and Audrey are reunited he compliments her for taking advantage of the opportunity to talk with his boss. If his perception was correct, Audrey will respond affectionately to his compliment. If his perception was wrong and she was flirting, Audrey will probably feel bad about her behavior and respond affectionately because of Ben's non-critical, understanding behavior. Whatever her intention, in either case they go home and make love.

Let's look at the fact again. What was Audrey really doing? Whatever, it constitutes an objective reality: a fact that exists independently of subjective interpretations. Ben's perception of what Audrey was doing is his personal, subjective reality, which may or may not agree with Audrey's actual intentions. What determines whether Ben will make a negative or a positive perception of her behavior? There is a cliché about perception that suggests we see what we want to see. An extension of this cliché is that we see what we expect to see. In the latter case, for example, we tend to look for and accept only information that is consistent with what we already know about events, objects, or persons being observed and discussed. This is what happened, for example, in the warm-cold exercise I described in Chapter Five. However Ben perceives his wife's behavior, everything that he subsequently says or does will be based upon his perception of the behavior in question and the meaning he attaches to it.

How we perceive and assign meaning to events, objects, or other persons is unique and personal. Since no two people are alike in terms of their needs, values, and expectations, no two people perceive a particular event, object, or person in exactly the same way. What one partner thinks is beautiful, the other may think ugly. The most pervasive difficulty in marital communication, in my experience, is the fact that each partner thinks his/her perception is the correct perception--that it is reality. The possible negative consequences of an erroneous or distorted perception can easily be imagined. People who work with computers have an expression that seems to apply here. It is "GIGO," an acronym for garbage in, garbage out. An erroneous perception (garbage in) inevitably leads to inappropriate behavior (garbage out).

When our background experiences--what I will refer to as memory--are cluttered with faulty learning, prejudices, stereotypes, and unconscious needs and values, our perceptual accuracy necessarily is distorted. Since every act of communication is preceded by an act of perception, it is critical for us to develop insight into how accurately we perceive our world.

A woman client shared a joke with me that illustrates the possible consequences of partners having different perceptions. According to her story, a husband and wife had been kissing and embracing several minutes when the husband whispered, "Let's make love." The wife, reflecting a moment of confusion, replied, "I thought we were." Although my client would not admit to being the involved wife, I really appreciated her joke. It shows what can happen when two people who are engaged in the same activity have different perceptions about what they are doing.

What is reality? How can we know it? In one sense, reality is only a stimulus--something that can be noticed or detected by one of our five senses. When our sensory mechanisms are well developed and we have an adequate background of cognitive experiences relative to particular sights, sounds, touches, tastes, and smells we can perceive various stimuli with only minimal error or distortion. But without some prior experience of, say, smelling a rose it would be impossible for us to identify a particular flower as being a rose by its smell only.

In a similar manner a two-year old who has just learned that the new household pet is a "dog" may also point to a kitten and say, "Doggie." The child cannot yet discriminate; the presence of four legs, fur, and a tail calls for the label "dog." As vocabulary and experience increase, so do perceptual abilities. The point I want to make here is that partners will always view things from different perspectives and with different perceptual abilities. What is reality for them? Is it what they perceive it to be? Or does it have an existence apart from their individual perceptions? The fact that there are no easy answers to these questions is the source of frequent marital misunderstandings and conflicts. Can they be alleviated? I will offer a brief, qualified answer.

Our errors in perceiving events, objects, and persons are caused more by our own characteristics than characteristics of the things being perceived. Thus, it would follow that the more we know ourselves the more accurately we can perceive things outside ourselves. And how do we get to know ourselves? Ironically, we can never know more about ourselves than we are willing to let others know about us. This is the challenge and the reward of love, trust, and openness in marriage.

Russ Holloman, Ph. D.

Love, Trust, and Openness

In Chapter Five, I discussed the marriage relationship as interactive and interdependent. In describing marriage as interactive I wanted to emphasize that partners become married in a psychological and sexual sense only when they are in each other's social and physical presence. It is through interacting that their marriage is made real; without this interactive relationship, their marriage is never truly consummated. When the partners do interact, they quickly realize that their relationship is also interdependent. By this, I mean that the motivation and behavior of each partner both affects and is affected by the motivation and behavior of the other. This characteristic of their relationship dictates that they are always adjusting, hopefully growing and becoming. The dynamics of an interdependent relationship cannot be captured with a box-type, still camera; a movie camera is required. As the behavior of one partner affects the other the other partner is changed in some way. In turn the new behavior of the changed partner affects the other partner in a new and different way.

Imagine a scenario of a husband wishing to please or have a positive effect on his wife. He wants her to think well of him, to accept him, to love him. Having this goal, he behaves toward her in ways which he feels will produce the desired effect. Whenever he interacts with her there is necessarily an effect. Is it the effect he desires? The only way he can confirm or disconfirm his desired effect is through her feedback. In the absence of feedback about the actual effect of his behavior, he can do little more than blunder on, hoping he's doing everything right.

Why wouldn't his wife want to provide him timely, descriptive feedback about his behavior? Maybe the effect of his behavior is negative and she doesn't want to hurt his feelings. Maybe she is unsure how he would react to potentially negative feedback. Or, maybe she is fearful of and frightened by her own feelings and tries to repress them. Or, maybe, as I often hear partners say, "I don't know how I feel." Whatever her reasons, she is denying her husband valuable information that he could use in determining the appropriateness of his behavior toward her. If, for example, he received confirming feedback that some particular behavior had a positive, desirable effect on her he would continue that behavior, perhaps trying to behave that way more often. On the other hand, if he received disconfirming feedback about his behavior, he likely would refrain from that behavior. So, since his wife either doesn't care enough or is unwilling to risk enough to provide him feedback, there is a blind-spot in their relationship. Still desiring to impress his wife, the husband shares only complimentary information about himself which he feels will produce that effect. More than merely concealing unfavorable information about himself, he might behave in nontraditional ways which differ from his usual behavioral patterns. Remember, he's trying to present an image he thinks she will like. He pretends, hoping she will see him in positive ways he knows he is not. He has two goals: (1) don't reveal possibly negative information, and (2) pretend to be something he knows he is not, if necessary, to achieve the desired effect. He wears a mask to conceal possibly negative information; he builds and maintains facades of a person he thinks she will like. Because of his deceptive behavior his wife can never know him as he really is. When she becomes aware of his concealing behavior, realizing he is presenting a false picture of himself, she becomes suspicious. "Why does he do this? Can I trust him?"

Ironically, the more successful the husband is in mask-wearing and facade-building behavior the more he loses contact with the reality of his being. When he can no longer relate to his wife in terms of his true being, he is driven to even greater extremes of the behavior that caused his predicament in the first place.

The result of the blind-spot and the facades and masks is that the channel or artery of communication between the partners is blocked. Remember our cholesterol analogy in the previous chapter? This psychological cholesterol can be just lethal as the physiological kind. When partners don't know the thoughts, feelings, and motivations of the other, when they engage in a lot of deceptive behavior toward each other, they lose faith in their ability to communicate. "Why bother?" they ask. Do partners have to suffer these self-inflicted wounds? No. Their relationship can be changed. It's not always easy, but it can be changed. Wanting to change it is half the battle.

In real life, it is often difficult to remove the barriers to more effective communication. To facilitate our discussion, let's magically remove them so we can look at the relationship from another critical perspective.

Have you ever thought about how unguarded you are when you are sleeping? I remember Lenora once saying to me at breakfast, "Russ, you were smiling in your sleep last night. What were you dreaming about?" I couldn't remember dreaming, and I didn't know why I was smiling, if I was. I was left wondering, however, why she had taken note of my smiling. Why did she mention it to me? As unguarded and vulnerable as we are while sleeping, the moment we awaken fences are erected to protect us from others. Yes, even from our partner. These fences aren't made of wood, wire or concrete--they are made with behavior: how we relate to our partner, what we share with them, how open or closed we are in discussing relevant aspects of our relationship. The reason we build these fences (defenses) is to protect the self from all the fire-breathing dragons out there that can hurt us.

Partners who erect and maintain these fences do great harm to their relationship, they suffer privately in a sinister and damaging way. This is the essence of my argument: it requires sustained effort to build these fences and keep them up. Both psychological and physiological energy is required to keep one's guard up against any inadvertent disclosure of information about themselves that might result in embarrassment, ridicule, or loss of esteem. Recall how you typically behave toward someone whom you don't want to know certain information about you. Most likely you try to keep the conversation on safe subjects. Any effort by the other person to discuss something that you feel you must protect is immediately rebuffed--the fences go higher as the flames of the dragon get closer.

In 1959, I was a young Air Force officer stationed in Germany with my wife and daughter. I had received two quick promotions and was often told by my superiors that I had a promising future in the Air Force. I liked this kind of talk and began to visualize myself as a future colonel, or even as a general. My job provided frequent access to important people who could run interference and open doors for me. I was investing a lot of time and effort in building favorable work and social relationships with these people.

Everything was coming up roses for me until that morning when the chaplain came and told me that my father had committed suicide. Everything--I mean everything--changed at that moment. My grief was mixed with feelings of embarrassment, anger, and confusion. Then I started feeling guilty. Thoughts of how my father's suicide might affect my career began to dominate my thinking. In my youthful naiveté I reasoned that only crazy people took their lives, and I knew the Air Force would never promote me to the high rank to which I aspired if there were questions about my mental stability. I was plagued by the ancient question, "Do the sins of the father really fall upon the son?" I couldn't let that happen to me. As soon as I consciously entertained that possibility, I unconsciously decided that no one would ever know how my father died. Without being fully conscious of what I was doing or why I was doing it, I started behaving in bizarre, injurious ways, all designed to protect my secret. My colleagues began to ask questions about me; my superiors began to criticize my work. My wife and daughter later told me how they, too, were affected by my defensive behavior. Without realizing it I was destroying the very relationships I should have been building. I was investing so much of my available energy in buying psychological protection that I had little energy left to perform my Air Force duties and to attend to my family. The fences I erected to keep other people out had become a jail that was locking me in.

It was inevitable that a breakdown would occur. And it did. I was hospitalized, and you can easily imagine what my diagnosis was. With the patient counseling of a wise, insightful therapist and the support of my family and friends I was helped to understand what had happened to me. The greatest help in accepting what I had done, however, came from my superior officer. He came to visit me in the hospital and I felt obligated to explain things to him. I wanted him to understand. As I labored to do this, he interrupted me to say, "Russ, did you really think that I didn't know about your father? Of course, I did. Chaplain Williams discussed it with me before he told you."

At that moment I felt like a fool, but I also felt relieved--I felt free. I didn't have to protect my secret any longer. What I had thought was a fire-breathing dragon turned out to be an Easter bunny. It wasn't easy, but as I recovered from this dark experience I began rebuilding relationships and performing my work at the quality level I previously had enjoyed. Within my family, I realized how much I had alienated myself from them. It saddened me to realize that I actually had thought of them as enemies. From both Lenora and my daughter, Suzanne, I received nothing but love and forgiveness even when they couldn't understand why I had behaved as I did. I promised them that, with God's help, I would never let that happen again. Looking back, I can now see that the seeds of my present work were planted at that time.

I hope that my story helps you to understand the possible consequences of overly rigid, exaggerated defensive behaviors. The more time, energy, and attention we invest in maintaining defenses, the less we have to devote to other more meaningful activities such as building family relationships, working, reading, and growing roses. I'm not arguing that people don't need some minimal level of psychological protection. Defensive behavior is often needed to help up cope with changing, ambiguous situations we encounter. But these fences should never be higher than they absolutely have to be.

What is an appropriate height? How is it determined? An adequate answer to these two questions requires more space than these pages permit, but I do want to suggest a rule or two. First, try to develop an awareness of the kinds of defensive behavior you are prone to use. Try to identify what it is that you are protecting, and then ask yourself, "What is the worst thing that could happen to me if this information were known by my partner?" Sometimes you will find that the possible consequences are not all that bad. You might discover, as I did, that what I thought was a firebreathing dragon was no more threatening than an Easter bunny. Again, I'm not arguing that there are no dragons out there. Whether they are real or only imagined, the effect is the same, and we feel the need to protect ourselves from them. For me, after understanding my need to lower the fences so I could communicate more honestly with others, I began to take small, prudent risks. When nothing bad happened, I was encouraged to risk more, to trust more. My fear of being vulnerable began to moderate as I was able to understand that vulnerability was preferred to withdrawal from every social situation containing any possibility of danger. More openness in my relationships with others, especially with Lenora, helped me to become more sensitive and concerned about their feelings and circumstances. With increased trust, I found that my behavioral flexibility also increased. I was no longer locked into rigid, repetitive, inappropriate patterns of behavior. I could choose behaviors that were congruent with my intentions toward others. As I sensed the freedom to make choices, and saw that I could produce good outcomes in my relationships with others, my confidence increased. And other people started relating to me in ways that reinforced my emerging behavior. It was another case of the self-fulfilling prophecy: we make happen those things we expect to happen. Referring to this time in my life, Lenora always said, "What goes around comes around." What she meant was that if we react to others with secretiveness and mistrust that is what we get in return. Others will respond with trust and openness when that is what we show to them.

Living in the Loving Room

In this section, I will review some of the ideas discussed above and will present them in a different way, using another model to help our understanding of communication between partners. This model has been

Making Marriage User Friendly

of great help to me, both in understanding my own relationship with Lenora and in helping partners in therapy. It involves a technique known as the Johari Window (Luft, 1969). It resembles a window with four panes, and the basis for dividing the window into quadrants is the amount of information each party has of the relevant thoughts, feelings, and motivations of the other. Figure 6-1 is a graphic illustration of the model and the descriptions I have given to each of the quadrants. My discussion will be from the perspective of Partner W.

Figure 6-1

Partner W

	Known	Unknown
Partner H. Known	Quadrant 1 Free Arena Loving Room	Quadrant 2 Blind Spot Denied Arena
Partner H. Unknown	Quadrant 3 Masks/Facades Hidden Arena	Quadrant 4 Unconscious Unknown Arena

Quadrant 1 is the arena of marriage in which partners are able to relate with openness and trust. In this arena, they are more spontaneous, more creative and more productive. There is no need to be secretive or to engage in destructive game-playing. In this arena, which I like to refer to as the loving room, is all the information about Partner W's behavior, feelings, and motivations that is known by both partners. It is conscious, verbalized, public, and contiguous in time and place. When two people first meet, quadrant one, compared to the others, is very small. This is because they are unknown to each other. Gradually, both before and after marriage, quadrant 1 grows larger as Partner W shares information which previously was hidden in quadrant 3, and Partner H shares information previously held in quadrant 2. Thus, quadrant 1 can be larger by making quadrants 2 and

3 smaller. The size and shape of quadrant 1 is an indication of the overall quality of the marriage. Quadrant 2 contains bits of information known to Partner H, but unknown to Partner W. This information generally consists of conscious but non-verbalized feelings and expectations Partner H has of Partner W. For reasons known only to him--lack of trust, fear of rejection or defensiveness, or the suspicion that his information is not germane or valid--he has never shared these feelings with Partner W. The more Partner H guards against disclosure of this information, the more preoccupied he becomes with the possibility of negative consequences of such disclosure--also, the more distant and impersonal he will be in the relationship. Since all the information in quadrant 2 is denied to Partner W, it is a blind spot for her. She doesn't know how she is perceived by her partner. The existence of this blind spot always will have an adverse effect on their marriage.

Quadrant 3 contains information that is known to Partner W but is unknown to Partner H. Since this information is under the direct control of Partner W, the shape and size of this quadrant is a function of her willingness to disclose. Why would she let this circumstance persist? Possibly she feels vulnerable to disclosure and doesn't want to prejudice the relationship. Or, she may wish to create a certain mystique or preserve a power base by keeping some things to herself. Whatever her reasons, this hidden area constitutes a barrier between her and her partner.

As with the blind arena, all partners have hidden arenas. When quadrant 3 is small it offers few obstacles to effective communication and understanding. However, to the extent that Partner W is defensive, insecure, or distrustful of her partner's responses to her, she will be less willing to take risks. Thus, Partner W can let this quadrant become large and rigid, isolating her partner in the process. This quadrant can be referred to Partner W's hidden area; she hides any information about herself she does not want known to her partner. She hides her real self behind a mask of her own choosing, presenting a facade of a person she knows that she is not. The negative consequences of Partner W's defensive behavior are easily imagined.

Quadrant 4 is a repository of information unknown to Partner W. It includes her unconscious feelings, thoughts, and motivations. Unfortunately, the content of this quadrant is also unknown to Partner H. You might question why anyone would be interested in this arena if they don't know what it contains. But that is exactly why we must be concerned with it. This quadrant is filled with possibilities--potentials, skills, and insights not yet discovered. It is the arena of growth. All the information now contained in quadrants 1 and 3 originally was in this unknown arena. Over time, through courtship, marriage, and the continuing process of adjustment, this information was moved from the unconscious arena into quadrant 3; some of it was further moved through the disclosure process into quadrant 1.

It is this sense of discovery that Dr. Scott Peck wrote about in *The Road Less Travelled* (1978). Dr. Peck, a psychiatrist, describes a technique he uses with patients in which he draws a large circle on a piece of paper. At the inside boundary, he draws a smaller circle. He explains that the small circle represents the patient's conscious mind. The remaining area of the large circle represents the patient's unconscious mind. This vast area, containing what Dr. Peck calls riches beyond our imagination, lies waiting to be discovered and understood. An individual's willingness to explore this arena is the key to growth and learning. Many partners choose to do this in therapy, learning to share the information previously hidden in quadrant 3, and inviting feedback to remove the blind spot in quadrant 2.

Let's look again at quadrant 1 and consider some of its properties. There are no secrets in this quadrant--it is the loving room. From the perspective of Partner W, it contains information about her that she previously has shared with her partner. Since she has let herself be known to him, both partners can behave toward each other in more caring, spontaneous ways; trust and acceptance are high. Their behavior is uninhibited, self-acknowledged, and congruent in terms of their honest sharing of their awareness of private thoughts, feelings, and motivations.

A difficulty with this model is that we have no accurate way of determining either the size or the shape of the quadrants for partners. This limitation does not diminish its usefulness, however, since partners are constrained only by their willingness to introspectively examine the content of quadrant 1 and to develop the trust required to share information contained in quadrants 2 and 3. The partitions between the quadrants are flexible and can either contract or expand, depending upon how interpersonal data stored in quadrants 2 and 3 are processed. Two basic processes are available for this purpose. The first of these, the exposure process, can be used by partners to reduce the size of their hidden areas. As information formerly hidden in this quadrant is shared, the area gets smaller and the loving room (quadrant 1) is made correspondingly larger. Their willingness to enlarge the loving room is reflected in their disclosure of information germane to the marriage. Frothy, empty, beguiling utterances-

-however plentiful--act only to fill the air with minutia and inconsequential chatter. Careful listening to this kind of sharing reveals that all it does is obscure a lack of real disclosure.

A second process is to solicit feedback from your partner about information in quadrant 2. Through this means, each partner can tap into the unspoken reactions, feelings, evaluations, doubts, etc., of the other. Successful use of this process depends upon each partner's ability to ask informed, seeking questions. Partners also must indicate a readiness to use the required information in efforts to improve their relationship. Finally, partners must feel that it is psychologically safe to share quadrant 2 information. An essential part of this feeling of safety is the belief that the receiving partner will not react defensively. As partner W invites and receives feedback about the content of quadrant 2, it is made smaller and the loving room grows larger. I will conclude my discussion of this aspect of marital communication by sharing an experience in which this model was acted out.

Several couples from a local church asked me to staff a communications workshop for them. I made arrangements through a realtor to use a cottage at nearby Clarks Hill Lake. The floor plan of the cottage somewhat resembled the four quadrants of the Johari Window. We gathered in the room representing quadrant 1 and everyone sat on the floor in a large circle, using pillows and blankets brought for that purpose. Before I sat down, I gave each person two 3" x 5" cards. I asked them to describe on one of the cards a feeling or other bit of information they had about their partner which had never been shared with them. Although no names were used, completion of the task took several minutes. The cards were collected and strewn over the floor in the room which corresponded to quadrant 2. Then, on their remaining card, I asked them to describe something about themselves which they considered germane to their marriage but which they had never disclosed to their partner. Completion of this card took even longer. These cards were collected and scattered across the floor in the room corresponding to Quadrant 3, the hidden area.

As I took my place in the circle, I offered some introductory comments. "This group will meet for many hours tonight and tomorrow. It will serve as a laboratory where each of us can gain a better understanding of the forces which influence the style, frequency, and content of our communication with our partner. There is no structure, rules, or agenda we have to follow unless we so choose. It will be up to us to fill the vacuum created by the lack of these familiar elements and to observe and try to understand what happens. My role is to help us learn from our own experiences. I will not, however, act as a group leader, nor will I suggest how we should proceed. With these few comments I think we are ready to begin in whatever way you feel will be most helpful."

A long silence fell upon the group as I finished talking. Aside from some of the participants shifting to a new sitting position, nothing happened. Everyone was seemingly waiting for someone else to speak. Finally, I asked, "Did you folks come up to the lake tonight so you could sit here and contemplate your navel?" Again, silence.

After another long, uncomfortable wait, Harmon, a middle-aged school principal who had recently remarried after a difficult, strife-ridden divorce, broke the ice. "I don't know about you folks, but I would like to get my cards back." Sensing the possibilities in his behavior, I responded, "They're yours, get them if you want to." Instantly, his wife, Vida, jumped up and blocked his path to the door. "No you don't," she shouted. "My cards are in there, too." After a few exchanges between Harmon and Vida about their lack of readiness to share what was on their cards, other members of the group began sharing their feelings. "Isn't this what we came up here to do?" one member asked. "Yes, but not so quickly," another responded. As Harmon and Vida sat down with us, I suggested that we take a look at what was happening to the group.

"You seemed so occupied with what was on those cards that you could not think about what we came here to do. With all your suspicions and fears about what might happen if what you wrote on those cards was made known to your partner, you were spending all your attention and energy on building fences. Let's experiment a bit and see how much of this information really needs to be protected. Let's see if it's not more rewarding to re-direct our attention and energy to building our marriage."

What followed that night and all day Saturday was a richly rewarding learning experience. We didn't want it to end.

Intermission

In the first part of this chapter I discussed two common but unbelievably difficult problems which must be overcome before partners can effectively communicate. The first, perceptual distortion of reality, is more treacherous and resistant to change than the second: the question of whether partners desire to communicate. Consider the following exchange.

Wife: You never help me around the house.

Husband: I certainly do, and I don't think you should say a thing like that.

This kind of disagreement is almost impossible to resolve as long as the partners respond to each other in terms of their own subjective perceptions of what actually happens. It is only when they are able to talk in terms of their expectations and the behaviors they consider appropriate to their expectations that they can begin to understand and resolve their disagreement. What I am suggesting, of course, is that they first have to get their relationship in order before they can effectively communicate and resolve their problem situation.

The idea that partners might not want to communicate surprises many people. "Here we are trying to learn how to communicate, and you're telling us that many partners actually don't want to communicate. I don't understand."

"It's a tangled web of ability and motivation," I explain. "Look at all the usual reasons partners communicate. Not all of these reasons are present in every marriage, i.e. not all partners want to disclose; they are fearful of the intimacy that more open communication could bring. Many partners don't trust their spouses and avoid sharing information that would make them vulnerable. Finally, many partners think of information as power. They equate knowing something their partner doesn't know to having power over them."

Even under ideal circumstances, when partners are reasonably aware of their perceptual tendencies and profess their desire to communicate more effectively, problems still abound. In the remaining pages of this chapter, I will discuss some of these problems and offer some suggestions you can use not only to resolve communication difficulties but also to help you and your partner achieve new levels of growth, understanding, and closeness.

Understanding Begins With Communication

As the language of high-tech becomes more a part of our everyday communication, marriages are increasingly being described as information processing systems. By this is meant there is an indeterminate amount of information of all kinds available to partners. Some of this information is known only to Partner H; other information is known only to Partner W; some information is known to both partners. Only when all the available information is known to and understood by both partners can they adequately process it in improving the overall quality of their marriage. To help you better understand the complex nature of marriage as an information processing system, I have stressed its diverse but interdependent nature. Although partners have a separate, distinct existence, marriage brings them into a systemic relationship with each other. It's like having a circle or boundary drawn around them. Everything the partners do inside the circle has an effect upon the other. This effect can be neither evaded nor ignored. The boundary separates the partners from the outside world. Behavior that is both permissible and expected inside the circle is not publicized outside the circle. Partners can choose how much they will let behavior outside the circle affect them in their private world inside the circle. The boundary can be closed or permeable. When it is closed, partners are a system unto themselves. When the boundary is permeable, they are interacting with the outside world, which is a larger social system.

As critical as the relationship between shared information and successful adjustment is, we can never fully know our partner. I could never get inside Lenora's body and know her mind and see things the way she did. In this sense, we are doomed to an existential loneliness. This separateness can be overcome, however, to the extent that the marital system permits and facilitates the exchange of information. As partners exchange germane information, their understanding of each other is improved. They can anticipate each other's actions; they understand the other's reasoning processes; misunderstandings are minimized.

While communication can improve understanding, it doesn't necessarily lead to agreement. Even if it were possible, I don't feel it's beneficial for partners to agree on everything all the time. Within limits, disagreements are wholesome and can be productive. Partners often gain new understandings of each other as a result of working through disagreements. Even though we might conclude that total agreement in marriage is neither possible nor desirable, we would, with equal certainty, argue that total communication is desirable. Or is it?

There are two questions related to the idea of openness and total communication that continue to bother me. The first question asks, "Could I ever know all there is to know about Lenora?" The answer, obviously, is no. One reason for this answer is the large unknown arena in the Johari Window model discussed above. Another more pervasive reason is that Lenora was always changing, growing, evolving, becoming. The person she was one day would be different from the person she was the day before and the person she would be the day after. Her life was like a book that was being written, and each new day was a new page to be studied and understood. Although I could never know her completely it was important that I understood everything that was known. My understanding could be improved by sharing with her and asking her to confirm or deny my understanding of what she had shared. I might not agree with everything that she shared with me, but it is important that I understand it.

The second question related to total communication is actually a reservation about its advisability. In a workshop I was conducting I asked the participants, "Suppose you had a brief affair in the past that is now ended. Would you, in the interest of being honest with your partner, reveal this information?" Many of the responses were guarded but the majority answer was no. Then I asked a related question. "If your partner had such an affair, would you want to know about it?" Again, the majority answer was no, but it was much more decisive than were the answers to the first question. Without doing too much harm to the numbers, I concluded that one-half of the partners would want to confess a past affair, but two out of three partners would not want their partner to confess. Interestingly, some of the same people who said they would want to confess would not want their partner to confess. Our discussion of this outcome evolved around two issues: (1) whether a confession would help or hurt the marriage, and (2) the issue of forgiveness. It's dangerous to generalize from this one experience, but when I am working with a client who presents this issue I try to help them understand their reasons for wanting to confess and the possibly adverse effects such disclosure could have on the marriage. The question of whether to confess is best answered by, "It all depends."

Understanding Communication

Many people believe that communication is nothing more or less than just doing what comes naturally. Because they spend a majority of their waking hours in various forms of communication activity they naturally feel they know a lot about it. It does not follow, however, that mere repetition of an activity results in improved performance. Even under ideal conditions, highly motivated, articulate partners sometimes will experience communication difficulties. This happens because successful marital communication involves two people--one sending a message and another receiving the message. Neither partner has control over the entire process. Communication is effective when the receiver interprets or responds to the sender's message in the same way the sender intended it. In other terms, communication is successful when the reality of the receiver is isomorphic with that of the sender. This simplistic definition of communication makes it seem easy, doesn't it? Why, then, do partners have so much difficulty communicating. Perhaps the most common source of difficulty results from the receiver not understanding the message the way the sender intended it. Senders, on the other hand, do not always send the actual message they intend. Since the sender's intentions are private, they are unknown to the receiver. I knew my intentions, for example, but I had to make inferences about Lenora's; she knew her intentions but had to infer mine. Whenever we make inferences we consider the message from our, not the sender's, frame of reference. When we consider the many ways we can misunderstand each other, it's a wonder we can communicate at all. Effective communication might deservedly be called a miracle.

Communication failures caused by the gap between what the sender meant and the receiver thought the sender meant are created primarily by psychological factors. Two of the most important of these factors--perception and motivation--already have been discussed. Now, I want to briefly discuss another category of problems: word usage, grammatical form, and verbal ability. All these problems constrain the effectiveness of marital communication.

An interesting story from the *Bible* (Genesis 11:1-9) provides insight into a part of the problem. The people of Shinar decided to build a tower so tall that it would reach up to heaven. Because this displeased God, he mixed up their language so they could not understand each other. Unable to communicate, they could not finish building the Tower of Babel and it crashed to the ground. Today when persons with different educational and cultural backgrounds attempt to communicate it often appears that their tongues are confused. I am not referring only to the different languages people might speak but to the meanings they give to situations and to the words used to share these meanings. A good example is the difficulty in interpreting the word "links," as it was used in Iraq's initial proposal to withdraw from Kuwait in February 1991. Recall, too, the debate over the shape of the table that the officials used to draft the document attesting the end of the Korean War. Are these subtleties important? Yes. Do they occur in marriage? Yes.

Lenora often would phrase a request in terms such as, "Russ, would you like to vacuum the carpet?" Early on my response was, "No, I wouldn't like to, but I will." I now realize she didn't like to ask, "Please vacuum the floor," and I respected that difficulty. Then, my answer was simply, "Yes." There was no reason to make an issue of the way she phrased a request.

The more alike people are, the more they accept and respect each other's idiosyncrasies, and the easier it is for them to communicate. The more unlike they are the more difficult communication will be.

A different kind of problem can occur when partners have different levels of fluency in use of the language. Words are symbols--they are the tools we use to think, speak, and write. When our vocabularies are limited, both our ability to think and communicate our thoughts and feelings are diminished. It has been reported, for example, that twenty-five per cent of the daily vocabulary of people twenty-five years of age or older involves only nine words. Add thirty-four more words for a total of forty-three and you have fully half of an average person's daily use of vocabulary (Funk and Lewis, 1971). This circumstance can be fully appreciated only when we realize that our English language includes approximately half of a million words.

This was probably Moses' fear when he tried to dissuade God from sending him to Egypt to free the Israelites from the Pharaoh. Moses argues, "No, Lord, don't send me. I have never been a good speaker.... I am a poor speaker, slow and hesitant." (Holy Bible, Exodus 4:10) An amusing story about President Calvin Coolidge also demonstrates how people use or do not use words. President Coolidge was a man of few words and often was referred to as Silent Cal. According to the story, the President returned from church one Sunday and was asked by his wife what the sermon was about. "Sin," was the President's one-word reply. "What did he say about it?" Mrs. Coolidge asked. "He was against it," responded the President.

With certain partners in therapy I often inquire how frequently they use such expressions as, "Thanks," "You look great tonight," and "I love you." Regrettably, use of these terms of appreciation and endearment is often low. And the explanation partners offer is pitiful. "Jean knows I love her. Why do I have to tell her every day?" When partners defend their non-use of these terms with these explanations, it's because they are lazy, uncomfortable with the subject, or insensitive to the needs of their partner. Whatever their reasons, partners who do not show courtesy, gratitude, and love, are denying their marriage a source of richness and enduring pleasure.

Partners in distressed marriages seem to know what they want to say, but their lack of confidence in using words to communicate often causes them not to try. Although these skills are an important part of communication, something far more important--more basic—is wanting to communicate. With this attitude comes a willingness to accept whatever risks that might come with being more open and sharing.

Listening

Listening is hard work. Hearing is easy, but real listening is difficult. Hearing, like seeing, is a physical process. But listening, like reading, is an emotional, intellectual process. It is also an activity of the heart--a process which demands, in addition to desire, particular skills to understand the real meaning of what was heard and what was not spoken. It is only when these inputs are effectively combined that we have the basis for successful communication.

There are many kinds of listening skills. One with which I am not concerned is the skill a lawyer uses when questioning a witness. My daughter, who is an attorney in Atlanta, told me that she listens for contradictions, irrelevancies, errors, and weaknesses. She does not listen in order to help a witness adjust or cooperate. What I am concerned with is just the opposite of what she does in the courtroom. I'm advocating a kind of active listening that shows respect to our partner, which encourages and enhances their feelings of acceptance and esteem. Again, this kind of active listening is not easy. This difficulty is unfortunate because listening is more important in marriage than talking. Talking does not guarantee that the other partner is listening, but as long as one partner is actively listening, the other partner is encouraged to continue their efforts to communicate. When we actively listen, we show respect to our partner and, by implication, we are saying that our listening is more important than any other possible use of our time.

My mention of time points to one of the pervasive difficulties in listening. It has to do with the difference between rates of speaking and rates of listening. Most people talk at a rate of approximately 125 words per minute, yet they can listen at a rate of up to 500 words per minute. Because it is difficult to slow down listening or thinking speeds, people have to commit about four times as much thinking time for every minute of listening time. What partners do with this extra listening time determines whether they are good listeners. Obviously, patience and a willingness to wait enhance listening skills.

To engage in active listening we must have a sincere interest in our partner. Faking interest is perhaps our worst listening habit. We all live in glass houses as far as our attitudes are concerned, and they always will show through. We think we already know what our partner is going to say so we pretend to be tuned in. Consider the following scenario:

Wife: "The Jeffersons are going to vacation in Arizona this year. Is Arizona a nice place to visit?"

Husband: "That's fine, dear."

Wife: "Do you mean that Arizona is fine?"

Husband: "That's fine, dear."

Wife: "I'm having an affair with the postman. He's coming at seven tonight."

Husband: (Guess the husband's response.)

For selfish reasons alone, one of the best investments we can make in our marriage is actively listening to our partner. To insure successful communication, one partner must take the responsibility for setting a pattern of active listening. When we show interest and caring by actively listening, our partner is encouraged to communicate more openly with us. Like other behaviors, listening behavior is contagious. In Biblical terms, interest begets interest, trust begets trust, and listening begets sharing.

By actively listening to our partner, we convey the idea: "I'm interested in you as a person and I feel that what you want to share is important. I respect your thoughts and feelings, and even if I don't agree with them I know they are important to you. I won't try to evaluate or change what you are saying, I just want to understand you."

Still, many people are unwilling to actively listen because of the risks involved. If we relate to our partner's needs, aspirations, sorrows, joys and, indeed, their life experiences as though they were our own, we run the risk of being changed in some way. If we listen our way into the psychological world of our partner, we risk making their world our own. It can be threatening, however, to give up, even momentarily, what we believe and start viewing the world through our partner's eyes. This phenomenon is common on many of the so-called talk shows on TV. Several people are trying to talk at the same time. No one is listening; no one wants to listen. Each wants the last word.

Over the course of our lives, listening is the communication skill we learn first. It begins in infancy. Next comes speaking, followed by reading and writing. In my many years of college study I have had numerous courses which emphasized reading and writing skills. I also took courses in oral communication or speaking, but I have never had a course in listening. My college experience suggests the dilemma many partners face: listening is the communication skill we use the most but it is also the one we have prepared for the least.

Nonverbal Communication

Ken and Faye had been married less than a year when they requested an appointment with me. They had a frightening argument a few nights earlier and were concerned about what was happening to their marriage. Midway into their first session, I was trying to get them to share with me the history of their spat. But Faye was insistent in wanting to tell me about a more recent confrontation, which occurred after they had gone to bed the night before. I let her talk. She stated that she had not believed some excuse or explanation that Ken had given her so, as she explained, "I told him I was going to get up and turn on the light so I could see if he was telling the truth."

In telling her story, Faye revealed that she knew something about body language that is unknown to many people. That is, little goes on inside the mind that doesn't show in the eyes. Some recent research reveals, for example, that the pupils of our eyes will grow larger when we view something pleasant; our pupils contract when something unpleasant is experienced. It was also found that when we try to mask our feelings--in lying, for example--our eyes will both dilate and contract. This is something Faye and good poker players know well.

We can adjust what we say to conform to what we are willing to reveal, but we have no control over the way our bodies respond. I could decide to lie about a matter to achieve some advantage or to protect myself from discovery or criticism. That is an intellectual or cognitive decision to lie. However, my autonomic nervous system, which governs a wide range of body functions, is independent of my central nervous system and does not know how to lie. Any wonder that non-verbal communication is often referred to as listening with the third ear?

It is not only the eyes that communicate what is going on inside. Facial expressions, hand and arm gestures, body posture, and proxemics (psychical proximity) all communicate inner feelings more accurately than does speech. Even our clothing and status symbols are remarkably revealing to people who have sensitivity to these aspects of our behavior. Is all this important? In a nutshell, yes. It has been estimated that body language accounts for over half of the communication process, particularly in the area of communicating feelings.

Can you tell when someone is lying to you? Most of us tend to think we can. How do we know? Most of us will answer something like, "I don't know how I know, it's something I feel." Most likely it's because we observe certain signals or cues by people that suggest a deceptive intent. It is likely, too, that we are no more conscious of what signals we're reacting to than we are of our behavior when we intend to deceive. Some tattle-tell behaviors I take note of include covering the mouth, scratching the eyebrows, pulling the ear lobes, touching the nose, and rubbing the cheek. Over the past several years I have made frequent use of my camcorder to help clients become more aware of their unconscious, dysfunctional behaviors while communicating. When we review the film I can point to mannerisms that seemingly reflect what they are feeling as they respond to their partner and to me. When they see themselves in the monitor, they realize that others see what they are now able to see. Their efforts to conceal are very transparent.

There is no such thing as no communication. My use of the double negative is intentional because I want to emphasize that we are always communicating. The absence of spoken words does not mean that we aren't communicating in other ways. When we stop talking, when we sulk and pout, when we angrily turn away from our partner, we are still communicating--we are still sending messages. When we withdraw either emotionally or physically, we are telling our partner that we are unwilling or unable to accept responsibility for our present behavior. Rather than engage in any of these withdrawal behaviors, it is more loving and helping to stay in the arena and try to understand what caused us to want to withdraw.

Because others respond more to our nonverbal signals than to the verbal content of what we are saying, it is critical that our verbal and nonverbal messages be congruent. The best way to achieve congruency is to be honest in all our communications. This way we don't have to worry about what our body is saying. When we rid our mind of all thoughts of anger, revenge, and fear we can become more congruent because we are internally congruent--there is agreement between what we know (intellect) and what we feel (emotion). Sometimes, however, we have feelings which we don't like or which conflict with our image of our self. In these situations, the value of honesty dictates that we share both feelings: the disliked primary feeling and our secondary feeling about having it. In doing this we accept full responsibility for all our feelings. We are thus seen as being honest by our partner, and this perception enhances trust and more open communication.

Anger is an emotion that used to frighten me. I had observed the terrible things people do and say when they are angry. Further, anger always seemed to be accompanied by a loss of self-control. Feeling this way, I always tried to conceal or contain my anger. Gradually, I was forced to realize that I couldn't hide it. Understanding this, I then wrestled with the question, "What can I do with my anger since I can't conceal it?" One possible, but improbable, answer was to never get angry. But I couldn't do that; I didn't want to do that. Things like hunger, injustice, child abuse, and ignorance still anger me. So what I now try to do in all my interpersonal relationships, but particularly in my marriage, is to be as honest as I can. I learned to say to Lenora, "I feel angry but I don't like feeling this way. I don't like feeling separated from you. Will you help me to understand and resolve this feeling?"

In this chapter I have avoided sharing long lists of rules to follow in our efforts to communicate more effectively with our partner. Although rules--lists of dos and don'ts--can provide us a feeling of well-being, they also have a deceptive quality because the feeling of well-being is often false. Moreover, the reasons for a rule are not always understood. Another disadvantage of rules is that they are often followed indiscriminately. We experience disappointment and frustration when following the rules does not produce sought-after outcomes. My objective has been the development of an attitude of love and acceptance of our individual responsibility to listen and to share with our partner all information that is germane to our marriage. Having this attitude, our concern is always to act according to it.

Congruency in Relationships

Dr. Carl Rogers (1961) has used the term congruence to define the situation in which there is an accurate matching of our experience, our awareness of that experience, and our communication of that awareness. Although he presented his theory as a way of determining the authenticity of a counselor-client relationship, it is helpful to apply it to marital relationships. Congruence depends upon a state of equality between each of the three states of our being. Perhaps this theory can be more easily understood by observing, say, an infant who is experiencing hunger. Since infants accept hunger as a natural physiological state without any stigma attached to it, they immediately accept in into their awareness, i.e., they are conscious of their hunger. And, almost simultaneously, they communicate their awareness (hunger) to anyone who might furnish food. With their accurate matching of experience (hunger), their awareness (hunger), and their communication (hunger) they are seen as being congruent, honest, authentic, real, etc. One reason we respond to children so warmly is that they are genuinely honest or congruent about whatever they are experiencing. As Rogers might suggest, "Children are their experience."

You and I once behaved like children--completely open and honest about everything that went on inside us. But as we grew older we gradually learned that being honest was not always to our advantage. We learned to distort the reality of our experiences, to lie when it was to our advantage, and to deny or repress, even to ourselves, any experience which threatened our self-image. Why? Unfortunately the congruency we admire in children becomes a source of conflict and rejection as they grow beyond childhood. It seems that as parents, we're always producing another generation of liars. Let's look at some ways we can be incongruent.

A husband came home from work to find paint sprayed on the sidewalk in front of the steps. His face flushed, his voice communicating anger, he rushed inside, demanding to know who the culprit was. His wife quieted him, pleading that he not show anger in front of the children. His response, with some evidence of sincerity, was a denial of being angry. Yet, it was evident to all the family members that he was angry in spite of his denial. Evidently there was a breakdown in communication within himself between the experience level (anger) and the awareness level (calm). The husband/father explained later that he had always been repulsed and frightened when he saw his father angry and he vowed never to get angry in front of his children. In his way of thinking he does not get angry; it is too painful for him to accept anger into his awareness. When he denied being angry, he was strangely communicating the truth as he knew it. The only emotion he would let himself accept was calmness; he had successfully repressed his anger.

In cases like this when we experience someone feeling a certain way but denying that feeling, we are left wondering why. Why must we go away wondering if we can trust people who don't or can't own up to the feelings we experience them having.

One other example--one which we have all experienced--shows how we deal with unpleasant feelings of which we're aware. We are guests at a party. Not having a good time, we begin thinking of going home. We look at our watch as we stifle a yawn. As we depart early we politely say to our hostess, "Thanks for a really wonderful evening. Exciting guests;

stimulating conversation. We must get together again. Real soon." In this common example, we were experiencing boredom, and we were aware of it, but we communicated joy. The breakdown occurred between our awareness and our communication. The incongruence in this case is thought of as denial or dishonesty. We justify our "white lies" to protect the feelings of others.

With these examples to ponder, consider the role of honesty in our marriage. Although it has many complexities and extenuations, we tend to recognize congruence or incongruence in individuals with whom we interact. The greater the perceived incongruence of marital communications, the more the ensuing relationships will be plagued by suspicion and mistrust. Conversely, the greater the perceived congruence of experience, awareness, and communication in marital relationships the greater the likelihood the communication will be accepted as open and honest, resulting in increased trust, openness, and mutual satisfaction in the relationship.

If we are serious about becoming more congruent in our marriage--helping it to become more user-friendly--honesty must become both a value and a goal in all our communications with our partner. Without this kind of honesty there is no basis for building and maintaining a relationship.

A Final Thought

Before I conclude this chapter I want to share with you the result of an assignment I gave to some partners in a group therapy session. On a chalkboard I drew a large box with four quadrants or sections. Labels were given to the quadrants to help the participants identify the kinds of behavior they could place in each quadrant. Figure 6-2 graphically shows what I'm referencing. Study their responses. Ask yourself, "Do I sincerely want to be helpful in all my communication with my partner?" If your answer is yes, try to behave in the helpful ways suggested in the figure and avoid the hurting behaviors. You might have some suggestions to add to the lists.

Russ Holloman, Ph.D.

Figure 6-2
Forms and Effects of Marital Communication

	Verbal	Non Verbal
Helpful	**Quadrant One** - Shares feelings, provides information about self - Is honest - Does not judge - Reflects sensitivity and consideration - Attitudinal and behavioral flexibility - Attitudes of warmth, caring, liking, interest, respect - Is nondefensive - Shows a sense of humor	**Quadrant Two** - Listening - Touching - Good eye contact - Smiling - Close physical proximity - Overall attitude of approval and acceptance - Makes physical and emotional investment in marriage - Recognizes mutual rights, needs, and responsibilities
Hurting	**Quadrant Three** - Advice giving, overprotection - Blaming, placating, cajoling - Extensive probing and questioning - Directing and demanding - Patronizing attitude - Unpleasant tone of voice - Talking about self too much	**Quadrant Four** - Physical sneers and frowns - Yawning, closing eyes - Avoiding, withdrawing - Aloofness, air of superiority - Not listening

Chapter Seven

Helping Through Acceptance and Attending

As I begin this chapter, three concerns are guiding my thoughts. Each of them must be resolved satisfactorily before we unconditionally can accept and incorporate attending behaviors into our marriage.

The first of these concerns can be presented best as a question. It's a disturbing question. It might make us uncomfortable but it has to be asked, if only to be answered and forgotten. The question is, "Did I marry well? Would I marry the same person again?" This question has to be answered "Yes" before our love can ever be unconditional. To have any doubt about this question causes us to withhold our full commitment to our marriage. Our love for our partner will be conflicted; it will be a conditional love.

If your answer to this question is "Yes," you can skip the remainder of this discussion and go to my second concern. But what if your answer is not "Yes"? Let's suppose you say, "No. My marriage has been disappointing from the beginning." Or, you say, "Yes, but I could have done better. The old adage about love being blind is true." To be plagued by a negative answer to this question is, figuratively, to live in a hell on earth. This hell forces people to look for a way out of their predicament.

Divorce is a frequently chosen way out, but it is less a solution than a form of escaping or running away from the problem. Learning to live with the mistake of a bad marriage but always in an unforgiving, grudging manner is another solution. Neither is this behavior a viable solution; it is more a submissive, passive acceptance of a bad circumstance. A third solution is to accept your partner in the manner that Adam and Eve accepted each other. It wasn't a matter of their not having a choice, but, rather, that they believed in the wisdom and goodness of God. To hold your partner to a higher standard of physical attractiveness or personal excellence than you're willing to apply to yourself is to live by a double standard. To let doubt persist about this concern is to live under the specter of a question that has no final answer.

A middle-aged, professional man in therapy with me sought to justify a sexual liaison with the excuse, "When my wife and I married we were both virgins. For fourteen years she was the only woman I had sex with. I was curious, I wanted to know what it would be like with another woman."

Referring to a physically-attractive, socially-prominent woman who was known to both of us I asked, "What would it be like to do it with her?"

"I can't go around having sex with every woman in Augusta," he said, somewhat angrily after a long pause.

"Even if you wanted to try, there would always be another woman with a prettier face and a sexier body. You could never have a final answer to your question. So, why begin? As long as you seek to satisfy your sexual needs outside marriage, your love for your wife will never be whole. It will always be a conditional love. You will be robbing your wife and yourself of the love and sexual fulfillment you both want."

My second concern is about the unknown area (Quadrant 4) of the Johari Window that I discussed in the previous chapter. At the time of marriage, there is no way for partners to know what is in this arena--neither their own nor their partner's. The boundary of this arena is both permeable and flexible and the amount of unconscious information contained in it is indeterminable. As willing as partners might be to explore and disclose the content of this arena, it never can be completely known.

After seven years of an often-conflicted, sometimes-disappointing marriage, Raymond was sharing his feelings with me about his fear that he and his wife, Juanita, were growing apart. "She's changed in ways that I never thought possible. Before we married, and for a long time afterwards, she was always fashionably dressed. Always had what I call a tailored, Lilli Ann look. Now, she's overweight and doesn't seem to care how she looks. Sometimes I am embarrassed to be seen with her. That's just one example of how she has changed. See what I mean? She's certainly not the woman

I thought I was marrying. Was she always this way? Was I unable to see it?"

I encouraged Raymond to tell me more of his side of their problem. As he talked, he gradually backed off the idea that he was still the same person he was at the time of their marriage. He also was able to admit, in a later joint session, that he had been unwilling to let Juanita change from his first image of her. Finally, both Raymond and Juanita were helped to understand that, compared to fourteen years ago, they necessarily were changed people and that this process of change would continue. Their problem was learning to accept its inevitability--even the necessity of change. Understanding this, they could either do nothing and, passively, let change happen to them, or they could intervene and direct it toward desired ends. But before they could change what was happening to them, they first had to accept the idea that they indeed were changing. It also was necessary that they accept each other as they change. This was my third concern: that the adjusting process must and will continue, requiring partners to accept and affirm change in each other.

Acceptance

Acceptance is more than saying "Yes" to the question of marriage; it is more than the "I wills" and the "I dos" of the marriage ceremony. Acceptance is an attitude or state of mind in which we unconditionally accept rather than question, doubt, or resist. Acceptance is an expression of our willingness to go along, to cooperate, and to be receptive. It does not mean passivity, resignation, or detachment. Unconditional acceptance is an active, thoughtful, and deliberate state of mind.

The need for acceptance becomes critical the moment partners realize that they do not measure up to each other's wishes and expectations. When the glow of romantic love fades, acceptance means loving your partner in a more mature kind of relationship. It means giving up dreams and fantasies for a reality of blemishes, failures, shortcomings, and weaknesses. Although we might have imperfections, being accepted by our partner helps us to feel perfect. Such acceptance does not mean being blind to each other's shortcomings. What it does mean is that we are willing to work to resolve any problem that interferes with closeness or otherwise complicates our relationship. Acceptance means finding joy in what is rather than what was or ought to be. Finally, acceptance facilitates intimacy, equality, and happiness. A lack of acceptance makes love conditional.

A matter of practical importance at this point is the relationship between self-acceptance and acceptance of our partner. Generally, the available evidence suggests that before we can accept our partner we have to accept ourselves. If we think well of ourselves we tend to be more open and accepting of our partner. In therapy, I often have expressed the thought that we can't give to our partner something we don't have. Acceptance of our partner begins with and depends upon our having a healthy sense of our personal identity. Self-acceptance does not mean that we are blind to our faults and shortcomings. It does mean that we accept ourselves in spite of our imperfections. Recognizing that there always will be room for improvement, the self-accepting person focuses on growing and becoming rather than a resigned acceptance of what is.

Acceptance of ourself and acceptance of our partner can be expressed in the language of transactional analysis (Berne, 1961; Harris, 1969) as "I'm O.K., you're O.K." With these words, we declare that we are worthwhile, valuable, and loving and that our partner is equally worthwhile, valuable, and lovable. This is a necessary condition for the development of an intimate, satisfying marital relationship. Although acceptance opens the door for partners to help and attend to each other, it does not create in itself the substance of the relationship. It is made real as these personal qualities and behaviors are used to build and maintain the relationship.

Lully and Claude had been living together for four months, when, at Lully's insistence, they came to see me. Lully wanted marriage; Claude didn't. "I like Lully a lot," Claude explained. "We have lots of fun together and the sex is good, so why can't she let it go at that. I don't want to lose her, but I'm not ready to make the commitment she wants from me. Marriage could be a trap for both of us. No, I think things would be better right now if we weren't tied to each other." Claude was unwilling to come back for a second session.

About three years later I received a late-night call from Claude. He was crying as only a man can, and he wanted to talk. I determined that there was no emergency and suggested an appointment the next day. As he talked, I compared his words with what he had said years earlier.

"When I got to my room last night--yes, I'm living alone--it caught up with me. I realized how tired and lonely I was. I was tired of all the empty talk, the fakey people, the drinking, everything. It was exciting at first, but somewhere it all went wrong. I was wrong; Lully was right. Did you know that she's married? Finished her masters degree and is teaching in Columbia County. Back to me, I didn't want to be bogged down;

Making Marriage User Friendly

didn't want to be committed. I didn't want a relationship if it had strings attached. Well, that's what I've got: no strings, no attachments. Who do I really know or care about? Who cares about me? It's all narrowed down to nothing."

Several months after we terminated Claude's individual therapy, he called again. "Dr. Holloman, Bettye and I have been dating since Christmas. We love each other and have talked about marriage. We want to go into this with our eyes open, and we both feel that we should get some counseling before we commit ourselves to each other. Will you see us?"

In some ways Claude understood the meaning of commitment better than the many people who never question their motivation or readiness for marriage. He understood it well enough to avoid marriage before he was ready for the responsibilities that go with it. One conclusion that I made after many years of counseling with distressed couples is that in the euphoria of romantic love and the excitement of marriage, many people sincerely believe they are committed to the relationship. I also concluded that many of these same people, while professing a strong commitment to their marriage and to each other, still have reservations about the future or the quality of their relationship. Commitment clouded by fears, doubts, and mistrust is little more than wishful thinking. Unconditional commitment means staying the course.

Commitment is not just a feeling, it is an act of the will, a choice. It is equivalent to saying, "I accept the responsibility for making this marriage work." When I was commissioned as an U.S. Air Force Officer, I took an oath. Some words from that oath reflect the essence of what I mean by commitment. I will paraphrase them into a comprehensive statement about marital commitment: "I accept this commitment to our marriage without any mental reservation or purpose of evasion."

In therapy, clients sometimes describe how they use fear, intimidation, and threats to get something they want from their partner. Wives withhold sex; husbands threaten to leave. Is this commitment? Hardly. The commitment of these persons is of a lesser type. They seem to say, "I'm committed only as long as things go my way." Real commitment doesn't depend on getting one's way; rather, it seeks full expression and satisfaction in a mutuality of interests. Real commitment is intentional with respect to the maintenance and growth of the marriage, although it can be flexible and collaborative as to how these goals are reached.

Russ Holloman, Ph. D.

Equality

A satisfying and enduring marriage is a relationship between equals. If one partner in a marriage feels unequal, the relationship is based more upon power and dependency than upon love and intimacy. Unfortunately, too many people uncritically accept the argument that because men and women are different they are *ipso facto* unequal. This argument might have some validity on the athletic field, for instance, but when used as a defense against marital equality I strongly reject it on two different grounds. First, if it is to be valid it must apply to the differences among sexes as it does to differences between the sexes. This is something proponents of that argument don't like to admit. Second, the argument simply is not relevant to the idea of equality in marriage. Men (husbands) and women (wives) are different but are equal as individuals, both in and outside marriage.

Marital equality, in my view, is both a social and a spiritual concern; it refers to the equality of individuals as persons--it is personhood. Wholeness requires equality. Further, equality is not something that can be given to one person by another. Neither is it something that can be taken from them. It is something that must be claimed, felt, and expressed in terms of one's own circumstances. It must also be accepted by the other.

Equality in marriage can exist only when there is a single standard for both partners concerning both rights and responsibilities. This is not a contradiction of my earlier statement. Equality belongs to the person; however, it can be and often is surrendered for security or for the promise of reduced friction in the marriage. Partners can be unequal in many ways without compromising their ability to contribute to and benefit from their marriage. Equality does not mean being like or the same as your partner. Likeness and sameness may suggest equality but, in actuality, they are achieved at the expense of equality. Likeness and sameness evidence conformity, and conformity means surrender of one's individuality.

There are two ways that partners can relate to each other. First, they can see each other as objects--what Martin Buber (1970) has referred to as an "I-IT" relationship. In this kind of relationship, which explicitly reflects a lack of equality, we talk about our partner, thinking only of how they can be useful to us. Whenever our partner does something for us, there is little concern about how they might feel about the transaction. Buber argues, and I agree, that a person should never be treated as an IT, a thing to be used or experienced, nor as an object of mere interest or fascination.

The second way of relating to our partner is in terms of an "I-THOU" relationship in which we recognize our partner as someone who is unique, equal, and irreplaceable. We accept our partner as an individual with private feelings and a personal world view. Instead of talking about our partner we talk to them with a full awareness of their presence. When we accept our partner as a THOU we reveal something about ourselves that is associated with a higher level of psychological maturity and interpersonal adjustment. The I of an I-THOU relationship obviously is different from the I of an I-IT relationship.

Nothing is more vital to marital intimacy and love than a feeling of equality and adequacy. Yet, it is possible for us to behave in ways that actually undermine our partner's feelings of equality. We may, for example, zealously strive to prove our own adequacy without realizing that we may at the same time undermine similar efforts of our partner. Sometimes, too, we can become so preoccupied with our own feelings that we neglect the needs of our partner. When we help our partner to feel more accepted, more adequate, and more secure in the relationship, they are enabled to help us more with our needs. It is another application of the adage that what goes around comes around.

Individuality

In my high school there was a set of identical twin girls. They were so much alike that even their mother confessed to being confused about them at times. It is my understanding that, biologically, what began as one person divided into two separate people--identical twins form when an ovum splits into an identical pair soon after conception. Thus, Carlene and Charlene inherited the same genes and shared the same genetically determined characteristics. They also had a common environment which tended to reinforce their hereditary similarities. However, in spite of all their physical similarities and temperamental closeness each was very much her own particular, individual self.

Although they were separate selves, when they wanted, they could be nearly carbon copies of each other. In their dress, speech, and mannerisms they seemed to enjoy stressing their alikeness and playing games with others by confusing their identities. A friend and I once double dated with them. Neither of us was certain that the person we asked was the one we were with on the date.

Often, when they were stressing their alikeness, teachers and friends would have to ask, "Which one are you?" The response would always be, "I am me." Then, after a short pause punctuated with silent amusement, "I am Charlene." The "I am me" part of their response relates to this section on individuality. When partners can make "You are you; I am me" statements in marriage they are recognizing and accepting both their partner and themselves as individuals. The personality of our partner is something of intrinsic value and they are worthy of love and respect in their own right. This love and respect never must be conditional on one partner becoming a looking glass self of the other. To be an individual, in this sense, means one is autonomous, personal, distinctive, and self-directing. Thus, each partner in a marriage has a separate and distinct identity and brings to the marriage a unique personality including distinctive intellectual, emotional, physical, and social competencies.

Acceptance of our partner's individuality is recognition of their separateness, which includes rights to personal opinions, political preferences, and spiritual sentiments. When Lenora and I married, we were different in many ways. She was Democrat; I was Republican. She was Baptist; I was Methodist. Reconciliation of these and other differences was never a condition of our love or our marriage. Even though we were joined in one church, I suspect that we sometimes canceled each others vote on election day. Our differences always enriched our marriage and I cherished and benefitted from her uniqueness. I delighted, for example, when she studied an issue and arrived at her own opinion about it. Further, I always tried to show regard for her individuality by encouraging feelings and behaviors which reflected her own predispositions.

There are at least three aspects or dimensions of our partner's individuality that have to be accepted unconditionally. They are the physical self, the social self, and the spiritual self.

The physical self, beyond the body, includes everything that is physical: clothing, automobile, jewelry, house, etc. All these things are purchased not only because we find them useful and pleasing but also because of the image they project. Lenora would rather invest in good furniture, home improvements, and quality clothing than, say, a high-priced automobile. I liked to travel, had a weakness for electronic gadgets, and often fantasized about owning a sports car. But I really appreciated the tasteful way Lenora furnished our home, and her taste in clothing always made me feel good when I was out with her. On a couple of occasions, I suggested that she get a pair of jeans. "That's not me," was always her reply. She was expressing her individuality.

With respect to Lenora's physical self, the matter of financial security was especially important. I would never demean her by trying to exercise exclusive control over our financial resources. Having to ask me for money or my permission before she made a purchase would violate her individuality. It would make her an extension of me and she couldn't be an individual and an extension of me at the same time. Our financial affairs were arranged so that they reflected her need for psychological autonomy and security. Only when she felt secure in her physical self could she feel free to express herself in other areas of our marriage.

Lenora's social self was probably not as diverse as mine, but her feelings about and commitment to those things that were important to her were felt deeply and were unwavering. While I interacted with a wide range of colleagues, she had a smaller circle of valued, close friends. She was a gifted conversationalist, comfortable with persons from varied backgrounds, and was spontaneous and sincere in her laughter and show of affection. Her honesty, patient understanding, and loving attitudes influenced and shaped the lives of both me and our children and significantly determined the social relationships within our family. She knew who she was and was comfortable with herself. I accepted and loved her as she was.

The spiritual self is often difficult to understand because it is more private, less observable. We can observe only outward behaviors and make inferences about the spiritual self. Lenora did a lot of volunteer work, served on several committees in our church, and was responsive to the needs of others, particularly in times of illness, grief, or disaster. When questioned why she did those things, she responded in terms of her values and religious beliefs.

Although partners refer to it by different names, many of the difficulties in distressed marriages are related to their needs for privacy and psychological space. Privacy, as I use the term, refers to the need for occasional aloneness for whatever reason or purpose. It is more related to solitude than loneliness. While both are chosen, solitude brings solace, loneliness brings despair. Privacy, in my view, is a basic condition for personal security and psychological well-being.

After a day of appointments, the most rewarding thing I could do was to retreat to my greenhouse for some time alone. It was an effective way of ridding myself of any signs of stress or pent-up feelings. Being alone for even a short while was therapeutic in the sense that it renewed me and provided a boundary between the activities of the day and my time with Lenora in the evening. It was important, however, that I explain my need for time alone. Otherwise, my need could be misinterpreted as avoidance behavior. Fortunately, Lenora understood my need and protected me from telephone calls and other intrusions. She, too, needed time alone for activities and rituals that were meaningful to her and I always respected her needs at these times.

Why do we need privacy? Why do we sometimes feel imposed upon when our privacy is invaded? Privacy serves our need to get away from everything. It provides an opportunity to be alone with our thoughts and our feelings. When I'm having some difficulty thinking through a problem or decision that I'm facing, I often walk around the lake in front of our house. Being alone for this purpose enables me to clear my mind and block out distractions and interferences.

We are both private and social creatures, and we fluctuate between our need for solitude and our desire for social interaction. Although our needs for social interaction and togetherness are ever present and persistent, it is in our moments of solitude that we can renew our energies, and prepare ourselves psychologically for meaningful interaction with our partner. Unfortunately, we often experience guilt and the fear of being misunderstood when we express our need for alone time.

The mother of a two-year old child expressed her feelings this way: "This sounds terrible but sometimes I just want to get away from her (child's) crying for attention. Just a couple hours is enough. But I don't dare mention this to my husband; he'd think I resent our daughter. It's not that at all, I just need some time for myself." As valid as this need is, it can come up lacking when one partner doesn't understand or accept the other's need for privacy. It also can be ineffective when the needs of the other partner are for togetherness.

Our own secular experiences provide evidence of there being two pathways to psychological and spiritual growth and fulfillment. One of these is social interaction with significant others; the other is the path of self-discovery, self-reflection, and prayer. One of the most indescribable experiences I ever had was spending a weekend in a monastery in Colorado where I had to observe its rule of silence. Although I was happy to see Sunday afternoon arrive, the weekend was an unparalleled growth experience. And my relationship with Lenora and our children was elevated to a higher plane of consciousness and meaning. The Bible describes numerous instances when

Jesus sought to be alone for meditation and prayer. After being alone, Jesus always returned for significant encounters with the people around Him.

It's not a matter of either togetherness or aloneness; we need both. Since togetherness is the presumed natural state of being in marriage, it is often an act of courage (and risk) to express our need for privacy. It is an act of love to grant privacy when it is requested.

An extension or application of our need for privacy is our need for personal space. This need expresses itself in both a physical and a psychological sense. The physical space that I enjoy most is my study. It's where I do my writing and also where I saw clients. My study is also my retreat. To paraphrase a popular expression, "My study is my message." It told clients and others who visited me there a lot about me. It's furnished the way I want it. The pictures and memorabilia on the walls and tables all are of my own choosing and there is a story or message associated with each one. Lenora, too, had her own needs for personal space--space that reflected her personality and responded to her needs--space where things were arranged exactly as she wanted. While we have private space needs, we also have shared space needs, and the time we spend together in the shared space is always more prized and rewarding when we go there from our private space.

Our need for psychological space is a need for privacy of our feelings, thoughts, and dreams. Again, this need is not a denial of our desire to share private information with our partner. It is, rather, an explanation of our need to be alone with our thoughts without unwanted intrusions from others. It is not necessary to be physically apart from each other to be psychologically alone. Lenora and I developed the ability to be in the same room and yet be alone. She would read or work crossword puzzles while I read or listened to classical music. We did this by choice and I felt that we were showing respect when we allowed each other to be totally involved in our own private activity.

A final dimension of our need for personal space is our need for personal possessions. Closely related to this need is the idea of territoriality, or having our own turf. For Lenora and me, it meant respecting what belonged to or was predominantly used by the other. For me, it meant not using her bath, opening her mail, or looking in her handbag or wallet.

Attending

Throughout this book I have emphasized the interdependence of partners' behavior in marriage. Since marriage is a bound relationship between two people, the behavior of each partner is sharply focused in terms of its effect on the other partner. It is, in fact, hard for one partner to escape the effect of the other's behavior. I'm not suggesting that we are responsible for the behavior of our partner--behavior always is the responsibility of the actor. What I am suggesting is that we become more aware of the total, actual effects of our behavior. With this awareness, we then can do those things that encourage and reinforce mutually desired behavior. Attending is the path to both accentuating the positives and eliminating the negatives. Whatever we do in attending behavior becomes the essence of a helping relationship.

I use the generic word "attending" to include five specific behaviors and attitudes we can use to help our partner. The word attending suggests being sensitive to, or paying attention to, the needs of our partner. It can vary from saying the right thing at the right time to being present when it is desired or needed. It often involves nothing more or less than empathic listening, holding hands, or hugging. Being in our partner's physical presence is not necessary for successful attending, but we always must be in their psychological presence. When we engage in attending behavior we are showing our love; we also are showing our concern to help our partner grow emotionally, socially and spiritually. Attending behavior is our answer to Elizabeth Barrett Browning's question, "How do I love thee?" Each act of attending is another way of saying, "I love you."

Affirmation

Affirmation is the act or process of declaring our continued commitment to or belief in something that we earlier had professed. In courtship we professed our love of our partner; in marriage our partner needs to know that our love continues undiminished. Feelings of love and affection, which are freely shown during courtship, can and often do fluctuate when faced by the realities of marriage and the cooling of infatuation and passion. When this happens, partners often reassess their situation and ponder whether they might have made a mistake in marrying. If questions or doubts about the wisdom of continuing the marriage emerge, they undermine the security and psychological well-being of the other partner. When commitment to the marriage becomes conditional, the glue that holds the partners together is weakened and their closeness, intimacy, and security are threatened.

When we affirm our love for our partner as the years pass, we are helping them to feel accepted, approved, and secure. In married life, the roles we play and our behavior in those roles, unfortunately, often are taken for granted unless they are in some way extraordinary. As a result, many partners do not receive the recognition and appreciation they need to bolster their self-esteem and satisfy their need for approval. This circumstance is inexcusable in view of the overwhelming evidence that people are motivated to repeat any behavior that earns them praise and acceptance.

Even in situations when, say, the behavior of our partner hurts or disappoints us, it is necessary that we separate our disapproval of their behavior from any disapproval of them as a person. By making it clear that we accept and approve of the doer while rejecting the doer's behavior helps our partner to deal with our feedback in a non-defensive manner. By showing our continued love, we are attending to our partner's needs for acceptance and security.

When I inquired into the history of Phil and Anne's seven-year marriage I was amazed to learn that they had physically separated five times. Both of them, in evident embarrassment, seem to say, "We can't live with each other, and we can't live without each other. Can you help us?" Anne had started the sequence of separations by twice moving out and getting her own apartment. Then it was Phil's turn to voluntarily move out on two separate occasions. In the most recent instance, Anne asked Phil to move out.

Their courtship had been equally stormy and disrupted by breakups during which each of them had dated other persons. After a while, as though they were guided by some strange force of destiny, they would start dating again. It was in between two of their separations--while they were dating--that they married. Thus their marriage became a continuation of intermittent periods of being together and being separated. They were apart--separation number five--when they came to see me.

Phil offered what he described as an easy solution to the problem of their off-and-on marriage. "I think we should get a divorce and then get married again. That way we could start out fresh." Although I advised against that extreme action, I saw in Phil's suggestion a light at the end of the dark tunnel from which they were trying to find their way. In their own unmellowed way Phil and Anne loved each other and wanted to find a way of living together without all the ups and downs they thus far had experienced. I was able to help them build upon their love feelings as they relived their courtship and the expectations they had of marriage and each other. We then concentrated on resolving some of the remaining bothersome questions of adjustment. Phil and Anne had wanted to ride the wave of euphoria and cotton-candy romance forever. Having inordinately high expectations of their marriage without any accompanying commitment to make it work, even small shocks to the stability of their marriage drove them apart. Their therapy involved unlearning a lot of old, inappropriate beliefs and attitudes and learning new ways of relating that contributed to their needs for stability and security.

Human love, if it is to exist, must be strong enough to overcome the frailties and shortcomings of the loved person. When we concentrate on the faults and minuses of our partner we are judging; when we look past these imperfections and see the person we love we are reaffirming our love for them. Affirming partners build each other up and concentrate on what is good rather than dwelling on minor faults. Affirmation also means offering understanding and support instead of criticism and withdrawal when our partner faces problem issues. It does not mean that we solve the problem for our partner. Finally, affirming partners understand their need for and dependence upon each other and let the beacon of acceptance and commitment guide them along the often tangled path of marriage.

Tenderness

I comfortably could have substituted words like kindness, consideration, thoughtfulness, or politeness as the title of this section. Forgiveness, which I will discuss later, also shares a kindred relationship. Notice how the Apostle Paul tied them all together in Ephesians 4:32 "...be kind and tenderhearted to one another, and forgive one another...." Although these words are near synonyms, there is a particular quality of refined behavior suggested by each. Each adds a dimension of civility and propriety to the social code that should be the standard of all marital behavior. It was this big picture of polite behavior that my mother always had in mind when she encouraged me, as a child, always to be a gentleman. "Always say 'thank you,' respect your elders, open doors for ladies, and don't get in line in front of others," she constantly reminded me. Later she added admonitions against picking my nose and scratching my itch.

When I was seven years old I had to have hernia repair surgery and in those days a long recuperation routinely was prescribed. During my recovery I was attended by four of my father's sisters while my parents worked. Their care--the things they did for me and the attitude of love they displayed as they cared for me--encouraged me to use all of the above words and to show the kinds of behavior that each suggested. In school, however, I found that behaving this way often was met by sneers and derision from my peers. I became confused because of their tendency to point to my behavior as a sign of weakness, even femininity. My doubts about the correctness of my behavior increased when I saw their rudeness and flippancy being rewarded by attention from girls. Again, my aunts--especially Aunt Lucille--came to my rescue. They helped me to see that what we would today call machismo behavior was not strength at all, but instead was an effort by people to compensate for the love and acceptance they didn't receive at home. They also suggested that maybe I should get some new friends.

While I was teaching at the U. S. Air Force Academy, I saw further evidence of the "tenderness equals strength" equation. Some members of the varsity football team were selected to play in a post-season charity game for the benefit of a children's hospital. One of the chosen players was an advisee of mine and upon his return from the game he gave me a picture of himself holding a young infant. He explained that during a pre-game practice session, the game sponsors held a picture-taking session. In the picture he gave me, all that I could see of him was his big arm. But perched securely on his arm was a young infant whose clothing had been removed for this particular photo. So what I saw in the photo was the delicate, pale buttocks of an infant sitting on the big, tanned arm of the cadet. What a contrast! His arm seemed as big as my leg. What strength it suggested. He easily could have crushed the infant against his strong, muscular body but what I saw in the picture was only tenderness and concern for the infant's well-being. Perhaps that was what the publicists had in mind when they staged this particular shot. The overall message of the picture was that there is no tenderness like that shown by strong people.

Tenderness is not the opposite of toughness or crudeness. It is a positive attribute of a person; it is an act of the human will. In its effect it is the icing on a cake; it is Mary Poppin's spoonful of sugar. Being tender--kind, considerate and polite--is something we do because it adds to the quality of human life. It makes us more human. But, if we do it only in public, to others, it is artificial and lacking in sincerity and ease. Strangely, it sometimes seems that married people are more considerate of others than they are of their partners. It also can be observed that considerate behaviors, so evident during courtship, seem to be regarded as unnecessary in marriage. This is unfortunate since it makes courtship behavior seem contrived and designed only for the short-term goal of winning a marital partner.

Tenderness and kindness are qualities which never go out of style, even though teachers and writers often are embarrassed to talk or write about them, especially in adult relationships. By their omission, it seems that these behaviors are best left for children. I have several so-called marriage manuals on my bookshelf. The emphasis of these books mostly is on technique: what to do, how to do it. References to feelings such as love, tenderness, and consideration are rare. When they are found, they are treated as though they were peripheral concerns and that no good could come from discussing them.

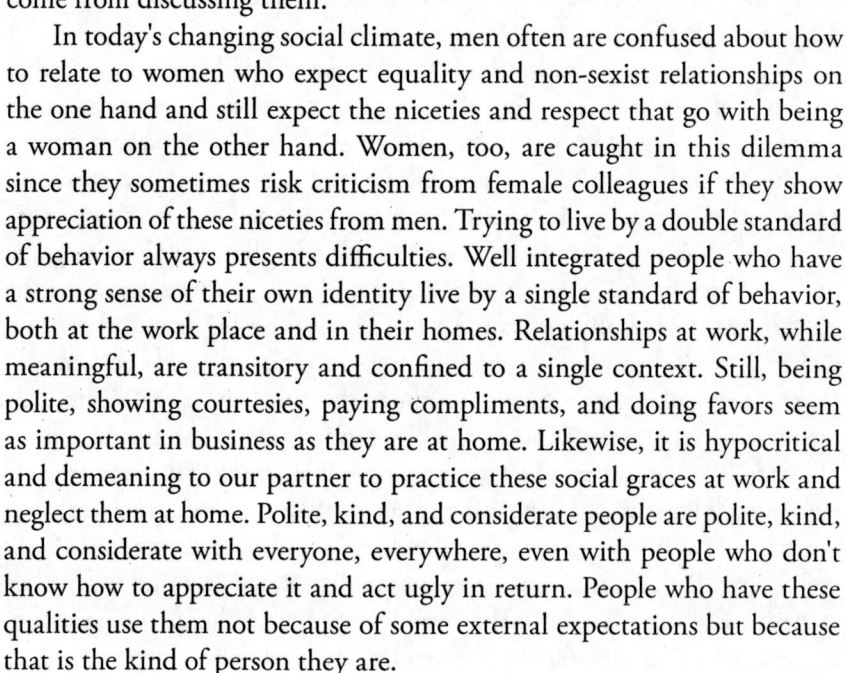

In today's changing social climate, men often are confused about how to relate to women who expect equality and non-sexist relationships on the one hand and still expect the niceties and respect that go with being a woman on the other hand. Women, too, are caught in this dilemma since they sometimes risk criticism from female colleagues if they show appreciation of these niceties from men. Trying to live by a double standard of behavior always presents difficulties. Well integrated people who have a strong sense of their own identity live by a single standard of behavior, both at the work place and in their homes. Relationships at work, while meaningful, are transitory and confined to a single context. Still, being polite, showing courtesies, paying compliments, and doing favors seem as important in business as they are at home. Likewise, it is hypocritical and demeaning to our partner to practice these social graces at work and neglect them at home. Polite, kind, and considerate people are polite, kind, and considerate with everyone, everywhere, even with people who don't know how to appreciate it and act ugly in return. People who have these qualities use them not because of some external expectations but because that is the kind of person they are.

Tenderness, for me, was the discovery and celebration of the love the little boy within me had for the little girl within Lenora. Although I was an adult I had to respect the child within me before I could show tenderness to Lenora. I could not give her tenderness unless I could first give it to myself. For adults this is sometimes hard to do; for children it is always easy. Jesus taught that "Whoever does not receive the Kingdom of God like a child will never enter it." (Mark 10:15) The point I want to make can be expressed with a similar metaphor: Our tenderness must be genuine, like that of a child.

I liked to hold Lenora's hand--it pleased both of us. She always thanked me for the cut flowers I kept on her bedside table. We exchanged valentine cards and unashamedly shed a tear or two watching a sad movie. She grew old with me but she never lost her beauty, and I like to look at her. I did whatever I could to cause her to stay glad that she married me. Not unexpectedly, the more tenderness I show to her the more I was rewarded with love.

Intimacy

When we are unable to be intimate with at least one other person we are doomed to an existential loneliness. But it is not only because of our desire to avoid loneliness that we seek intimacy; intimacy is sought for its own benefit. In every kind of ongoing human relationship, from business partnerships to marriage, closeness, openness, and trust play an important if not a decisive role in determining the quality of the relationship. During a luncheon speech to a group of senior citizens, I asked, "What is important to you now, at this time, in the present circumstances of your life?" Although expressed in different ways and with varying degrees of eloquence, their answers could be summarized as, "Wanting to be close to someone." For some, it involved children or grandchildren, others wanted to be close to their spouse. All expressed their need for closeness to God. In my therapy work with clients, young and old, male and female, I got similar answers when this question was asked. They also were heard in premarital counseling.

Intimacy is not a now-and-then, sometime thing; nor is it restricted to certain times and places. Although intimacy requires effort, it is not something that you do--an activity. Necessarily, activities have a beginning and an end. Intimacy is more a state of being; it is not something that can be taken off the shelf and used Saturday nights and Sunday mornings. It is more correct to say that we are intimacy than to say we do intimacy. To associate intimacy with and expect to find it only in some form of peak experience is to overlook our moment-to-moment, day-to-day relationships. It would be like trying to satisfy our eternally recurring hunger by eating one big meal. Intimacy is an ever present need in all ongoing relationships. In close, valued marriages the partners are intimacy. Notice that I did not say that partners are intimate. As an attitude, value, or attribute, intimacy is not something you do, it is something you are.

Russ Holloman, Ph. D.

As a state of being, intimacy is given and received, in continuing moments of risk and trust, openness and disclosure, discovery and acceptance. In marriage, our goal is not to think of intimacy as some kind of ultimate, top-of-the-mountain experience, but something that fills all our days, making each moment a valued experience. It cannot be reduced to sharing the same bed or living in the same house. Nor can intimacy be equated to an act of sexual intercourse. Two people can live in the same house, share the same bathroom, sleep in the same bed, engage in sexual intercourse and still not share intimacy. Fear, shame, and lack of trust and openness, which can be found to some degree in all people, are formidable barriers to intimacy.

The essence of intimacy is feelings. While intimacy may be expressed with both words and actions, they promote intimacy only to the extent that they represent and are an extension of feelings. Our words and actions, although well intentioned and expressed in situations conducive to intimacy, are nothing more than perfunctory gestures if they are not rooted in and supported by feelings. Dr. Isaac Rubin (1983) capably has expressed the emotional nature of intimacy as a dual, reciprocal process. For him, intimacy attends when we feel close to our partner and feel our partner's closeness to us. We accept and respond to our own feelings while, at the same time, we are receptive to our partner's feelings for us. This dual process is reciprocated by our partner. It is the totality of this two-way process that constitutes intimacy. In bottom-line thinking, we cannot be intimate alone. Intimacy is the difference between being with our partner and merely being in our partner's presence. We can be in our partner's presence and yet be emotionally distant. From a men's locker room comes the explanation that wives enjoy sex more when they are lying on their left side--this way they can watch the television.

Another way to capture the essence of intimacy is to reflect on the difference between the prepositions in and into. Frederick Buechner (1988) has furnished a good explanation of that difference. A person is in architecture or in teaching, we say, meaning that is what they do during work days. That is how they earn money to pay their bills. But it is another story if we say they are into these things. When we are into something, we live and breathe it; we identify with and internalize it. It goes with us wherever we go; we can't get enough of it. To be into books means that the sight of a signed first edition of *Alice in Wonderland* sets our heart pounding. To be in books means only that we sell them at the local bookstore. See the difference? Intimacy is withness; intimacy is into; intimacy is I-THOU.

I have identified five kinds or dimensions of intimacy. Each in some way is different from the others; not better, just different. In some cases the difference is great--it is a difference of kind. In other instances, the difference is small--it is a difference of degree. Each is included because it is exclusive in some way. Yet, they all are complementary to each other. I will clarify their seemingly complex relationship as I discuss each one.

Emotional intimacy is not one of my five kinds of intimacy. Rather, it is the essential ingredient of all five kinds. It is the emotions or feelings we have about an idea, person, or activity that makes the association or relation intimate. Without emotion, there is no intimacy. Thus, emotion is a common, critical ingredient of each of the five dimensions. Think of a potato. Let's compare emotion to a potato. A potato can be cooked in numerous ways all by itself. It's the same way with emotion: it can be experienced in many different ways. A potato can also be cooked into a casserole, a soufflé, a soup, or a salad. In a like manner, emotion is found in each of the five dimensions that I will discuss. In fact, it is the presence of emotion that makes these various kinds of intimacy possible.

Social Intimacy: This kind of intimacy grows from common bonds, values, and expectations that are shared by people as members of various social groups. It can be found in a car pool when the values of promptness, safe driving, and equitable sharing create a sense of togetherness. Members of a bowling team unite around the expectation that each member will always do their best. Loyalty and a commitment not to let your buddy down promotes a cohesive closeness in military organizations. In marriage, the common values of fidelity, home, family, and God bond partners to each other in social intimacy.

In each of the above settings, the members share certain values and ideals which bond them together. In military parlance, all will say, "We wear the same uniform." There must also be a commitment made as a condition of membership. In turn, holding common values leads to positive feelings of belonging and interdependency which, in turn, equal intimacy. Without the accompanying feelings, the relationship is perfunctory.

Intellectual Intimacy: We are attracted to persons who can think in stimulating and creative ways. This intellectual attraction, for some people, can be stronger than sexual attraction. My graduate philosophy and psychology classes are remembered easily because of the kindred relationships that developed between students and professors as we discussed the theories of prominent persons in the fields.

Thinking in the same way is not a condition of intellectual intimacy. Rather, a commitment to an atmosphere of independent thought and intellectual objectivity is the essential requirement. Intellectual intimacy develops easily among members of problem-solving groups; people cooperating to solve a mutually felt conflict also can experience it. In both instances, it is the sense of accepting responsibility (not blame) for the problem or conflict and offering insightful solutions that promote intimacy. It is the feeling "This is tough, but we can solve it" that causes members to share their ideas and to respond to the ideas of others. Surprisingly, intellectual intimacy is a prerequisite to sexual and marital intimacy. What is not surprising is that many married people complain about their partners' lack of intellectual ability. "My partner is great in a lot of ways but taking part in an intellectual conversation is not one of them," typifies an often-heard complaint from both husbands and wives. When partners fail to stay informed about significant social, economic, and political events, they can become dull and uninteresting conversationalists. When partners do not grow intellectually, when they refuse to re-evaluate their thinking in terms of new information and developments, there is a corresponding emphasis on keeping things the way they are. When this happens, intellectual intimacy is unlikely.

I met Lenora in a college classroom. I always sat up front and typically got to know only the three or four people sitting around me. In a sophomore literature class an attractive woman, who usually sat in the back of the room, consistently made insightful, informed comments and interpretations about the subject being studied. She often gave answers and insights that escaped the other class members (all of us). Without any personal knowledge about her except her participation in the class I was attracted to her. I sought her out and soon we were dating. After two years of courtship and fifty-nine years of marriage, I continued to value the intellectual intimacy I felt with her. This intimacy was valued all the more because it complemented our marital and spiritual intimacy.

Intellectual intimacy can be attained more readily and with less risk than other kinds. The ease and respectability that goes with intellectual intimacy cause some people to harbor it as a substitute for other kinds of intimacy. A fear of physical or sexual intimacy also can cause them to seek refuge in intellectual intimacy, attributing a higher level of worth and satisfaction to it than normally justified.

A friend invited me to lunch explaining that he wanted to talk over a personal problem. Before ordering, he suggested that we have a glass of wine. While waiting to be served, he started talking about the wine. "This wine won't be as good as the '85 Chardonnay I had the other evening," he said. He continued, talking about the origins, culture, etc., of various wines. I listened. Through my salad and his soup, he talked. Well into our main course, he was still talking about wines. Again, he apologized for the wine we were having, repeating his wish that we could have had a glass of the premium Chardonnay. All the time I was wondering, "Where is the personal problem?" I also wondered about the wisdom of his wanting to discuss a presumably serious problem at lunch.

Finally, seeking to force the issue, I said, "Tom, I can never have a glass of the wine you had the other evening. It is gone. Finished. Let's enjoy the wine we do have." My intervention caused him to stop talking. Silently, he started randomly moving his food around in the plate. Finally, he said, "Russ, this is the hardest thing I have ever had to talk about."

Tom had unconsciously sought safety in his monologue about wines; it was his way of avoiding the problem he really wanted to discuss. My purpose in sharing this story is to point out that couples will use this same technique or strategy to talk about intimacy rather than experience it. Their conversation is sincere enough, but it is filled with "should's" and "ought's." Talking about intimacy is once removed from experiencing it--being it--in the here and now.

Physical Intimacy: Included here is such physical closeness as touch, eye contact, voice whispers, and body warmth and aroma. Hugging, kissing, and caressing also come to mind as aspects of physical intimacy. All sexual intimacy has a physical dimension but not all physical intimacy is sexual. This difference can be explained, first, by the fact that sex ordinarily is performed in private and, second, by our belief that sex should occur only in the context of marriage.

Lenora and I were enjoying a picnic lunch on Augusta's Riverwalk when a young couple arrived and sat on a blanket not far from us. "More picnickers," Lenora casually observed. It was soon evident, however, that the couple had not come to eat. Instead, they started embracing and, occasionally, kissing. We noticed that people walking by demonstrated an apparent discomfort and tried not to look at the couple. I suggested, "If that couple started fighting, all these passers-by would stop and gawk." Not really expecting an answer, Lenora asked, "Why is that?" She understood, it seemed, that the physical intimacy of the couple was disapproved by the passersby. A place where a certain four-letter word really fits is the societal admonition, "It's O.K. to fight but don't make love." It reflects the split personality of our value system when we tolerate violence with an air of approval but frown upon any public showing of physical intimacy. People seemingly are more threatened by the psychological and spiritual nakedness of showing tenderness and sharing feelings than they are of the physical nakedness in sexual intimacy.

It often is argued that physical intimacy is, necessarily, a prelude to sexual intimacy and should be avoided when sexual intimacy is not intended. This is unfortunate, at least in marriage. Physical intimacy, like the potato, has value and can be cherished for itself. It does not have to be limited to those situations where it is a prelude to sex. To think this way cheapens physical intimacy and makes sex a non-rewarding act of obligation. An often heard complaint from wives is, "Why can't he just hold me? Sometimes, I'd just like to hold him but I don't dare do it unless I am also ready for either sex or a fight." Then, paradoxically, I hear husbands say, "I resent being trapped in an image that I hug my wife only when I am interested in sex. I am more than a sex machine that turns on whenever we touch."

It's tragic that in cases like these, when both partners want the same thing, that they cannot communicate their wishes and preferences. It is not a case of them being in conflict but, rather, not being able to articulate their agreement.

Sexual/Marital Intimacy: I will discuss these two dimensions as though they are one. This presumption reflects my moral belief that marriage is the only sanctioned context for sexual intimacy. But I also believe that sex between an unmarried but loving, committed couple is more moral than sex between a married but unloving couple. How can I hold and defend these two incongruent beliefs? It's simple. Sex, apart from love and commitment, whether in or out of marriage, is exploitative and self-serving. It's certainly not intimacy. Thus, the sexual intimacy I will discuss here is the kind that can be equated only to marital intimacy.

For someone who has never known the joy and comfort of sexual intimacy in marriage, no description or explanation is adequate. For those who have, none is needed. So if my words paint an unreal or unbelievable picture of marital intimacy, please remember that I am writing against the background of my own marriage and the sharings of hundreds of couples in therapy. Marriage sets sexual intimacy apart from other intimate relationships. It elevates sexual intimacy above sexual involvements outside marriage. Casual or uncommitted sex, in or outside marriage, is mere physical activity; it falls into that one percent of our being that I discussed in the previous chapter.

The emotion--openness, trust, vulnerability, and commitment--that precedes and accompanies sex in marriage is all in the ninety-nine percent of our being. It is for this reason, perhaps, that our brain has been called our biggest and best sex organ.

It is only in marriage that the four loves described by C. S. Lewis (1960) are merged together. The first of these is <u>eros</u>, or passion. It is a love that seeks to fulfill its own hunger. Outside marriage, this kind of love is manipulative and self-serving; it inevitably produces a win-lose relationship. In marriage, eros is joined by <u>agape</u>, a love that seeks to give. Complementing eros and agape are <u>storge</u>, love expressed as affection, and <u>philia</u>, love expressed as friendship. Marital intimacy rises to its highest when partners freely accept their giving and receiving roles of commitment and surrender, of disclosure and discovery, of risk and trust, and of stability and growth. Marriage is the focal point of a variety of human needs; marital intimacy is both the source and means of satisfying these needs.

Spiritual Intimacy: Numerous religious leaders have suggested that the ultimate concern of people about their lives is a religious concern. If this is true, and I believe it is, there will come a time in our lives when the most important questions we will face will be religious and deeply theological in nature. Whether the word ultimate is defined as that which is most important or as that which comes at the end of life, the ultimate concern about life is a question to which only religion can furnish answers.

Lenora and I believed there is a spiritual dimension to human life and that in order to be fully human we must acknowledge and worship God, who created us. Thus, we have membership in both a human family and in the family of God. By birth we received the physical attributes of our parents and a family name. Through our baptism we received the spirit of God into our lives and were given a Christian name which identified us as unique persons loved by God. Being created for communion with God, Lenora and I found in that relationship a meaningful orientation for the integration of our spiritual and secular lives. Living our lives as members of the priesthood of all believers under the fatherhood of God demands and provides intimacy with each other and with God.

Esteem

Let me suggest an entertaining, productive way to spend an evening when the TV is offering only reruns. Ask your partner to answer in three or four sentences the question "Who am I?" The initial response will probably be something like "Why are you asking that question? I'm me. I'm myself."

"Yes," you say, "but <u>who</u> are you?" With more thought and encouragement, your partner will typically try to explain some of the key words in their initial response: the words me and myself. What is it like to be me? What does it mean to be myself? If you try my suggestion, be prepared for a long evening.

When we describe our "self" we are painting a picture of what we look like to ourselves. The description we offer is our self-image or self-concept. While we paint a single image of ourselves, it is always influenced by the image we think others have of us. Also involved is the image of how we would like to be seen. Indeed, by comparing these three images, we get some understanding of how accurately we are describing ourselves. Our evaluation of our self-image--how we feel about what we see--is referred to as our self-esteem. Although outside influences can play an important role, our sense of self-esteem or personal worth ultimately is derived from inner sources. This is my basis for urging clients to take responsibility for their own self-esteem.

Self-esteem is a gift from the self. No one can give it to us nor can they take it away without our permission. Esteem from others is nice to have but it is not a substitute for our own sense of well-being. The more confident and self-directing people are, the more independent they are of outside influences in determining their sense of worth. These people are inner directed. Outer-directed persons, on the other hand, depend upon favorable evaluations by other people for their sense of self-worth. They are less free to grow and develop their potentialities--they are too busy trying to conform to the expectations of others.

We should never accept uncritically the evaluations of other people--particularly family members. Close family members are usually too ego-involved to be subjective and are less able to see us as clearly as a perceptive, helpful friend. However, when others, family members or not, consistently see us differently than we see ourselves, we should seek help from others to either confirm or disconfirm their feedback. If, however, feedback from others generally confirms our self-image as a mature, competent, and productive person, a single instance of negative feedback should not cause us to doubt the more favorable generally-held image we have of ourselves.

There is a widely held view that feelings of inferiority--low self-esteem--are deeply rooted in childhood experiences. People who believe this way and use it to justify their lack of improvement efforts are often heard to say, "It's not my fault I'm this way; I had a bad childhood. Someone else has to accept the responsibility for changing me." I cannot accept their argument.

Low self-esteem is a common complaint from people in unhealthy marriages. Typically, one partner makes the complaint while trying to point the finger of blame toward the other partner. Fortunately, this is a circumstance that is easily changed. I always begin therapy with people presenting this complaint by having them look separately at the word "self" and the word "esteem". I point out that the two words are joined with a hyphen to form self-esteem. "Since it is your "self" esteem it is your evaluation of your self-image. Whether high or low, your self-esteem reflects a choice that you have made. You chose to feel the way you do about yourself. Why did you decide as you did?"

Let me illustrate my point by describing an imaginary scene on a basketball court. A couple of inexperienced people are asked to come onto the court and shoot the basketball through the hoop. Both shoot one time and both miss. One of them says, "Let me get closer until I get the hang of it. I'm sure I can do it." The other person says, "I'm embarrassed. I knew I couldn't do it." Both people had the same experience, but they chose to interpret their experience differently. One responded in a determined, confident belief; the other with a negative, irrational belief. It is our interpretation of our experiences, not the experiences themselves, that do such far-reaching damage to our self-esteem and, thereby, our ability to lead productive, satisfying lives.

I once was asked by a local middle school to work with a group of seventh graders who had been classified as high-risk students. By this term, it was meant that these students most likely would fail the year's work and not be promoted to the next higher grade. Although it was only early April, they already had been "written off" by their teachers. "Why bother now?" these teachers reasoned. "They will be back next year and we can start over."

These children showed all the classical symptoms of low self-esteem as they communicated their generally negative views of themselves to others. They were not yet old enough to understand what I have argued above about the essence of self-esteem, nor did they yet know that they had a choice as to how they might feel about themselves. I asked them to think of some reasons they might have for liking themselves. For more than an hour I was privy to some of their most intimate revelations.

"I like myself because I can play the violin."
"I like myself because I can operate my uncle's computer."
"I like myself because I can build crossword puzzles."

The children who made these statements--children who could perform these skills--still thought of themselves as failures because of low grades they had made and the perceived judgments of their teachers. As I worked with and learned more about these children, I began to suspect that it was the teachers who were failing. The teachers, naturally, tended to blame the system.

I suggested to the school principal, "Since these children have already been written off for this school year, let's take them out of their regular classes and the seventh grade curriculum they are supposed to be studying and put them into a special, experimental group. Then let's select a caring teacher to work with them the rest of the year to help them develop a more positive self-image. Let's help them to make some small achievements so they will feel more confident about tackling math and English next year. Let's help them to feel more confident; let's help them to believe in themselves."

"Can't do it," he replied. "First of all, Atlanta would never let us deviate from the prescribed curriculum. Second, I doubt if any of my teachers would want to work with this group on a full-time basis."

I left the school wondering why children who can play the violin, work with computers, and build crossword puzzles have to be branded as failures and suffer the resulting dysfunctional consequences of low self-esteem.

Children aren't the only ones who suffer these consequences. Adults also need a sense of personal achievement; adults also need to be recognized; adults also need to be confirmed. While low self-esteem can begin in childhood, there is no age limit on raising it. In marriage, partners have a two-part responsibility in helping each other to develop and maintain a healthy self-image. First, it is unloving to criticize and blame our partner in ways that cause them to doubt their own self-worth. Second, it is loving to confirm our partner in ways that cause them to value themselves more highly. When we are confirmed by our partner we feel an increased sense of self-acceptance and self-worth. It is hardly necessary to have a psychologist tell us that for good mental health we need these feelings of self-worth and the consequent positive self-esteem.

Lenora always shared such positive feelings about my work that I never would be able to repay her. Still, I tried by confirming her opinions, her decisions, and her behavior in all aspects of her life. I complimented her dress, her food preparation and homemaking skills, and her many involvements and accomplishments outside the home. Even when I felt that some aspect of her behavior might have been more effective had she done things differently, I tried to approach the matter in terms of possible clarification. "Did you consider . . .," or "Were you free to . . .?" I would never knowingly do or say anything that might cause her to doubt her worth and competence as a person.

I'd like to emphasize one caution before I finish this part. Confirming responses to our partner always must be honest and never used to artificially manipulate their self-esteem. As partners in a helping relationship we never must engage in false flattery just to make our partner feel good about themselves. Neither am I suggesting that we become "yes" people and routinely confirm every bit of behavior. What I am suggesting is that we develop sensitivity to our partner's involvements and always express our agreement and support when they are genuine and warranted. When our partner knows we are concerned and genuinely are interested in helping them, even disconfirming feedback can be seen as helpful and caring.

Forgiveness

As I sat across my desk from Nelson, my mind was doing flashbacks, trying to recall and put into perspective the chain of events that had led to our meeting. Two years earlier, Nelson and Margot had what appeared to be a happy, fulfilling marriage. They were financially secure with Nelson's six-figure income and seemed to enjoy spending their money on the family and worthwhile community causes. In their middle forties, they were involved in a number of community and church-related activities and projected a common-folks image in spite of their otherwise affluent lifestyle. Their two children were talented tennis players and participated in numerous youth competitions throughout the state and region. On these trips, the children always were accompanied by their mother. When possible, they were joined by their father.

After returning from one of their competitions, the older boy made a comment to his father that suggested the possibility of some questionable behavior by his mother. Although Nelson thought it highly irregular, he discounted the matter and did not mention it to Margot. His suspicion was later renewed, however, when Margot insisted that she alone accompany the boys on one of their trips even though Nelson had planned to go. Nelson's insistence on going caused Margot to withdraw angrily, leaving only Nelson to go with the children. Telephone calls from the tournament location to his wife were not answered. When he and the boys returned home Sunday evening, Margot was not there. She had left a note on the kitchen table offering her apologies for the ugly scene she had created in front of the boys on Thursday. She also explained that she had gone to the beach for the weekend.

A month or so later an anonymous telephone call to his office confirmed Nelson's worst fears. He immediately went home where, before the boys got home from school, he confronted Margot with the accusation that had been made in the telephone call.

"Yes. It's true. Don't pretend that you didn't know. I do want a divorce. Also, I want the boys, the house, one of the cars, and enough money for the boys and me to continue living the way we have been. Since Georgia has a no-fault divorce law, there's no need to mention what has happened."

Nelson did not want a divorce and begged Margot to let bygones be bygones and not think about a divorce. He was willing to forgive and forget. She was adamant, however, and a long period of legal consultations and divorce mediation followed without resolution of their differences and without their divorce being finalized. Finally, Nelson accepted the fact that Margot was determined to divorce him. He also agreed not to mention her admitted adultery for the boys' sake. He suggested selling the house and splitting the proceeds. Margot would not agree. He then suggested deducting one-half of the value of the house from the sum of money she was asking. Again, she refused, claiming that would not be fair to the boys. The hassle had now been going on for over a year with Nelson living in a convenience apartment and paying all the bills at what he called the big house.

As I studied Nelson's face and hands and listened to his sometimes repetitive speech, I saw a man who seemingly had aged several years during the past twelve months. Alcohol, cigarettes, an inadequate diet, and lack of sleep and exercise were taking their toll.

"She had no right to do this to me and the boys. She's the guilty one, but she is making me look like the villain. It's not fair. Why is she so inconsiderate, so greedy? I'll never give in to her. I'll never give her what she wants. Don't you think I'm right?"

"I gather that it's important for you to be right?"

"You bet it is! She had no right to do what she did."

"She did it though, and you can't change what has been done. It's history. Yes, you have a right to continue fighting her if that's what you want to do. You also have the right to settle with her, and get on with your life, if that's what you want to do. Have you taken a long look at yourself in the mirror lately? It's costing you more to be right than it would cost you to accept her wrong."

"Are you suggesting I settle with her?"

"Yes, I am. You can afford it. And one more thing: throw in a little extra. That would be your way of saying I forgive you. It's also a way of forgiving yourself."

Nelson had been hurt by Margot's infidelity, but her unwillingness to attempt reconciliation coupled with her demands for custody of the boys and what he viewed as an unfair financial settlement, were even more devastating to him. As their conflict continued without any signs of a viable resolution, Nelson began to express both contempt and hate for Margot. Feelings of guilt accompanied his negative feelings about her. Gradually, he accepted the reality that the reconciliation he wanted and had thought possible was unlikely. His realization that his marriage could not be healed helped him also to realize that he had to go on with his life. Before this could happen, however, he had to rid himself of his negative judgments of Margot, his anger, his hate, and his consuming desire for revenge. His bitterness, he realized, was hurting only himself. Forgiveness was the only way out of the self-destructing circumstances that surrounded him--circumstances that were darkening and threatening his life.

It is a part of our folklore that a good marriage consists of two good forgivers. The logic behind this adage lies, perhaps, in the recognition that marriage involves two well-intentioned but imperfect people. Mistakes will be made, disappointments will occur and feelings will be hurt. No one, in marriage or out, can be expected to be perfect. We have to be forgiven, in a sense, for being human. Because of our imperfections, forgiveness is the only way we can be reconciled to our partner and start over. In our fifty-nine years of marriage, I often had to say to Lenora, "I'm sorry that I.... Please forgive me." She must have loved me a lot because she forgave me a lot, and her forgiveness was always complete. She might not have been able to forget my offense or failure but she never mentioned it again. As the Apostle Paul suggests in 1 Corinthians 13:5, she kept no record of my wrongs.

It is both good theology and good psychology to forgive those who wrong us in some way. The most powerful and memorable example of forgiveness is Jesus praying for those who were crucifying him. From the cross he prayed, "Forgive them, Father, they don't know what they are doing." (Luke 23:34) Jesus' prayer for forgiveness of his torturers and taunters fully was consistent with his mission of love and reconciliation. I always have been able to understand and accept the first part of his prayer: "Forgive them," but the second part, "They don't know what they are doing," was for a long time difficult for me to understand. But when I was helped to understand it, I was amazed at its simplicity. Simply, those who were crucifying Jesus were so filled with rage, hate, and fear that they were blinded to the reality of their actions. They truly did not know what they were doing.

Can partners in marriage hurt each other without knowing it? Unfortunately, yes, although the reasons are not always clear. Faulty communication and changed expectations are two often-cited culprits. Unwilling to accept the responsibility for our behavior, we try to blame our partner for having made us do it. Whenever we act in our own self interests without considering the needs and desires of our partner, whenever we fail our partner, whether by the commission or the omission of an act, we violate their trust in us.

The things we can do which separate us from God and from our partner are infinite. Whatever we do, however, God is faithful to forgive us as long as we truly repent of our wrongdoing. As we are forgiven, we must forgive those who wrong us. How many times? Jesus' disciple, Peter, asked if seven was an appropriate number of times. "No, seventy times seven," was Jesus' reply. (Matthew 18:21-22)

In our marriage, as in all secular relationships, we must be forgiving in order to be forgiven in our spiritual relationship with God. This is the spiritual or theological reason we must forgive. There also are sound psychological reasons for forgiving. To hold a grudge and insist upon retribution for an offense against us is to be held captive by our judgment and desire for revenge. To forgive our partner is to release them and us from our desire for punishment as a way of making things right. Forgiveness also means letting go of our self-righteousness and feeling of being blameless. This was part of Nelson's problem. "Margot's to blame. She's the one who ruined our marriage. It's not my fault." Holding on to his belief of her wrongdoing was a punishment of himself. It communicated hate and revenge, not love. It revealed his deep-seated resentment, not forgiveness. It held him captive.

What we must understand is that holding negative feelings and judgments against our partner does not change them. Neither does it improve the relationship between us. It only isolates us from our partner, like a wall or a broken bridge would. Once we are able to forgive and rid ourselves of our negative feelings and judgments we then are free to start rebuilding our relationship. The wall is removed; the bridge is repaired.

Such is the nature of a new beginning.

Chapter Eight

Helping in Decision Making and Problem Solving

Mark Twain once told a story about a policeman who was making his rounds on a particularly dark night. He came upon a drunk who was on his hands and knees under a streetlight searching for his house key.

"Where exactly did you lose it?" asked the policeman, trying to be helpful.

Pointing into the pitch-black night, the drunk mumbled, "Over there."

"Then why are you looking over here?" asked the policeman.

"This is where the light is," replied the drunk. "I can't see over there."

This story is old, but it has a lasting appeal because it can help us to understand not only the process but also the psychological consequences of marital decision making. In our efforts to understand how partners make decisions and how they are affected by their decisions, we tend to look only in the area that has been illuminated by prescriptive writings and our own personal experiences. But, like the moon, marital decision making has both light and dark areas. It also has a gray area where it is neither light nor dark. In this chapter I will discuss both the lighted and dark areas; however, primary emphasis will be given to the dark area. My purpose is not to review the mechanics of decision making, but to explore the effects of decision making upon partners. A decision should do more than simply solve a problem. It also should improve the quality of the partner's relationship. This is the concern of the dark area.

Three Views of Marital Decision Making

In the light area everything is neat, orderly, and well structured. Decision making is logical and rational--it prescribes the way decisions are supposed to be made. Two plus two always equals four, and one partner, given the same set of facts about a problem, should reach the same decision as the other partner with the same set of facts. A well-known representative of this approach to decision making is Science Officer Spock, a member of the crew of the United Star Ship Enterprise. As depicted in the television series, *Star Trek*, Mr. Spock characteristically thinks like a computer; he is unemotional, logical, and precise. Sergeant Friday of the television program *Dragnet* also comes to mind. Remember his cryptic words, "Just the facts, just give me the facts."

In the dark area there is a lot of marital decision making that is neither neat, orderly, nor well structured. Intuition, judgment, and emotion characterize this area more than do analysis and evaluation. Past experience and personal preferences are mainstays. Here, two plus two always equals four, but partners often are at a loss to explain how a particular decision was made. This approach, too, is epitomized by a character from *Star Trek*. Commander McCoy, the warm and caring ships surgeon, is emotional, intuitive and human-relations oriented.

In the light area, decision making is supposed to be rational and objective. Decisions which conform to these criteria supposedly provide a maximum amount of goal accomplishment or personal benefit and satisfaction. In the dark area, decision making is subjective and intuitive. Decisions on this side tend to be good-enough decisions. Two personal experiences illustrate this difference.

Recently, my daughter, who lives in Atlanta, called to tell me that she had four orchids I could have if I could drive over the next day to get them. She explained that she was leaving on a business trip and had no one to care for them. I quickly reasoned that taking the necessary time away from my work plus the expense of driving three hundred miles round trip to get the orchids would not be cost effective; it would not be rational if viewed from the light area. But when I realized that I would like to see her before she left Atlanta, my decision to go seemed imminently rational. My reasoning here was from the dark area. The thing that made the difference was substituting a new purpose for the old. Would I have wanted to visit her at that time if the orchids were not involved? Probably not. The point I want to make is that my decision was subjective--it expressed a desire or preference. Was it rational in the sense of being cost effective? Probably not. Was it rational in terms of satisfying a personal desire? Yes.

My second experience involved our purchase of a new automobile. Lenora and I had decided it was time to trade in the family sedan for a new one. We quickly agreed on the make and model and the various equipment options we wanted on the new car. After some comparative shopping we found what we wanted. However, when we went to close the deal we encountered a problem we had not anticipated. The sales person told us that he had several cars like what we wanted. "They are all alike except for the color. Which color do you want?"

I knew that Lenora didn't like red, and I didn't want green. But, eliminating these two colors did not solve our problem. Lenora suggested that I make the decision. I declined, explaining that she would be the primary driver of the car. I then countered with a suggestion that she make the decision, assuring her that I would be happy with whatever color she chose. Apparently tiring of our indecision, the sales person invited us to lunch so we could talk it over. Our decision, when we made it, was strictly from the dark area. We chose taupe, a color that matched one of Lenora's favorite dresses. Again, my point in this personal story is that had we made our decision according to the rational model of the light side, we would have had to consider such things about the various paint colors, ease of maintenance, durability, visibility under different weather conditions, etc. Our decision expressed our personal preference. For us it was a rational decision.

Neither of these two approaches to marital decision making is superior to the other. Both are good when used in the right way to solve the right problems. Intuition need not be distrusted simply because it lacks the sacrosanct quality of analysis. Neither is it rational to refrain from making a necessary decision when confronted by the limitations of the analytical method. It never simply is a matter of choosing between being analytical and being intuitive. Rather than being exclusive and independent of each other, they can and should be used as complementary components of any decision-making process. In our decisions about the orchids and the new car, rational considerations played a part, but these were overshadowed by personal feelings and subjective judgments.

When Lenora and I made decisions about money matters we tried to be as rational as we could. We were concerned about the rates of return on our investments, their safety, and our access to them in case of an emergency. To make these decisions on any other basis, in our view, would have involved a lot of imprudent risk-taking. On the other hand, our decisions about vacation spots were made in terms of personal preferences. But this doesn't mean we were not rational. We knew what we wanted; we knew what pleased us. We made choices that gave us the most of what we wanted. Effective marital decision making depends upon partners being analytical when it is necessary and feasible, and being intuitive when analysis is no longer feasible.

In my discussion of the light and dark areas of marital decision making, I was primarily concerned with two matters. First, the light area reflects the way decisions should be made; it is prescriptive. The dark area is more descriptive since it reflects how partners actually make many of their decisions. In the dark area, which I will discuss in detail later, my concern will be with the psychological consequences of decision making. Whether marital decisions are good or bad, effective or ineffective, the marriage always should be enhanced. A couple of questions can perhaps bring my concern into clearer focus. Does the process of making a decision help you and your partner to understand and accept your togetherness and interdependency, or does it leave you questioning each other's motives and lack of mutual concern? Do decision-making experiences increase your sense of confidence and control or does it leave you disillusioned and fearful of the consequences of future decisions? As you ponder the range of possible answers to these questions, you easily can see that decision making is a critical part of a helping relationship in marriage.

The basic premise of this chapter is the idea that through our decision making we can create and sustain a marriage that provides a high measure of emotional, intellectual and spiritual fulfillment, contrasted with failure, frustration, and disappointment. While the test or standard of quality might vary from one couple to another, the means of attaining this kind of marriage is the same for everyone. It is the process and result of intentional decision making.

Who Makes the Decisions in a Marriage?

The question "Who makes the decisions in a marriage?" is, by implication, a question about the bases for decision making. It is a question about who has the right or power to make a decision. Are decisions made unilaterally by one partner or are they made jointly by both partners? If they are made by one partner, what is the basis or justification for this arrangement? Is it a recognition of some special competence that partner has, or is it based upon a power that partner is able to force upon the other? Does it reflect an agreement giving that partner the authority or right to make certain decisions. Figure 8-1 identifies several bases of marital decision making and provides some examples of decisions appropriate to each.

```
                        Figure 8-1

                Bases of Marital Decision Making
_____

        Made by One Partner on Basis of

            A. Power (without approval or right)
                 - All decisions included
                   if power is great

            B. Personal (individual right)
                 - Political preferences
                 - Tastes in dress, food, etc.

            C. Competence (by agreement)
                 - Auto maintenance
                 - Food preparation

            D. Entitlement (legal and moral right)
                 - Personal inheritance
                 - Care of parents

            E. Crisis and opportunity (right and obligation)
                 - Medical emergency
                 - Quick action situations

        Made Jointly

            F. Conjoint (right of vested interests)
                 - Purchase of house
                 - Rearing of children
```

Power

In all arenas of society, including marriage, the power to make decisions is viewed as an ability. Correlates of power are coercion, force, control, and domination. A partner who is able to use any of these correlates has power over the other partner. The powerful partner is dominant and controlling; the less powerful partner is submissive and must defer to the wishes of the other. Ability, as I have used the word, is not the same as competence, which I will discuss later, Neither does one partner's power to unilaterally make marital decisions mean that partner has a right to decide. A partner gains the right to make a decision only after demonstrating a relevant entitlement or competency. Even then, the ultimate right must be granted by the other partner. While authority and rights are voluntarily granted to one partner by the other, power is seized or gained through negotiation with a less powerful partner. Thus power is neither given nor sanctioned. The unwilling partner goes along because they have to—they are not free to do otherwise. There is, in my opinion, no place or justification for the use of power in a helping relationship.

Personal

It is widely argued that personal decisions affect only the decision maker. Under close scrutiny, however, this argument becomes tenuous. Let's consider two relevant examples. A couple has decided to go out for dinner. Each partner is free to make a personal selection from the menu. But suppose that before leaving their home one partner expressed a desire for Chinese food. Let's further suppose that the other partner does not like Chinese food. The desire of the first partner will definitely affect the opportunity of the other partner to choose what that they desire, unless they can find a multi-ethnic restaurant. In a like manner, each partner has a right to his/her own religious preferences. But what if they express different preferences? In order for them to have a common religious identification, one of the partners must change. Or, as is often the case, there might be a compromise on a third choice. The point I want to make is that in an interdependent relationship such as marriage, there are few situations where a decision by one partner does not have an effect upon the other. Only when there is a premise of a single effect is there a defensible right to a personal decision.

Competence

As our society becomes more differentiated and specialized, there is a tendency for peoples' knowledge and skills to be restricted to one or, at the most, a few areas. There is no way for a person to be skilled or knowledgeable in all areas of human activity and fields of knowledge. One consequence of this specialization is that the more a person concentrates in a particular area, the more expert that person becomes in that field. From medicine to interior design, people acquire specialized skills that earn for them the recognition of being a expert in their particular field. People who lack these particular skills seek the expert's advice or recommendation. This is something we all do when confronted by a problem outside our area of skill and knowledge.

In marriage, expertness is more often a function of gender than recognition of competence. Wives traditionally defer to husbands on questions of, say, maintenance of the family automobile. In turn, husbands tend to defer to wives on questions of how best to handle social situations. In both instances, the acts of deference might follow the recognition of a relevant competence possessed by the other partner. However, one partner's expertise or knowledge seldom is so complete that is does not warrant scrutiny by the other partner. Particularly onerous is the claim of a partner that his/her personal competence should not be questioned. When this happens, personal needs are being satisfied at the expense of the marriage.

In most marriages, there is a division of responsibility for decision making that reflects claimed or recognized competencies of the partners. These arrangements operate very successfully and conveniently for simple and routine decisions. In making more complex, non-routine decisions, however, consultation between the partners seems both desirable and beneficial.

Entitlement

A bout with gallstones confronted me with having to make a decision unilaterally. After the initial, painful attack, several weeks passed without any further pain or difficulty. Wanting to know the prognosis of my situation, I scheduled an appointment with my doctor. I was told that it was possible that I would have no further problems. He quoted some statistics about the number of people who remain asymptomatic after a single gallbladder attack. He also told me that removal of the gallbladder would be considered elective surgery. Lenora and I discussed my problem. "What should I do?" I asked. "Are you comfortable with the sixty-five/thirty-five probability?" Being neither a surgeon nor a statistician, she could answer only in terms of "What if . . . ?" Throughout our discussions she reiterated the idea that the decision must be mine alone. I elected surgery only after considering the possible consequences of each alternative. The most persuasive factor was my belief that surgery could be more complicated if required later in life. I didn't want to take that chance.

In a somewhat similar situation, Lenora was confronted with numerous decisions related to the care of her aging parents. She often asked my opinion on various matters, knowing that I earlier had faced the same problems with my mother. I could and did offer her opinions on various matters, but I never could know completely her feelings of love for her parents and her desire to provide for their needs in the most dignified and comforting ways. The final decision was one she had to make. Whatever it was, it would have my support.

Crisis and Opportunity

During my service in the Air Force I often was separated from Lenora for long periods of time. During some of the absences--which had a habit of occurring on short notice--I was working under circumstances where she did not know where I was. Contacting me would have been very difficult. Because of this circumstance, we often engaged in various kinds of emergency planning. In addition to giving her my power of attorney, we tried to identify and plan for all problem situations that might confront her during my absence. Problems as diverse as an emergency hospitalization to the breakdown of the washing machine or family car were considered. It gave me peace of mind knowing that Lenora was knowledgeable about these matters and would make any necessary decisions in my absence.

As hard as we tried to anticipate the various problems which she might have to resolve, there always were unexpected problems for which we had made no plans. Lenora faced a problem of this type when our house was damaged by a hail storm during my absence. Emergency repairs had to be made. Our insurance company had to be notified; assessments of the damage had to be made. These and many other decisions had to be made. She was there; she made the decisions.

Apart from crisis situations, there are opportunities that might slip away if timely decisions are not made. Several years ago, while I was attending an out-of-town professional meeting, our stockbroker called Lenora to share information about a company whose stock we owned. He explained that a news release contained a negative evaluation of the company and that it possibly could cause a sell-off of its stock. Although Lenora liked to leave these decisions to me, she realized that this time she had to decide. "Sell," she told the broker. Her decision protected our paper profits in the stock. Later, after the market had discounted the adverse news about the company, I asked her opinion about again investing in the stock at its then lower price. "You made the decision to sell and it was a good one, do you want to buy it back at its lower price?" Her decision to buy also proved to be good as the stock later recovered its losses.

Partners are more willing to make quick-action decisions when they know the other partner will not be critical should the decision prove faulty. Even when one partner has less expertise or experience in making certain decisions, they should be encouraged to make them to gain experience and to increase their decision-making confidence. This is especially true when the possibly negative consequences of a decision are minimal.

Unfortunately, there are partners who will claim or create a crisis situation as a justification for making a unilateral decision. "I didn't have time to call you; a decision had to be made," is an often-heard justification for a decision made by one partner without consulting the other. Partners who use this ruse not always are convincing; partners who use it too often are even less believable. Use of this deceptive strategy also shows disrespect for the other partner. Inevitably, the motive behind such behavior becomes transparent to the other partner and introduces distrust and suspicion into the relationship.

Joint Decision Making

In marital decision making the adage, "Two heads are better than one," is its own justification. There is a vast body of psychological evidence supporting the conclusion that qualitatively better decisions result when both partners participate in the process. Both partners draw upon their individual knowledge and background experiences to make suggestions about possible solutions. There also is the advantage that each partner can evaluate possibly erroneous or inappropriate judgments made by the other. Another equally important benefit of joint decision making is the commitment partners give to a decision they helped to make. When we participate in making a decision which affects us, we want it to be good. It is our decision; we are committed to it.

Joint decision making requires the mutual agreement of both partners--with only two people involved there is no possibility for majority voting. If either partner has any doubts or reservations about a proposed decision, their discussion should continue until their doubts are resolved or an alternative decision is substituted. Naturally, this approach to marital decision making has its critics. In addition to requiring more time, critics argue, it works best only when partners have faith in it and are willing to compromise in order to reach a decision. Otherwise, either partner can block a decision from being made.

Supporters of this approach argue that its benefits far outweigh its shortcomings. In addition to producing better decision with higher levels of acceptance and support, the partners' interaction in the process produces a sense of togetherness and cohesion. Each partner gains a better understanding of the values and goals of the other. Finally, because it gives each partner an opportunity to test the worth of their ideas in an uncritical, supportive environment, there is an affirmation of their self-esteem.

Joint decision making, admittedly, can be less efficient in terms of time than decision making by a single partner. Individual decisions also can be better if the partner making them has some relevant, demonstrated expertise. But if partners desire the intangible benefits of increased psychological understanding, and if they want to increase their self-confidence and confirm their interpersonal competence, joint decision making alone offers this promise.

Patterns and Bases of Marital Decision Making

Figure 8-2 identifies three patterns of one-partner decision making. For each of these patterns I have indicated the applicable or permissible bases for decision making. Each of these bases was discussed in the previous section. What I want to emphasize here is that there are few decisions which do not affect both partners. This effect does not have to be equal for both partners. It can, at times, be subtle and indirect; it can be minimal in terms of a single decision but additive in terms of repeated instances. When there is a mutual interest in a decision, when there is a possible common effect, then both partners justifiably need to participate in making the decision. Business organizations--enlightened ones, at least--also are recognizing this need as they become more sensitive to employee concerns. In the political arena this need is supported by our right to vote against persons who ignore our needs and wishes. In marriage, where the effects of decisions by one partner cannot be escaped by the other, there is little excuse for ever making a decision in terms of Pattern A.

Making Marriage User Friendly

Figure 8-2

Patterns and Bases of Marital Decision Making

Patterns	Permissable/Applicable Bases (Refer to figure 8-1)
Made by One Partner	
A. Decides without consulting or telling other partner	Power and secrecy are antithetical to helping relationship
B. Decides without consulting but tells other partner	Crisis and opportunity
C. Decides after consulting other partner	Personal Competence Entitlement
Made Jointly	
D. Consensus of partners	Personal Competence Entitlement Consensus

Pattern B decision making is appropriate for situations which present genuine crises or opportunities. Caring, helping partners will make decisions in this manner only when they are fully justified. When they are justified, however, responsible partners will not refrain from making them. This is being responsive to the demands of the situation and the needs of the marriage.

The difference between Pattern C and Pattern D is more a difference of degree than a difference of kind. Partners who consult each other before making decision are showing the same respect and achieving most of the benefits normally associated with joint decision making. Critical to this conclusion is the extent to which the concerns and opinions of the other partner actually are incorporated into the final decision. With the possible exception of crisis and opportunity decision making, all the bases of decision making are included appropriately in the pattern of joint decision making.

As you can see, there are many bases and patterns of marital decision making. Whatever you practice in making marital decisions, it itself is a result of a decision by you, i.e., you decided how to decide. How did you decide? How do you feel about it today? Are there aspects of it you would like to change? In some marriages, decision-making practices simply emerge and remain fixed, unquestioned and unchanged, over long periods of time. This happens, unfortunately, even though partners' abilities, needs, and preferences change. Where a particular practice continues for a sufficiently long time, it can and often does gain the force of tradition. The argument, "This is the way we always have done it," gives the practice a sacrosanct quality, making change difficult. To insure effective decisions which also contribute to your emotional well-being and quality of life, the ways you and your partner make decisions should always be under review.

Head and Heart in Marital Decision Making
A View from the Dark Side

Marriage presents a never-ending succession of problems to be solved and decisions to be made. Like managers in an organization, partners in a marriage must respond to changes in their martial circumstances and to their innate needs and desires. To vacation at the beach of in the mountains, to join an inner-city church or one in the suburbs: these and a myriad of other decisions, ranging from the routine and simple to the critical and complex, are a part of every couple's life.

There are many aspects of our lives that are not of our own choosing: our sex, the color of our skin, the place and time of our birth, our parents, etc. These things must be accepted. Most of the things that really matter, however, are of our choosing. We do not always make these decisions consciously, but they are made-- albeit by default. In many areas of our lives, purposeful choices easily and eagerly are made. In other areas, for various reasons, we procrastinate and shy away from the agony and uncertainty of making decisions and simply let things happen to us. Sometimes, the doubt as to whether we can make good decisions prevents us from deciding. Other times, we are reluctant to accept the responsibility for possibly critical decisions and acquiesce in keeping the status quo. Our need to make decisions is so pervasive that our only escape is though incapacity, complete dependency, or death. Our efforts to escape this responsibility is a decision. Indecision--a decision not to decide—also is a matter of choice. Marriage is just one decision after another.

In this section I purposefully am viewing decisions as those actions we take for the purpose of improving the circumstance of our lives. Before decisions are made, there must be a motivation in the form of a need or desire. There also must be a belief that we don't have to be victimized by the present circumstances of our lives--we can change our life's circumstances by making different, more positive decisions. Often, there are dysfunctional aspects of our lives that are capable of being changed but they are unknown to us. In medical language, we are hurting but don't know it. In these cases, discovery and awareness must precede remedial decision making. In other instances, we may be aware of our hurting but have no control over the solution. Sometimes, even when we could stop the hurting, we do nothing because of the uncertainties of change. The greatest barrier to achieving a desired change is not believing that it can happen. Lacking faith, too many people do not bother to try.

When I refer to our life's circumstances, I have in mind any aspect of our marriage that has the potential to affect, for good or bad, our overall lifestyle, but especially our physical, emotional, and spiritual well-being. Janice, a twenty-seven year old divorcee had moved in with Jacob shortly after her divorce. "I couldn't stand the loneliness," she explained. However, she soon found that Jacob was treating her in much the same way her ex-husband had. Her explanation for moving out was, "I didn't have to take it from my husband, I certainly didn't have to take it from a live-in." After experiencing further frustration in responding to her need for a meaningful relationship, she began to raise questions about her relationships with men. These questions led her into a support group for divorcees. Several sessions later, she was beginning to understand how she unknowingly taught men to behave toward her in hurting, unrewarding ways. "I was my own worst enemy and didn't know it. Now I know what I want from a relationship and am able to communicate and stand up for my needs."

Barney was unhappy in his job of Director of Manufacturing for a local plastics company when he asked his wife to join him in exploring some alternative work involvements. His reasoning seemed well developed as he shared his desires with me. "If you look just at the externals, you'd say I've got it made. Looking at it that way, you'd be right, I guess. Some of the higher ups say things look even brighter for me down the road. But I'm tired of it; I want to do something else with my life. Jackie doesn't fully understand my feelings but, bless her heart, she is supportive. She knows that I would never recklessly jeopardize our future or that of the kids. We've got some savings and I have some stock options I can exercise at any time. We've also got a long-term mortgage, but we'll make it. If I don't change now I will hate myself later, and I don't want to grow old with regrets. I don't want to look back and say, 'Barney, you chased the dollar too long.'"

Barney was afraid his colleagues at work would brand him as being unappreciative. He also was afraid his family might think of him as being selfish and thinking only of himself. After a second session with Barney in individual therapy, his wife, Jackie, joined him. Finally, a few days after a session with the entire family, Barney called to tell me he had given notice of his resignation. Today, almost eight years later, Barney is a recognized and much sought-after expert in the art of restoring antique furniture. Jackie is a partner with two other people in a consignment shop specializing in sales of antique furniture. "I never realized we could make so much money doing something we really enjoy," Barney recently told me during a chance meeting.

The decisions Barney and Jackie made turned out well. Jackie supported Barney because she, too, wanted to move away from a recurring pattern of social activities that left her feeling frustrated and empty. Barney wanted to move toward a work involvement more in line with his interests and abilities. Neither acted compulsively; both fully accepted the responsibility for the decisions they were making, and they made their transitions with only a minimum of anxiety and stress. Jackie's success was particularly satisfying (and commendable, in my view) because she achieved it without the total family support system that Barney enjoyed.

Although it is tempting to say that a good marriage is a result of good decision making, the critical question is how to make good decisions. An equally important consideration is feeling good about a decision after it is made. Feeling good about the decision, in turn, helps the partners to feel good about themselves. Our decisions reflect not only the choices we make but also how we feel about them. Over time, they show their effect on us.

A good decision, in terms of the rational model, is one that maximizes the goal or desired outcome. But the rational model assumes that partners have only one goal and that they know the outcome of all the available alternatives. These constraints help us both to understand the limitations of the rational model and to accept the idea that every decision has some elements of judgment and personal preferences in it. Every decision also incorporates a mixture of both factual and value premises; it is the product of both a reasoning and a psychological process. Once we accept this fusion of analysis and judgment, our criteria of a good decision might also include the question of how the decision was made and whether both partners were committed to it. The goal or desired outcome typically is not maximized, but it is acceptable because it satisfies other enduring needs.

Making decisions and acting upon them alter our life situations and circumstances. Decisions--the choices we make--are the link between the way things were and the way they are now. Moreover, when we make a decision and act upon it, we not only produce a decision but also, we also produce decision makers. Whatever we are today is the result of numerous past decisions. In a like manner, the decisions we make today determine what we will be tomorrow. When our decisions are made inappropriately--when they fail to satisfy the criteria of being good decisions--negative consequences can result. These include increased dependency, increased interpersonal resentment and conflict, and lowered self-esteem. Decisions--every decision--should have the effect of bringing partners closer together and uniting their efforts to achieve something they both desire. Each new decision should elevate them to a higher level of goal accomplishment and psychological well-being. This is a critical dimension of the goodness of a decision.

Whether they are made by one partner alone or jointly by both partners, making decisions is, for many couples, a tortuous process. A significant reason so many people agonize over their decisions is the fact that decision making involves both an intellectual or reasoning process and a psychological or emotional response. Decision making is also plagued by the uncertainties of the future. Making decisions is never the simple, mechanical process it typically is described as being. Because our decisions affect our economic, social, physical, and spiritual well-being, they also have an emotional effect upon us. Our present state of well-being is the result of countless decisions from the past. It also is necessary to recognize that, in some cases, our emotional well-being is affected by decisions we did not make. Let me clarify this point. We cannot avoid making decisions. Even the decision not to make a decision, is a decision. We decided, in this case, not to decide.

Decision making is a problem for partners largely because of the uncertainties and risks involved. Can I make the right choice? Will it work? What will happen if I make a bad choice? Because partners don't have answers to these questions--because of unknown outcomes and risks--they procrastinate, they make excuses, they ask other people for help, and, when pushed for a decision, they try to blame society or some circumstance of their lives for the problem they are facing. For these people decision making truly is a problem. They make only safe decisions, e.g., those with little or no known risks.

For other people, the opportunity to make decisions is an opportunity for growth, change, and improvement in the circumstances of their lives. They realize that all people have problems. A good life, to them, is not one devoid of problems, but is one that results from adaptive solutions to problems. Problems, to these people, are inevitable, but anxiety and agony are optional. How competently they make decisions and how they feel about both what they decided and how they decided are the keys to their overall well-being. Instead of running away from or avoiding decisions, these people actually look for areas or aspects of their lives and relationships which can be improved through making new, better decisions. Am I eating properly? Am I getting enough exercise? Am I acting in ways that enhance my marriage? Do my personal and professional goals and my progress in reaching them need to be reconsidered? Am I focused in my relationships with my partner? Is our marriage what we want it to be? People who ask these questions realize that the quality of their lives can be improved only when they accept responsibility for it and make appropriate decisions. They are not afraid of the change their decisions produce--they actually look forward to it.

Making Decision Making a Growth Experience

Try as we may to prevent it, we realistically must expect a percentage of our decisions to turn out bad. A bad decision, unless it is very private, usually is known to our partner. How we react to it, however, can have a direct effect on our marriage, either positively or negatively.

If we face up to it, we can learn more from our failures than from our successes. A success typically is a time and cause for celebration; seldom is time taken to review a successful decision for possible improvement. We usually do not know nor do we care exactly what it was that made the difference between success and failure. But a failure provides an excellent opportunity for learning, if it can be reviewed in an objective, non-judgmental manner. Did we adequately understand our problem? Did we make some faulty assumptions? Did we overlook some critical bits of information? Did we consider all the alternatives. Could we have developed additional alternatives? These are hard, discomforting questions, but their answers, if they are truthful, can help us to approach future decisions with increased understanding and confidence.

Some decisions are of such relatively small importance in terms of long-range consequences that even if the worst happens nothing much is changed or lost. Recognizing this reduces the fear involved in making decisions. It also helps us to look at and learn from our failures. Most people have far more inner strength in dealing with bad decisions than they realize and, although they temporarily may question their competence, they can and usually do overcome their setbacks. This recovery and regrouping process can be helped greatly by an understanding, supportive partner.

Making Proactive Decisions

Through the years I noticed that my caseload predictably increased in January and February. So consistent was this trend that I began to ponder the reasons for it. Without going into a lot of detail, I found two different explanations--each pertaining to a separate group of couples. One group can be described as reactive. Their reasons for coming into therapy are related to the stresses and disappointments of the holiday season. Their decision to seek help was even more urgent when these stresses and disappointments spilled over and the marriage was suffering from unresolved tensions and conflicts. Reactive couples were hurting and they didn't want to hurt. Just as a person with a physical illness seeks help from a physician, these couples want relief from their psychological and emotional pain. They see the cause of their pain as a disease just as a person with a physical ailment does. They never think of themselves (their attitudes, values, and behavior) as being the disease--that their pain was self-inflicted. If the ailment had not affected them--if they were feeling no pain--they would not be seeking help. But the hurt and the pain were real--whatever the source or cause. This reality forced them to seek relief.

Opal and Hershel, who came for therapy in early January, fit this description well. Their case was a classical example of how we forget the purpose and meaning of Christmas. On Christmas Day, Hershel was still angry at Opal because she had to shop late on Christmas Eve for some family presents. The engine in their car was damaged during a Christmas Day trip delivering presents to Opal's parents because Hershel failed to check the oil level. They were late for a holiday dinner invitation because Opal had forgotten to get a baby sitter. Their marriage was a long, uninterrupted sequence of failures, omissions, and procrastinations related to their decision-making occasions. They had experienced an early, unplanned pregnancy because "Opal forgot to take the pill." They had to pay a penalty because their income tax return was mailed late. Hershel arrived late for work because he forgot to set the alarm. On and on, their failure to behave responsibly in making timely, effective decisions gave their marriage the illusion of being a comedy of errors. By their own admission, Christmas always seemed to bring out the worst in them. "What's wrong with us? Every year it's the same. We ruin Christmas for everybody: ourselves, our children, our parents. They always know when we've been fighting."

The second category of couples come for therapy because the partners view the new year as a time for new beginnings. For them it is a time of transition, an opportunity for renewal, for growth and fulfillment. These couples deny any conscious problems in their marriage. They are not hurting in the same sense as reactive couples; their goal or purpose is to improve the overall quality of their marriage--their decision is proactive. They decided to seek therapy not because something bad was happening to them, but because they wanted to make something good better.

In chapter five, I discussed in detail the case of Karl and Aretha--two of the most proactive people I have ever known. Spend a few minutes and read those pages again. Identify with Karl and Aretha; visualize what it would be like to visit with them for an hour or so. Ask yourself, "What makes them tick? What is the source of their vitality, their enthusiasm? Do they know something we don't?" Let me answer your questions. Their secret is their discovery that they already have everything they need for a vital, fulfilled marriage. They proactively decided to tap into their inner strength of positive, no-limits thinking. For them, success is an attitude. They rejected the idea that a good-enough marriage is good enough. If you could visit them, they would tell you, "What we have done, anyone can do. What we have, anyone can have. There are no limits on love, intimacy, or closeness. Enthusiasm and trust make the difference. Why settle for being normal when you can live on top of the mountain?"

Reactive decisions only help a couple to escape the pains and tensions of interpersonal living. Proactive decisions are concerned with becoming, growing, and actualization. Hershel and Opal were reactive; Karl and Aretha were proactive. After which couple do you want to pattern your marriage? The choice is yours.

Chapter Nine

Helping in Confrontation and Conflict Resolution

"Why can't people just get along? Why do they have to quarrel and complain all the time? Even fight, sometimes?"

These questions were asked by a forty-year-old business manager in his initial session with me. Thinking that his questions pertained to his marriage, I tailgated him and added, "And abuse each other and, sometimes, murder...."

Without any observable reaction to my comment he continued, "In my company, well, I can understand why conflicts occur. In business, it's every man for himself. In marriage, though, it's not supposed to be that way. Why...we're supposed to love each other. Sometimes when Marian starts one of her tirades...I know this is ugly but I just want to walk out and not come back."

"Marian is a strong-willed woman. Her mother says she has a mean streak in her. Whatever, she seems determined to get her way about everything. Some things she does don't amount to a hill of beans to me so I just let her have her way. Others really bother me. But instead of standing up to her I just withdraw and end up hating myself for not standing my ground. I love Marian and I think she loves me. But it confuses me and hurts, too, when she blames me for everything that goes wrong in her life. Can you help me? Where do we start, with my job or my marriage? It's my marriage that hurts me the most."

Feeling he wanted some assurance that help was available, I boldly answered, "Yes, I can help you." Then, responding in a manner that implied my understanding of his reference to his job, I suggested that we focus first on his marriage. "But it will be necessary for your wife to come with you; I want your marriage to be my client. Will she join you?"

Both Al and Marian had unrealistic views of the causes and consequences of their conflicted relationship, which caused them to behave inappropriately when conflicts did occur. Al found conflict threatening and divisive. It was important to him to get along, and he would go to great efforts to avoid conflict. To him, the best thing he could do for the marriage was to try to have a good relationship with Marian, whatever the cost. Differences drove him away from Marian and whenever she raised potentially conflicting issues with him he would retreat behind his wall of isolation, avoiding any situation that might arouse conflict. When he could not escape, he tried to smooth things over by discounting its importance. For Marian, assertiveness and confrontation were acceptable behaviors for resolving their conflicts. She could not believe that Al did not expect her to use them, and she strangely often questioned his love for her because of his unwillingness to confront her. She felt that conflict was to be expected and Al's refusal to recognize this frustrated her. She interpreted his passivity--withdrawal--to mean he no longer cared about their marriage. Feeling this way, she was prone to complain, "I'm the only one who cares enough to try to solve our problems." I'll return to the case of Al and Marian later.

Why Do Lovers Fight?

We're culturally conditioned to think of marriage as an emotional oasis, a refuge or retreat from the tensions and conflicts of the outside world, as properly, it should be. But too few couples ever attain this ideal state. It is not, simply, the absence of conflict that gives marriage this quality. All couples have disagreements and conflicts, and the presence of conflict in a marriage does not mean that something has gone wrong. Consider some of life's paradoxes. If there were no death, would we appreciate life? If there were no disagreements, would we know what harmony is? If there were no conflict, could we know the joy of "kiss and make up?" The fact that marriages can be improved through the renewing process of problem solving and reconciliation also is viewed as being inconsistent with common knowledge. People who feel that way fail to understand that both love and conflict get their energy from the same source.

In a nutshell, lovers fight because they care. Conflict would not occur if partners did not care about something--something they cannot get or something they cannot give. In marital conflicts, both partners seek an outcome they believe the other partner is unwilling to provide. Each partner reasons, "I can't get what I want or I can't give what is asked." In marriage, however, partners are in an interdependent, interactive relationship where they must give to and get from each other. Because the behavior of each partner both affects and is effected by the behavior of the other, the simplest and perhaps the only way to reduce or eliminate conflict is to stop caring or to terminate the relationship. When we withdraw from or refuse to interact with our partner we are withdrawing from the relationship. When we suppress negative feelings, we unintentionally suppress our ability to experience positive feelings, which is the psychological equivalent of falling out of love. It is a counterproductive, self-defeating approach to resolving conflict that has little to recommend it. A far better solution is to search for something both you and your partner care about--something that can unite you in a common pursuit. True intimacy and love are promoted more by quarreling and making up than by maintaining the myth of living in a conflict-free marriage.

You and your partner are unique persons and you show this distinctiveness in everything you do. No matter how hard you try to be considerate of your partner's feelings, you still look at every situation through you own eyes--your own psychological makeup. Included in your makeup is your unique combination of values, attitudes, needs, and expectations. Your partner, too, has a distinctive psychological makeup. Because you and your partner differ in this important dimension of your lives and your marriage, conflict is an inevitable consequence. Partners who have achieved a high level of marital adjustment in terms of having similar needs still experience conflict because their needs vary in intensity. Even when they are of comparable intensity they are not always synchronized in terms of their expression and duration. Whether between nations or marriage partners, conflict is a consequence of the differences in the values, attitudes, needs, and expectations of the parties.

The Nature of Marital Conflict

Conflict occurs in all life forms--from the simplest to the most complex. So pervasive is conflict that we might think of it as an integral part of the fabric of life. Indeed, much of our contemporary thinking about conflict views it not only as inevitable but also as desirable, claiming certain benefits from it. But conflict also can result in negative, undesired outcomes. The key seems to be in how we perceive conflict, how we feel about, and how we respond to it. In the case of Al and Marian that I shared with you earlier Marian was interested only in solutions; she had little understanding of how her forceful approaches to solving their problems affected Al. She felt she was right in her ideas about their problems and further felt a need and a right to defend them. Al, on the other hand, found conflict distasteful and in his words, "...learned to keep my mouth shut." He found it effective to agree with Marian even when he inwardly disagreed. Lacking any commitment to his passive agreements, he failed to behave accordingly. This only frustrated Marian further. "Frustration is better than somebody getting hurt," Al would counter.

An idea that today is gaining a lot of acceptance characterizes marriage not as an emotional oasis but as an intimate battleground. Rather than covering up differences and trying to avoid conflict at all costs partners need to learn how to confront each other. Conflict can be taken to extremes, of course, and the more intimate a relationship is the more likely conflict will occur. It also is likely that the conflict will be more intense. What I have in mind when I suggest that partners learn how to confront is that they learn to do it without endangering or hurting their relationship. In my work with conflicted marriages I always asked, "What kind of relationship do you want with your partner when this conflict is resolved?" Their answers to this question determine the parameters of the conflict. They might say, for example, "We don't want to do or say anything that will hurt our relationship. We love each other; we value our marriage." With this goal, they must confront in ways that do not hurt the relationship. On the other hand, if they say that their marriage is finished--that there is no way to save it--then all-out war is both possible and probable.

As is the case with most psychological terms, there is no universally accepted definition of marital conflict. My understanding of conflict--the one from which I operated in my therapy--viewed conflict as a condition or circumstance confronting partners in which they perceive incompatible goals and interference from the other in trying to achieve their goals. A necessary condition for conflict to arise is the interaction of interdependent, caring partners in a close relationship.

Goals of partners are incompatible when one partner wants to do something that is opposite to what the other partner wants to do. Because their goals are opposed to each other, both cannot simultaneously be achieved. One partner can give in to the other, permitting them to jointly pursue the other partners' goals, or they can compromise and pursue some substitute goals. If they are unwilling to compromise they might go their separate ways, each pursuing their respective, personal goals. Goals become incompatible because of the limited resources and opportunities available to partners. If enough money is available, both a new car can be purchased and an extra week of vacation can be taken. If opportunities are unlimited, partners can simultaneously satisfy both their maintenance needs and their growth needs. In the face of incompatible goals, conflict is reflected in the simultaneous struggle and resistance of the partners, which are opposite sides of the same coin. When one partner makes a demand or claim that is resisted by the other partner, their conflict will continue until the original demand is changed or until the other partner stops resisting or, preferably, it is resolved in a manner that is acceptable to both partners.

In every marriage, partners develop over time, rules or norms to govern their behavior. When one partner perceives the other behaving in ways that deviate from the rules, conflict is likely. Often, in the absence of such rules, conflict can take the form of a disagreement over who has the right to do what with respect to the other. Whether the perceived deviate behavior involves a violation of an agreed-upon rule or is an unacceptable behavior not covered by the rules, it is important to recognize that no one factor alone ever causes conflict. It seldom results from the simple fact that partner A is behaving contrary to an agreed-upon rule, but that in behaving that way partner A is blocking partner B's effort to satisfy a personal need or goal.

Fortunately, most of the minor disagreements partners encounter are resolved before they evolve into major ones, which is what I reference as conflict. Many couples are able to negotiate or otherwise resolve their disagreements through use of various problem-solving techniques or strategies. Lenora and I used the "scale-of ten" technique to resolving our minor disagreements. When an issue arose about which we had different feelings, I might say for example, "I feel strongly about this matter, say, a nine on a scale of ten." Lenora might then respond, "It's important to me, too, but my feelings are nearer to six or seven. I want to respect your feelings; they seem to be important to you."

People with whom I have shared our strategy will often ask, "What would you do if both you and Lenora said nine?" My usual response recognized the fact that our strategy would not work unless there is honest, open communication between us, supported by a sincere desire to resolve our disagreements. Its simplicity and straightforwardness do engender skepticism and mistrust, and partners willing to try it are not always successful in solving their problems before they escalate into more complex stages of conflict. If one partner has a strong need to win--even at the expense of the other--this strategy won't work.

In my definition of marital conflict, the process of perception plays a critical role. Marital conflict is not an objective set of conditions which exists apart from the partners. Rather, it is something that is perceived to exist or to be evolving. This process of perception is critical because one of the important steps in resolving marital conflict is to help the partners alter their perceptions of what is happening. Although this reasoning sounds simplistic, it can be much more difficult than changing the objective circumstances of their relationship.

Also implicit in my definition of conflict are the complementary ideas of interdependence and interaction. Conflict does not take place in a vacuum--certain preconditions must be present. One of these is the fact that partners are expressing different needs. Even when there is agreement about their mutual needs and wants, partners can disagree about how to best satisfy them. Almost without exception, I found that partners disagree more often and more strongly over the means to an end than they do over the end.

There is a widely held and strongly supported belief in our culture that conflict is bad, especially in the context of marriage. Behind this belief is the assumption that love (harmony) is the polar opposite of hate (conflict). The difficulty with this assumption is the fact that the opposite of love is not hate, it is "no love." In a like manner, the absence of hate does not mean the presence of love. Therefore, the opposite of conflict is no conflict, and the opposite of cooperation is not conflict, but is no cooperation. A zone of neutral feelings can be easily observed when, for example, partners declare, "We have no feelings at all for each other, neither love nor hate." This lack of feelings can develop because, in their efforts to suppress their negative feelings they suffered the unintended consequence of suppressing their positive feelings.

Beyond its dictionary definition, the word "conflict" has many connotations. Some people associate it with aggression, hostility, and violence. Conflict for these people is bad, and dangerous and should be avoided. For others, conflict is a milder term referring to disagreements, arguments, and quarrels. Although this latter view still conjures negative images, it does not demand an outright taboo against conflict. According to this view, conflict lies in a neutral zone between moral and immoral--that is, conflict is amoral--neither positive nor negative. It is how we view conflict and respond to it that gives us a positive or negative feeling about it. If we feel that only bad, harmful things can result from conflict, we will try to avoid it. Any overt behavior or expression of private feelings and thoughts will be avoided if it is capable of provoking conflict.

Admittedly, conflict can be and often is harmful, especially when it has no point, solves no problem, and contributes nothing to the quality of marriage. It is more likely to be harmful when partners fail to agree on a set of rules for resolving it. Without rules, conflict situations become a battleground where pent-up feelings are unleashed, coupled with accusations and name calling. Without a point or purpose, this kind of conflict rages on since it has no built-in limits or rules to guide it to a productive conclusion.

Conflict also can be helpful. It can alleviate or prevent more harmful issues, add a sense of drama to marriage, and provide an opportunity for sharing information partners otherwise might keep hidden. Many couples view conflict as therapeutic because it provides an opportunity for sharing private feelings and thoughts. More pointedly, conflict can be helpful if it clears the air of the latent effects of unresolved prior conflict and provides a stimulus for adaptive changes in the relationship.

I am not advocating that you purposefully create situations that breed conflict in order to achieve the claimed benefits. Conflict for conflict's sake is not what I have in mind. What I do believe is that some degree of change is essential for marital growth, and conflict can serve as a catalyst for change. Given the potentially beneficial role of conflict in a marriage, it should be managed instead of simply being resolved. This idea of managing conflict suggests that it can play a helpful role in the survival and growth of a marriage.

Do not be afraid of conflict. Accept it as an inevitable consequence of caring partners in an interactive, interdependent relationship; accept it as being beneficial when it strengthens the relationship by providing an outlet for addressing misunderstandings, resentments, bitterness, and misdirected aggression. In a marriage where the taboo against conflict is too strong, the groundwork is laid for partners' negative feelings to be expressed in unintended, hurting ways. When partners try to hide their negative feelings because they believe it is wrong to express them, they are more concerned with keeping their feelings under control than in changing the circumstances that gave rise to their feelings. Because it is nearly impossible to repress negative feelings, denying them always arouses suspicions and mistrust from the other partner.

Caring Enough to Confront

Throughout this book I have stressed the interactive, interdependent nature of marriage. When we understand and accept this characteristic of marriage, it is easily seen as an arena for expressing our love in helping ways. Accordingly, the most critical question we can ask about our marriage is, "What kind of effect do I desire or intend to have on my partner?" Our answer to this question always should be shared with our partner. After this information is shared, the next logical question is, "What is the actual effect of my behavior? Am I behaving in ways that are consistent with my intentions?" The answer to this question, necessarily, must come from our partner. When it is received, we are then ready to make appropriate changes in our actual behavior to make it more congruent with our intended behavior.

Unfortunately, this scenario is not possible in all marriages. The required good intentions, the trust, and the necessary openness are not always present. Often, even when these requirements are present, we might not be fully aware of the linkage between our behavior and the behavior of our partner. Even when we recognize this cause-and-effect relationship, we do not always behave in ways consistent with our intentions. Further, when we do try, we often conveniently assume that the actual effect of our behavior is what we intended. Making this assumption is all the more likely when we fail to receive disconfirming feedback. In the absence of confirming feedback there always is the likelihood that we are affecting our partner in ways other than what we intend. Instead of being loving and helpful, our behavior could be hurting and harmful.

If the above discussion were true of your marriage, what would you want your partner to do? Let's consider two possible responses. First, your partner says nothing about your behavior, either believing that it would do no good or fearing a defensive reaction from you. In the second response, your partner risks your defensiveness and rejection and confronts you with the actual consequences of your behavior. In which instance is your partner being honest? Helpful? Caring?

When your partner, in an effort to help you and the marriage, provides you information about your behavior, a helping technique I call confrontation is being used. I use this term to refer to any efforts by one partner to help the other partner examine the consequences of some aspect of their behavior. Confrontation, in essence, is an act of pointing out to your partner what you perceive to be an inconsistency between what they want to do or accomplish and what they actually are doing. It is an expression of your desire to be responsibly involved in nurturing the relationship; you are expressing your desire to free your partner to engage in more relevant, helping behavior and in less unintended, harmful behavior. It is your way of expressing concern--an outward expression of your inner feelings of love.

Unfortunately, the term confrontation also suffers a negative image, largely because people tend to confront others not about pleasant things but about painful, unpleasant things. Confrontation also can cause defensiveness and avoidance behavior. And if the goal and description of a confrontation are inappropriate, it can lead to conflict, which is why I chose to discuss it in this chapter. Confrontation, like conflict, is neutral--it is neither good nor bad. Its outcome depends upon the purpose and the style of the user, coupled with the trust and psychological safety partners feel in their relationship. Properly used, it is an effective technique for helping partners to change some unintended aspect of the other's behavior, thereby enriching the marriage. If it causes defensiveness or other retaliatory behavior, it is not helpful.

Confrontation also suffers from the stigma of being overly aggressive in both nature and intent. To its critics, it's a hostile action that produces only injurious, destructive outcomes. In my view, when it is used with care and understanding, it merely is assertive, never aggressive. It can remove barriers and open doors to improving the quality of any marriage if the partners are willing to assert their individual feelings in ways that do not cause defensiveness or alienation. Confrontation does not mean attacking your partner. Although it can be awkward and psychologically discomforting, you can show love and concern during a confrontation. When you don't care enough to confront, you are choosing a path of passivity, reflecting indifference and a lack of caring. When confronting, focus on your partner's behavior, not their personal attributes. Confront their concerns and behavior, not your own. Be descriptive rather than evaluative; be supportive rather than accusatory. Remember, the goal of your confrontation is to point out inconsistencies and contradictions between your partner's commitment to a goal and their actual behavior in working to achieve that goal. Remember, too, that you can benefit from your partner's confrontations only when you respond to them as acts of love and concern for you and your marriage.

When our children were young, it was usually my task to go upstairs in the morning and awaken them. Our daughter, Suzanne, always responded quickly. Mark, our son, liked to catch a few extra minutes of sleep, and it often was necessary to call him a second time. One day Lenora confronted me with a matter that was a surprise to me. "Russ, Mark asked me why you always seem to be angry with him in the mornings. I tried to explain to him that you were not angry, but I don't think I succeeded. Do you recall being angry with him recently?" Unable to recall a feeling of anger, I answered, "No. I've had no reason to be angry with Mark." Lenora agreed with my denial but offered the opinion that, possibly, it was the manner in which I called to Mark that caused him to feel I was angry. "Do I come across to you as being angry?" I asked. "I know you, Russ, I know you're not angry, but that is not the issue. What is important is that you are doing something that causes Mark to feel you're angry."

I felt a sense of sorrow and loss, and strangely, a feeling of gladness. I was disappointed in my behavior--in my failure to be more in touch with my feelings and for possibly communicating something of which I obviously was not aware and did not intend. My sense of loss resulted from the realization that I probably had caused Mark not to feel free to share his feelings directly with me. I thanked Lenora. Had she not cared enough to confront me, I would not have had the opportunity to make things right with Mark.

Strategies for Resolving Conflict

When partners are faced with conflict they generally respond in terms of two concerns. One of these is their concern for their own interests and goals. This is a self-serving approach since each partner seeks to force their desired solution upon the other. The second concern reflects the partners' awareness of and responsiveness to the interests and goals of the other partner, i.e., a concern for the relationship. This concern reflects a cooperative approach. What is important to realize about these two concerns is that they are independent of each other. A partner can be high on one concern and low on the other, high on both, or low on both. These two concerns or approaches are depicted in Figure 9-1. The vertical axis or line reflects the partners' concern for the relationship; the horizontal axis reflects the partners' concern for their individual solution.

Making Marriage User Friendly

**Figure 9-1
Approaches to Resolving Marital Conflict**

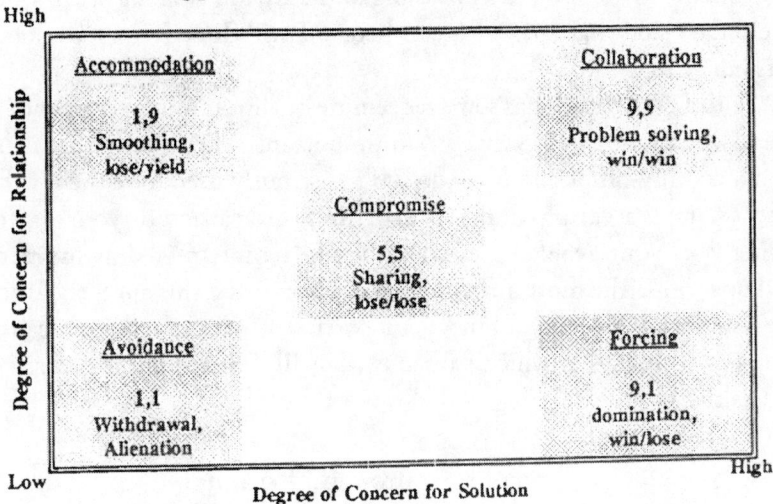

	Low — Degree of Concern for Solution — High
High Degree of Concern for Relationship	**Accommodation** 1,9 Smoothing, lose/yield　　　　**Collaboration** 9,9 Problem solving, win/win
	Compromise 5,5 Sharing, lose/lose
Low	**Avoidance** 1,1 Withdrawal, Alienation　　　　**Forcing** 9,1 domination, win/lose

Five different approaches to resolving marital conflict will be discussed. Each of these approaches reflects a particular combination of the two concerns described above. A standard format of discussion will be followed so that you easily can make comparisons between the five approaches.

The 1.1 Approach: Avoidance

This approach is characterized by a low degree of concern for both the relationship and the solution or outcome. Withdrawal is a benchmark of this approach and partners who use it, by implication, are saying, "I don't want to get involved." They feel that by remaining neutral they don't have to deal with the conflict. They treat both their partner and the conflict in an impersonal, detached manner--it is the ultimate form of withdrawal. Pontius Pilate, the Roman governor, used this defense when he was asked by the Pharisees to pass judgment on Jesus. (Matthew 27:24) As he washed his hands (of his involvement) he declared that he was innocent of causing Jesus' death. Today, we still hear people who follow the avoidance approach excuse themselves by saying, "I wash my hands of this matter, I don't want to get involved." Consider some of the other excuses partners give in defense of their avoidance behavior:

"I don't like to argue with Frank, so rather than express my point of view--which may lead to a fight--I just clam up."

"I want Liz to see me as pleasing and easy to get along with. I don't like the tension that goes with conflict, so I withdraw. That way, nobody gets hurt."

Still, this approach has some redeeming qualities. You can appropriately use it when the issue is viewed as unimportant, when the timing is bad, or if a cooling-off period is needed. If consciously used for either of these reasons, it is a caring thing to explain your reasons to your partner. Otherwise, your avoidance behavior could be interpreted as indifferent and uncaring. The most likely outcome, when using this approach, is that the problem between you and your partner won't get resolved, causing long-term frustration which subsequently will be acted out in a variety of unhealthy ways.

The 9.1 Approach: Forcing

This is a win-lose approach--it reflects a high degree of concern for one's desired solution outcome and a low degree of concern for the relationship. Partners using this approach seek to impose their preferred solution on the other partner. It is power-oriented and involves a lot of fault-finding and subtle, persuasive tactics designed to get ones way. The following comments reflect the essence of this approach:

"I'm willing to risk a few hurt feelings in order to get a good solution, especially when I know I'm right."

"Donna get's so emotional she can't see the problem as it really is. So I have to confront her with facts. And when facts don't work, well, I try to point out the holes in her thinking." On the negative side, a forcing partner may suppress, intimidate, or coerce the other partner into submission. Partners against whom this approach is used often become passive and fearful of sharing their feelings. Finally, this approach may prevent the real causes of a conflict from coming into the open and thereby create circumstances which aggravate the struggle, providing little incentive to search for mutually acceptable solutions to the conflict.

On the positive side, partners appropriately can use this approach in circumstances when they know they're right or when quick, decisive action must be taken. Even in these circumstances, partners should be careful to point out why they are certain about their solution. Lack of time is seldom an adequate defense for behavior which does not consider the interests and feelings of the other partner.

The most likely outcome of this approach is that the forcing partner will feel vindicated while the other partner will feel humiliated. And since the losing partner had no opportunity to express their needs, the conflict could erupt again.

The 1.9 Approach: Accommodation

This approach reflects a strong concern for the relationship with a low concern for finding a solution to the problem. Partners who adopt this strategy seek to avoid conflict for the sake of maintaining the relationship. Disagreements are smoothed over or ignored so that surface harmony is maintained in an assumed state of peaceful co-existence. Accommodators have the objective of not upsetting their partner. Their rationale can be explained as, "How can I help you to feel good about our problem? My position isn't so important that it is worth risking bad feelings between us." People in therapy with similar feelings offered the following reasons for their accommodation behavior:

"I dislike conflict situations and feel that confrontation is destructive in maintaining relationships. It is important for me to maintain a good relationship with Hank. Getting angry doesn't solve anything. Above all, I strive to control my feelings."

"I find it useful to make a joke now and then, it helps to release a lot of tension. Many times it actually causes us to forget our problem. So I agree with Evelyn (even when I inwardly disagree) so I won't be seen as a troublemaker."

Partners who use an accommodating approach to conflict resolution may be showing too little concern for themselves and their interests, which, in turn, may lead to a resolution without both partners sharing their feelings in a timely and meaningful way. An accommodator wishes to be seen as agreeable and cooperative, but the appearance may be more transparent than real. The accommodator's real motive may be a need for acceptance and affiliation. What an accommodator often fails to understand is that the marital relationship can be strengthened and renewed by working through conflicts.

Like the other approaches to conflict resolution, the accommodating approach also has its advantages. It is most appropriate to use when the conflict issue is more important to the other partner, when maintaining harmony is of great importance, and when the accommodating partner wants to let the other partner have the experience of winning. Finally, a partner may choose this approach when its disadvantages are outweighed by the disadvantages of the other approaches.

The 5.5 Approach: Compromise

This approach is best described as a lose-lose approach since neither partner gets what they really want. Still, there is the conventional idea that compromise is the way for partners to resolve all of their conflicts. If partners sincerely desire to reach a solution, compromising can be viewed as a variant of the win-win strategy which I will discuss next. But if compromise serves as a substitute for dealing with the real issues in a conflict, it can undermine the trust between partners. Again, some excerpts from case histories provide insight to people who use this approach.

"I always exaggerate my feelings. I ask for more than Glenn is going to agree to. But he does the same thing. Compromising lets both of us get what we wanted in the first place."

"Compromise is the best way for us. I've become a pretty good negotiator in getting Marcie to take a middle-of-the road approach on things. Settling for what you can get is a good rule to follow."

This approach, too, has its advantages and disadvantages. There are situations when it seems to fit and other situations in which it clearly is inappropriate. Although compromise may be the only practical way for two equally powerful and determined partners to resolve a situation, the word compromise often is viewed as being synonymous with weakness and a lack of commitment. It also invites a lot of game playing, including making unrealistic, improbable demands of each other. Compromise also is criticized because it most often results in a workable solution at the expense of a best solution, which is the goal of the collaborative or 9,9 approach.

The 9.9 Approach: Collaboration

My bias is for this approach. I like it because it is high on both the concerns depicted in Figure 9-1. More than any others, it enhances the idea of helping. It is not an easy approach to conflict resolution; its many advantages cannot be had without correspondingly greater efforts. First, it requires greater motivation, commitment, and patience. Second, its successful use depends upon more refined problem-solving skills. Critical to successful use of this approach are the following preconditions: (a) The conflict must be depersonalized, that is, both parties must concentrate on solving the problem in a win-win fashion rather than seeking to defeat each other. (b) Both partners must accept the desires and goals of the other as being legitimate and agree to respect them. (c) Both partners must believe that their relationship can be renewed and strengthened by working through their problems in a psychologically safe environment. Some clients in therapy shared the following insights as to why they used this approach:

"I don't want to give in to Mel and I don't want him to give into me. There's got to be a way for both of us to win. I value our relationship; I want the best for both of us."

"Sometimes it takes us a lot longer to reach a solution that we can both live with, but it's worth the extra time and the emotional investment. When Gwen and I finally do reach a solution, it gives us a good feeling. It confirms our love."

I always was more successful in using this collaborative win-win approach in working as a third-party mediator than in getting partners to use it in their own problem-solving efforts at home. It is the best way only when a number of special circumstances or preconditions are present. The most significant of these are the availability of time and the skills, patience, and commitments to make it work. When these conditions are not present, it would be imprudent to use this approach for the reason that the desired benefits cannot be otherwise experienced. It must be remembered that the long-range interests of partners are tied not only to solving their here-and-now problems but also to enriching their relationship. When the conditions which the approach depends upon are not present, partners need first to concentrate on developing them. There will be other conflicts and there will be a continuing need for a win-win approach to resolving them. As this approach is developed and refined through continued use, other congruent values such as openness, trust, and mutual respect for their differences are inculcated into the relationship. This is what the helping relationship in resolving marital conflicts is all about.

Understanding Marital Conflict as a Process

Earlier in this chapter I referred to conflict as something that "is." What I had in mind was the belief that conflict is neither good nor bad, neither right nor wrong--it just happens. Neither do I want to give the impression that conflict is a discrete event, beginning and ending in a moment of time. We can gain useful insight into the nature and dynamics of marital conflict by viewing it as a process. Process suggests an ordered sequence of stages or steps. Each stage in the process is directly affected by the content of the preceding stage; in turn, each stage affects the next following stage. Hence, the process can be thought of as circular consisting of five separate stages. When considered together, these five stages constitute a conflict episode. This is what we have in mind when we refer to a particular conflict situation.

Latent Conflict Stage

In this stage are found the necessary preconditions for conflict to occur. These preconditions can include, for example, unresolved issues from an earlier conflict. This particular circumstance is the most pervasive and invidious of all the adverse conditions that might plague a marriage. Disagreements not covered by the rules and norms of a marriage also can be troublesome. When they are not resolved in a particular conflict episode, they have a carryover effect which increases their potency and the likelihood for future conflict about the same issue.

For some couples, the presence of any of these preconditions results in immediate, overt conflict. Although these antecedent conditions must be present for conflict to occur, they do not actually cause the conflict. Partners decide to disagree; they decide to have conflict. Partners do not get angry over these conditions *per se*, they get angry because of the effects these conditions have upon their relationship. I often describe these people as having a short fuse. For other partners--long-fused people--these conditions can lie dormant for long periods without erupting into conflict. Long-fused partners can live peacefully with a powder-keg situation, not because they are fearful of conflict but because of their tolerance of the conditions that give rise to it. Short-fused partners live in almost continuous conflict, taking offense from minor disagreements and mildly bruised feelings that hardly would be noticed by long-fused partners.

Frustration/Awareness Stage

In this stage, the preconditions of the latent stage come into the open, being expressed in the form of pointed, accusatory questions and curt,

Making Marriage User Friendly

defensive responses. Partners feel frustrated without knowing the reasons; they only know that things are not going well for them. It is in this stage that the conflict episode actually is set into motion as partners become aware of blocked goals, disappointments, violations of marital rules and expectations, etc., that have been building up. Such awareness can occur, for example, when one partner engages in a particular behavior once too often. Like the straw that broke the camel's back, it is the instance that exceeds the tolerance level of the offended partner. Still, the offended partner has a choice of responses to this awareness. If they dislike conflict--a 1,1 style--the offending behavior will be down-played and treated as though it were not significant. The offended partner realizes there is the potential for conflict but they do not let it make them angry enough to confront the offending partner. A partner who is predisposed to a forcing style of conflict resolution (9,1) presumably would sense the possibility and the probability of conflict more quickly and draw attention to it by their efforts to impose their own solution on it.

Conflict Stage

In this stage conflict actually is experienced. It no longer simply is perceived; partners now realize that they are in a conflict situation. How they know they are experiencing conflict, what they might feel, say, and do about it: these aspects of conflict previously have been discussed. The conflict stage is mentioned here to establish it as a critical phase of the conflict process.

Resolution Stage

When partners tire of the pain, tension, and stress of conflict and begin trying to resolve it, they enter into the resolution stage. Five basic approaches which can be used by partners to resolve their conflicts were discussed in a previous section.

Aftermath/Follow-up Stage

It is in this stage that the circular nature of the conflict process becomes apparent. For this reason, I view it as the most critical of the five stages in the conflict process.

Unfortunately, when partners resolve a conflict they like to put it behind them and forget about it. This is a natural response since they want to return quickly to their everyday conflict-free, normal relationship. Moreover, once the conflict is resolved partners typically question whether any good could come from rehashing an unpleasant experience that has been resolved, for better or for worse. Each partner may claim that all is forgiven and forgotten, which is commendable, but their unwillingness to explore the residual effects of the conflict on their relationship leaves them less aware of existing conditions that can contribute to future conflict.

Finally, it is important to realize that conflict never happens in a vacuum--it has both antecedents and consequences. If, in the resolution stage, the antecedent conditions described in the latent conflict stage are altered so that they become less conducive to conflict the partners can feel good about the consequences of their conflict. But if the resolution of the conflict was reached in a manner other than a collaborative (9,9) approach the stage is set for future conflict.

Gender and Conflict

I previously have described marital conflict as a perceived condition between partners in which they have incompatible goals. Described this way conflict is subjective. It has no objective existence apart from the partners involved in it. Subjectively, two partners can respond to a particular interpersonal encounter differently. One partner perceives it as a conflict situation; the other partner, with equal honesty, takes an opposite view. Which partner is right? Both are right. Is there a conflict between them? Yes, at least in the form of a disagreement.

There are two questions about gender and conflict I want briefly to discuss. First, is there a difference in the way women and men perceive and respond to conflict? Do the views and feelings of women toward conflict differ from those of men? If differences do exist are they expressed in recurring, predictable ways?

Research on the question of gender differences in resolving marital conflict is being reported in research literature with increasing frequency. This trend is evidence, perhaps, of an increased societal concern with the often dysfunctional consequences of conflict. However, this research does not yet permit valid generalizations about the interaction of wives and husbands (females and males) in conflict situations. Some researchers have interviewed partners to learn what they say and do when they are in a conflict episode. These researchers also wanted to know how partners think and feel toward each other when they are conflicted. Based on the self-report data they received, these researchers concluded that women show a greater concern for the relationship while men show a greater concern for solving the problem. Other researchers, using different data gathering techniques, e.g., direct observation of partners in conflict, made different and often contradictory conclusions. Any overall answer to this question necessarily would be conditional; there are too many troublesome issues surrounding the available research to make valid, comfortable conclusions. One conclusion that does have some support in the research literature is that the behavior of women and men in conflict strongly is determined by situational variables. Primary among these variables is the nature of the conflict. Because situations vary in so many ways, even this conclusion is of limited usefulness.

Yet, in my counseling with partners in conflict I encountered more women than men who made accommodation (1,9) responses to conflict. Recall that this approach is more concerned with the relationship than with the solution. In a like manner, I saw more men than women using a forcing (9,1) approach, which is more concerned with solving the problem than with maintaining the relationship. I am not suggesting that female partners do not want to solve their problems, or that males are unconcerned with maintaining their relationships. The difficulty we face in interpreting all research findings on this subject is related to the independence of these two dimensions of conflict-solving behavior. Partners can show high concern for one dimension and low concern for the other. They can show high concern for both; they can show low concern for both. Because you are high on one dimension does not mean you are low on the other. The dimensions are independent of each other.

One other difference that I often observed is that men are more fearful of conflict than are women. Their discomfort easily is observed--they become more talkative, try to appear rational and deliberative in the conversation, and argue that the important things to be discussed are those concerned with resolving the conflict. These behaviors, especially the fear reactions, contradict the traditional stereotypes of women and men in conflict. Again, I don't have a good answer to why this happens. All I can do is to speculate that because of their fear of conflict, men feel they must resolve it in the easiest, quickest way possible, thereby removing the cause of their fear. In the heated give-and-take of the conflict, both women and men tend to forget about compromise (5,5) and collaboration (9,9) as more loving and helping approaches to resolving their conflict. Whatever gender differences I have observed, I attribute to cultural conditioning and situational factors. I am unwilling to accept the argument that women and men inherently are different in their views of conflict. Apart from situational factors, any differences that do exist are a result of social learning. If these views are socially learned, they can be unlearned and replaced by more socially appropriate and productive ways of feeling about conflict. This is one possible purpose and benefit of therapy.

A second question about the possible relationship between gender and conflict has significance for all of us. If gender differences do exist, should we take them into account, letting them guide our conflict-resolution efforts? Should they influence me in my work? My feeling is that we always must be sensitive and alert to any differences which might be encountered, but we should not routinely expect them to appear. Since both men and women theoretically are free to respond to conflict in an infinite number of ways, any effort to stereotype people and force them into an expected response mode would be prejudicial to effective problem solving. It would also be alien to good therapy. Looking for and expecting a partner to respond on the basis of gender could blind us to other more revealing, more insightful aspects of a conflict episode. Partners can differ in their perceptions of a particular conflict situation; they also can differ in their beliefs about the cause of the conflict, as well as what needs to be done to resolve it. These differences are rooted in the immediate situation as well as the outcomes of previous conflict episodes. They are intellectual and emotional and, in my opinion, unrelated to gender. Whatever differences they might express about how to achieve a goal, I usually find that both women and men are seeking the same goal: a balance of individuality, intimacy, and well-being in their relationship.

Suggestions for Managing Marital Conflict

In previous chapters I have stressed the importance of values and attitudes rather than strict rules as guides for behavior. Rules have a deceptive quality about them; they promote a false sense of well-being as the reward for some minimal level of compliance. Further, rules apply to specific situations and circumstances. When we try to behave according to predetermined rules, we have nothing to guide us when we encounter situations not covered by the rules. What I want to share with you in this part are suggestions, not rules. Although the word "suggestion" can be viewed as embodying values and attitudes, it is preferred to the word "rule." These suggestions are more guides to thinking and goal-setting than guides to behavior. Their worth is in both prevention and resolution of marital conflict. Taken together, they provide a structure or approach for managing conflict and disagreements under conditions that enhance the quality of the relationship.

Maintain a Marital Climate that is Open to the Sharing of Feelings about Problems and Areas of Disagreement

Prevention always is a better strategy than correction or resolution. The primary concern of this suggestion is on prevention of disagreements, but it also provides a pragmatic approach for solving problems when they do arise. When we are fearful of sharing feelings that possibly might cause disagreements or hurt feelings we suffer in a self-imposed silence. Bitterness and resentment are the inevitable consequences. They have an additive quality and can be viewed as a veritable volcano of hostile feelings waiting to erupt. All that is needed to precipitate an eruption is the experience of that one feeling; another case of the straw that breaks the camel's back. When an eruption does occur, the resulting conflict is more than a conflict of differences, it also is an outlet for expressing pent-up feelings.

Openness is the key idea in this suggestion. Individually, we want to be free to share our feelings and needs without fear that our partner will become defensive and critical or that they will demean and ridicule our feelings. If such openness is to exist, it must be felt and exercised by both partners. We cannot have it ourselves while denying it to our partner.

Accept the Responsibility for your own Feelings and Behavior

"If it weren't for you I wouldn't feel this way?"
"You made me do it. It's not my fault."
People who use these excuses are seeking to avoid responsibility for their feelings and behavior. Their actions reflect deep feelings of self-pity. They see themselves as victims, and believe their misery is not their fault. Blaming their partner for their problems, they reason that they do not have to change. When they argue, "I'm right, I'm a victim; you're wrong, you're the villain," they cast the conflict in win-lose terms. This forces the accused partner either to accept the accusation of being a villain or to

argue in defense against it. Neither action is conducive to a psychologically rewarding solution. Little is accomplished except a buildup of resentment and hurt feelings. Any solution to the conflict under these terms tends to be superficial and short-lived. Until people accept responsibility for their feelings and behavior little can be done change them.

Don't Dig up the Past

I purposefully have used the word "dig" because, hopefully, previous disagreements and hurt feelings were buried and forgotten when they were resolved. When we resurrect or recycle unpleasant experiences from the past, we really are saying that our forgiveness was not complete. If there was less than complete closure to earlier experiences, including forgiveness and reconciliation, there is the likelihood they will re-erupt. It is alright to remember and learn from past conflicts. It is another thing to relive them. Recalling past mistakes or errors in judgment of our partner has the effect of stacking the deck against them.

Ramona claimed to have forgiven Vernon for his self-confessed, single act of infidelity, but she continued to throw it in his face whenever she wanted something from him or wanted to punish him for refusing something she wanted.

"What do I have to do to stop you from bringing it up? Won't you ever forgive me? I made a mistake; I can't ever undo that. But do I have to do penance for the rest of my life? You say you've forgiven me, so why do you continue to punish me? And us?"

Ramona defended her actions by claiming that even though she had forgiven Vernon she could not forget her hurt and humiliation. She further defended her lack of remorse for her behavior by claiming that she could not help how she felt.

I asked Ramona to consider the possibility that it was more a case of being unwilling rather than unable to forgive. Although she resisted my reasoning, the commitment that kept them together after Vernon confessed his indiscretion was strong enough to keep her in therapy. Happily, they were able to overcome this traumatic incident in their relationship.

Attack the Problem—Not Your Partner

Let me rephrase this suggestion in the form of a question: Is it the problem or your partner you want to remove? This question seemingly begs its answer. If you did not care about your partner, I doubt whether you would try to solve the problem. I also believe that when you resolve a problem with your partner, you want to resume the relationship you had before the conflict. It is possible, however, that the relationship you resume will be better than it was before the conflict. But this possibility is less likely if the self-image and self-worth of your partner is attacked in the process.

When you seek to resolve a momentary difficulty in your relationship, avoid name-calling and accusations of blame. You never can build yourself up or appear to be more right by tearing down your partner or making them appear to be wrong. When you engage in such counterproductive behavior, you lose your integrity--you become less creditable. Use of these tactics indicates that you are more concerned with winning the argument than with maintaining the relationship.

Listen with Understanding

In chapter six, I discussed some of the differences between hearing and listening and some of the difficulties associated with each. Hearing was described as a mere physical response to an external auditory stimulus. In simple hearing there is no involvement of the self; there is no commitment to understand, accept, and respond to what is heard. A willingness to really listen requires involvement and commitment. There is involvement when we can say to our partner, "Tell me how you feel about this matter. Let's see if I can understand your feelings." There is commitment when we can say, "You've helped me to see things differently. I'm guilty, I guess, of looking at things only from my own viewpoint. Thanks for your help." A real benefit of listening with understanding is that it invites more sharing from our partner.

When we listen with understanding, we imply that we are willing to re-examine our thinking about the present conflict in light of what is shared by our partner. We imply, too, that we are open to the possibility of changing our thoughts and feelings about the matter. When we listen with understanding we show respect. Name calling and accusations in the heat of a shouting match destroy respect.

Identify and Focus on the Real Issues Behind Your Conflict

Athletic coaches often admonish players to keep their eyes on the ball. In resolving marital conflicts, this admonition can be rephrased to, "Keep your eyes on what is important; don't bring up extraneous, irrelevant issues." It also suggests that we not try to resolve all divisive issues with a single solution. What I am suggesting is that we try to resolve our conflicts with a rifle shot rather than a shotgun blast. This metaphor implies that with the rifle we can aim at the core problem; the shotgun blast, even with its many pellets, may or may not hit the problem. It may, in fact, hit everything but the problem. Bringing other issues into the target area seriously can complicate our efforts to resolve the core problem.

Mitch and Edwina had been in therapy with me for several sessions without any significant change in their pattern of relating. They had agreed on little beyond the fact that their marriage was no longer a satisfying experience. When I pressed for more specific complaints, we were able to identify and resolve several minor irritants. But when they seemed ready to focus upon the more troublesome aspects of their relationship, another seemingly irrelevant problem would be introduced. I suspected that the minor problems they continued to introduce were a subterfuge from getting to an as-yet unidentified core problem. The analogy of eating an artichoke, leaf by leaf, came to mind. Each minor problem that was resolved should have brought us closer to the heart of the problem. But, unlike eating an artichoke, each small problem was replaced by a previously unmentioned problem.

In a private session with Edwina, I asked her to imagine her house being on fire and that she could save only one item. "What would it be?" I asked. After a short pause she said that she would save the family photo album. As she shared with me her reasons for her choice I began to understand some of her feelings about Mitch that had escaped me throughout the conjoint sessions. Toward the end of the session I gambled and asked, "If you could solve just one of the problems you have with Mitch, which one would it be?" Her answer was not really an answer but it was revealing.

"I'm beginning to realize that I haven't been completely honest with you about my feelings about Mitch. And I haven't been honest with him, either. But I think he knows and plays along with me to protect my secret. I want to talk over this matter with him before I share it with you. Let both of us come next week and I think we'll be ready to get to what you call the core problem."

Edwina was right. Mitch did know of her problem but did not let her know he knew. He was protecting her secret. With these insights progress came quickly.

Avoid Either-Or, Win-Lose Attitudes and Behavior

The essence of this suggestion has been discussed in two previous chapters. Here, I want to add just a couple of thoughts. First, don't try to resolve disputes or conflicts in such a way that it causes your partner to feel that they lost or that they were defeated. It fosters a revenge psychology which can cause the losing partner to look for, or possibly create, another problem (opportunity) where they can win. The second point is a corollary of the first: it is impossible in a marriage for one partner to win and the other to lose. When one partner wins at the expense of the other, the marriage is the loser.

Maintain a Positive, Expectant Attitude

The experience of conflict in your marriage does not mean that it has failed. I previously have argued that conflicts (misunderstandings, disagreements, and quarrels) are an inevitable consequence of two people in a close, intimate relationship. While conflict does present a problem to be solved, to the positive thinker, it is an opportunity for improved understanding, new commitments, and increased intimacy. To the negative thinker, a problem is a problem. The Chinese expression for crises is "Wei-ji" (pronounced "way-ge"). Wei-ji combines the Mandarin characters for danger and opportunity to represent two aspects of a single situation. That is the way it is with marital conflict. Positive thinkers see an opportunity; negative thinkers see only danger.

Negative thinkers let problems defeat them. Expecting the worst to come from conflict, they unknowingly behave in ways that make happen the consequence they were trying to avoid. Negative thinkers concentrate on preventing marital conflict. They engage in a lot of accommodation (1,9) behavior to avoid conflict for the sake of the relationship. Positive thinkers are concerned with helping the marriage to become all that it can be. One way they do this is to accept and resolve in a collaborative (9,9) style all conflicts that emerge in their marriage. Expecting success, they search for solutions which satisfy the needs of both partners. Positive thinkers are realistic about the inevitability of conflict and do not view its presence as evidence of a marital breakdown.

Russ Holloman, Ph. D.

Reaffirm Your Partner, Your Love, and Your Marriage

One possible aftermath of a conflict episode is our partner's lingering doubt about their self-worth which, in turn, often is based on other questions they might have about the quality and durability of our love and the marriage we share. Whether or not our partner experiences these doubts, it is a concomitant responsibility of the helping relationship to reaffirm our partner as a person--a person we love in the relationship of marriage. Focus on the wonder of your partner; look for and express those things you admire about them. Express your appreciation of your partner. Learn to say often (and sincerely), "I really appreciate what you did." Or, better yet add, "I love you."

It is important that we always help our partner to feel accepted, approved, and secure: feelings that are important in the aftermath of a conflict episode. Being sensitive and responsive to the emotional, social, and spiritual needs of our partner is the essence of reaffirming behavior. Whatever form our behavior takes, its message is always, "I love you."

Chapter Ten

Maintaining the Helping Relationship

This final chapter will be brief. Its purpose, unlike the others, is to reflect and exhort more than to share. I will not repeat what already has been written, but I will reflect on it in terms of what I learned from some ongoing interviews I conducted with partners in both successful and unsuccessful marriages. I began these interviews as part of my research for another book I planned to write. As I listened and tried to evaluate the opinions and feelings they were sharing with me, I began to realize that the difference between what the partners in successful marriages and the partners in failed marriages were telling me was, in essence, the presence or absence of a caring, committed, and helping relationship. It was shown in many different ways, but in the successful marriages there was an active concern by the partners for the happiness, growth, and the psychological and spiritual well-being of the other. It was serendipity: I realized that what I was learning from the successful marriages was the payoff of a helping relationship. Few of the partners that I interviewed had ever read or heard the term "helping relationship," at least not in the context of marriage. But in explaining their reasons for the success of their marriages they described a relationship not unlike what I have chosen to call a helping relationship. I delighted in this finding.

In the preceding chapters, I discussed with you the characteristics and benefits of a helping relationship and offered some suggestions as to how it could be developed and practiced. In this chapter my concern is with maintaining the helping relationship. I have some reservations about the word "maintaining" in the above title but I have not been able to find a more suitable substitute. Maintaining connotes the idea of keeping a helping relationship as it is. Words like permanence, stability, status quo, and fixed come to mind. What I intend is more synonymous with words like dynamic, changing, and growing. I want to avoid the idea that a helping relationship, once achieved, takes a particular form and stays that way. Just as the partners in a relationship are always changing so must the relationship between them change if it is to remain helping.

A Look Backward

In chapter two I invited you to join me in a fantasy about two marriages. In our fantasy we made the partners and the circumstances of their lives as much alike as we could imagine them to be. We observed, however, that the two marriages had very different outcomes. One marriage evolved into a deeply satisfying, growthful relationship; it reflected many characteristics which offered the promise of continued growth and enrichment. The second marriage, with partners and circumstances similar to those in the first, began to show early signs of failing--a portent of lowered expectations and a waning commitment. I suggested that in both marriages the partners actually had decided what kind of marriage they wanted to have. In the successful marriage, the decision was intentional; in the less successful marriage the decision, perhaps, was made by default. I did not intend that the partners in the second marriage actually chose failure. No, what I meant was they did not choose success. Perhaps they did not realize they could choose the kind of marriage they wanted, or maybe, they were unwilling to pay the price of success in terms of dedication and commitment.

Throughout this book I have contended that a helping relationship is both the cause and a consequence of a growing, rewarding, and lasting marriage. It can help troubled marriages; it can make good marriages better. There is an important difference, however, in the motivation of partners to try it. In troubled marriages the partners want to solve their problems so they can be normal again--like other marriages. They want to remove a deficiency in their marriage; they are hurting and they do not want to hurt. In healthy, successful marriages the partners are not content to have just a normal marriage. "Why not the best?" they reason. Believing that there are no limits on the quality of their marriage except the limits they put on it, they eagerly and naturally show an active concern that promotes the happiness, growth, and well-being of the other. Choosing the high road for their marriage, they become helpers to each other. Through their commitment to a helping relationship, they communicate their desire to work together to nurture and strengthen their marriage to make it a continuing source of enrichment and needs satisfaction. This is one of their ways of saying, "I love you."

When I present my ideas on marriage and the helping relationship in speeches and workshops I always encounter some skeptical questions. "It's easy, Dr. Holloman, for you to feel as you do. You've been happily married for forty-plus years. Who can argue against you? Also, you've been trained in these things; you've got a lot going for you. What if you were just starting out like we (pointing to partner) are? Would you still feel the same way?"

To this kind of question I typically responded, "You're suggesting that a successful marriage is something for people who have everything else. If you feel that way, then I know that I'm the person you should be talking to." I tell them about the circumstances in which Lenora and I grew up--circumstances that did not promise a rosy future. "It is not the fact that Lenora and I have been happily married all these years that enables me to believe as I do. It's the other way around. It was living our lives according to these ideas that helped our marriage to survive and grow. It's not the absence of problems that makes a good marriage. Lenora and I have problems, just like you have problems. The difference comes from the way we respond to our problems. I can't emphasize this too much: we can choose how we respond to problems."

I try to assure questioners that the ideas and attitudes I advocate have nothing to do with age, education, wealth, or social standing. It is something anyone can have. The thought that these ideas can be held only by an elitist group has no merit with me. It's something that is available to everyone if only they will believe it--if only they will make positive choices about the kind of marriage they want. I have witnessed many "ideal" marriages flounder on the rocks of disillusionment and divorce. I also can point to many "risky" marriages that have survived all the obstacles and pitfalls that society and an uncertain future threw in their path. So, how can we explain the failure of ideal marriages and the success of risky marriages?

My answer to this question is always, "Let's look at the partners in each marriage. Did they let the circumstances of their lives determine what kind of marriage they would have, or did they believe they could have the marriage they wanted in spite of their circumstances?"

When Lenora and I married we had little going for us in terms of social, educational, and economic advantages, and preparation for marriage. What we did have was a lot of dreams and expectations. We realized that it was up to us. We could either blame the circumstances of our lives for whatever happened to us or we could take control of our lives and choose the kind of marriage we wanted. We found that believing as we did was really all that we needed. It was through our attitudes, values, and dreams that we sowed the seeds of happiness and permanence in our marriage. We made choices. You can, too.

Good News and Bad News About Marriage

Our local newspaper has a daily *Lifestyles* section which features news and stories about and of interest to the family. These stories run the gamut from engagements and weddings on Sunday to births on Thursday. Also appearing on Thursday are stories about couples who have recently celebrated their fiftieth (golden) wedding anniversary. Surprisingly, the number of golden anniversaries being celebrated is high--much higher than might be expected, given the age of the partners and the hazards faced by marriage today. Our paper also publishes a weekly *Legal Notices* section which includes, along with notices of other legal actions, a listing of people who have been granted divorces by the court system. This list, too, is long--too long.

Behind each of these various announcements is another, untold story. As a popular radio commentator might describe it, there always is a "... rest of the story." Not all of the engaged couples make it to the altar. Too many of those who do, do not survive the challenges and perils that lead to marital dissatisfaction, as well as separation and divorce. It is part of my mentality, I suppose, to want to know the rest of the story. After reading these good-news, bad-news stories, I always ask, "Why? Why do some marriages flourish while others fail?"

This question has been the topic of more sophomore sociology research papers, the subject of more after-dinner speeches, the brunt of more cocktail-party jokes, and the focus of more gossip over the backyard fence than might be obvious. What must be obvious, however, is that since the question continues to be asked, we do not yet have a satisfactory answer. I started out asking this question in a contemplative sense; recently I started asking it of the people involved in the newspaper announcements.

Making Marriage User Friendly

The more I thought about the good news of married partners celebrating their fiftieth wedding anniversary and the bad news of broken, dissolved marriages the more I wanted to know their opinions to my question of why some marriages succeed and others fail. I didn't intend a scientific, methodical kind of interview with questionnaires and statistical analysis of the responses. Rather, I envisioned being able to sit down with these people, in their living room or mine, and, with a cup of coffee, informally to talk about their marriage. From the goldies (married for at least fifty years) I wanted to learn their secrets for staying happily married; from the divorcees I wanted to learn what went wrong.

Meeting and talking with these people has been an enlightening, rewarding experience. Some of their stories made me happy, others made me sad. Some were sources of inspiration and encouragement; others caused feelings of consternation and disgust. There were moments when I felt I was treading on holy ground; there were other times when I wished I were somewhere else.

What I learned through these interviews helped me to better understand my own marriage and the possible effects of my behavior upon Lenora. It also helped me in my therapy practice. Not unexpectedly, I learned as much from the divorcees as I did from the goldies. Although I was more familiar with and understanding of the successes of the goldies and had heard much of what they said before I still learned a lot from them. Particularly significant were their understandings and feelings about love and commitment. Strangely, love was not mentioned as often as I had expected. They seemed to feel that without love there was little reason for a marriage to endure; it was a given for them. When they did mention love it was not in the usual sense of eros, or romantic love--it was more expressions of the warm affection that exists between partners who are very near and dear to each other. They had ways of expressing themselves that left me wishing that I had said that. Fortunately, in writing, as opposed to speaking, you can always go back and stick it in somewhere.

From the divorcees I heard sordid details of what can happen when partners do not play by the rules, when they have egocentric and self-serving expectations of marriage, and when marriage is viewed as a win-lose relationship. I learned how far one partner will go in trying to hold a marriage together while the other partner is seemingly bent upon destroying it. I learned about abuse, neglect, selfishness, lack of consideration, and other patterns of deviant behavior which still repulse me. I learned the full range of what can go wrong in a marriage.

The majority of the divorcees who agreed to talk with me were women. Because some of them lived alone, or because they could not come to my office, I had to interview them by phone. In spite of a lack of face-to-face contact they came across as having real, lasting feelings about what had happened to their marriage. Some admitted to being the culprit; others claimed to be innocent victims. Still, their responses were genuine and candid--they held nothing back. They seemed to appreciate what I was doing and, sensing that others might benefit from their failures, talked freely and intimately about their divorces. It was painful for them, however, and I repeatedly expressed my understanding of their circumstances and my appreciation for their willingness to share with me.

With the goldies it was like taking a trip through memory lane. With both humor and thanksgiving, they talked about their good times; with equal ease and candor they talked about their bad times. While they insisted they had tried to forget about the bad times, they admitted that it was the bad times that strengthened their relationship and cemented their love for each other. I observed many of them acting out what they were giving as responses to my questions. They respected each other; they apologized for unintended interruptions, misunderstandings, and inappropriate responses. They both attended and were attentive to each other. They listened with patience and understanding and were helpful and supportive in their interpersonal communication. They could furnish or correct details of a story being told by the other partner without causing them to feel they were being admonished. They often exchanged knowing smiles when they recalled intimate moments of their lives. They were gracious people and, although the social and economic circumstances of their lives differed greatly from one couple to another, all were hospitable, considerate, and loving in welcoming me into their homes.

In the remainder of this chapter I will share three simple but exciting and fruitful ideas that I learned from these interviews. These ideas are concerned with visualization, commitment, and giving something more. I could present more but these three seem to summarize all that is contained on numerous pages of notes and a like number of audio tapes. These ideas are more wisdom in nature than they are information. They integrate and transcend the many rules I might have written about had I not had the benefit of these interviews. Although the goldies and the divorcees responded from different perspectives, both contributed to the formation of these ideas. With at least fifty years of marital longevity behind them the goldies spoke with the authority that comes to successful people in all arenas of human endeavor. Still, it was from the divorcees that I received the most convincing support for these ideas. The divorcees spoke with the insight that is learned from failure. It does seem that we often enjoy success in some undertaking without being able to identify the real reasons for it. When we experience failure, however, we usually can point to the reasons. Thus, we are able to learn more from failure than from success.

Some of the interviewees were more articulate than others-they made my work easy. A few of them, for various reasons, not always were able to put into words the feelings they were experiencing and wanted to share. With them I had to ask many "Is this what you mean?" questions. What I will share with you may be my words but the thoughts and feeling are theirs.

Visualize the Marriage You Want

What is the key to a successful marriage? What must go right for a marriage to endure and grow? What are the things that can go wrong, even in well-intentioned marriages. These questions are being asked with increasing frequency as behavioral scientists seek answers to today's disturbing statistics about marital conflict and divorce. They are the same questions I asked in my interviews. I had expected a litany of the traditional, well-worn do's and don'ts about which I so often had read and had suggested frequently to my clients.

Much to my surprise and delight I found the majority of the respondents suspicious of rules. Rules, they felt, were too mechanical, too impersonal, too inflexible, and too general--something like "Take two aspirin and get a good night's sleep." Following simplistic rules can give a false sense of security. When people follow a set of prescribed rules they naturally expect everything to turn out alright. When it doesn't they experience frustration and disappointment, which often causes them to give up and stop trying. When they did admit observing certain recurring practices, they resisted my referring to them as rules. Rudy and Lena questioned the role of rules in marriage.

"I love Lena," stated Rudy. "Respect her, too. Is that a rule? A rule says 'You have to do it.' I respect her because that's the way she is, that's the way we are. When you love someone the way I love Lena, you don't need rules to tell you what to do."

Lena joined her husband in questioning the use of rules in a marriage in sharing the following incident. "Our granddaughter and her husband have all kinds of rules. One cooks dinner on Thursday, the other cleans the bath on Saturday. You can't imagine the hassles they have over who is supposed to do what. A few Saturdays ago their cat was chased up a tree. Lauren, that's our granddaughter's husband, refused to get up and rescue the cat because it was his morning to sleep late. Well, they live only a mile or so from us so Rudy and I went over and coaxed the cat down. With us, we do what has to be done. I couldn't keep up with a bunch of blamed rules."

Finally, another couple provided a helpful insight to what most of the other couples also were thinking. They talked of their dream marriage . "When you want something so much you dream about it, you naturally do all the things that make it come true. When you've done all that you can do, you do a little more. Don't worry about going fifty-fifty. That's not marriage--it's a contract."

This latter couple didn't use the word but they were talking about the technique of visualization. It is a technique that is being used successfully in many walks of life today. Jack Nicholas, I have heard, visualizes every shot he makes on the golf course, including the trajectory of the ball. Professor Higgins, of *My Fair Lady* fame, had a vision of the refined woman he had in mind for Liza Doolittle. What Professor Higgins did and Jack Nicholas continues to do, through the power of their thoughts, is to mentally create a picture of their goal or behavior. As simple and unscientific as it sounds, the success of this technique in other areas of life suggests that our vision of our marriage can point the way to its success or failure. Everyone has the capability to use this technique. It is the power of our own thoughts, it's the ability to envision or create in our mind an image of the kind of marriage we want, including the kind of marriage partner we want to be.

The generally accepted explanation for the success of this technique is that we tend to act out our dreams and vision. When we accept the idea that we actually can choose the kind of marriage we want, we then make decisions that are consistent with our choice. When our dream marriage is shared, we actually see ourselves in the desired relationship with our partner. As we share our dream we mentally act out the relationship. Rather than seeking or striving to have a certain kind of marriage we actually become that marriage. If we can imagine it, we can achieve it; if we can envision it, we can become it.

Commitment: Making the Vision a Reality

No matter how much we might want or wish for a more satisfying, rewarding marriage, wishful thinking alone will not make it happen. However, wishful thinking--what we often refer to as daydreaming--can be helpful if it involves the process of visualization and if it is followed with purposeful action. Otherwise, it is a waste of time, a retreat from the task of making our vision a reality.

Armed with a vision of the kind of marriage we want, we must commit ourselves to living--becoming--the vision. Commitment is an action step demanding faith and trust on the one hand and dedication and resolve on the other. It is through our commitment that we declare how much we value our vision of our marriage. For this reason our commitment is highly personal. It is an act of the will, freely made and freely given without stopping to count the possible costs. It depends more upon our strength of character than upon the stability of our emotions. Any holdout or reservation to total commitment is necessarily a lack of commitment.

Unconditional commitment easily can be a full-time, life-time endeavor. It provides the caring for a marriage to transcend the fickle impulses of early romantic love and then acts as an adhesive to weather marriage's inevitable storms later. It does not, however, guarantee an absence of problems. When problems do occur, it means that partners are willing to join together to resolve them. Commitment means staying the course, whatever happens. Only when both partners make this kind of commitment is there a real sense of security in their marriage.

An Example of Commitment

In chapter one I briefly discussed the case of Joanna and Harvey, which was still unfolding at the time of my writing. The rest of the story now can be told. It is a story of Joanna's commitment to her marriage and family; it is a story of her determination to look for a solution rather than to dwell on the problem.

As Harvey devoted more time to the business, Joanna became more persistent in her efforts to get him to spend more time with her and the children. Frustrated in these efforts, she suggested a reorganization of the business which would make fewer demands upon Harvey's time. Her suggestion was rejected by Harvey, claiming that it could be misunderstood in the business world, and if it was misunderstood it could adversely affect the company. Still, wanting to believe Harvey's promise that he would let go as soon as he could get things firmed up in the company, Joanna adopted a wait-and-see attitude. After what she called a reasonable time without any indication that Harvey was going to respond to her request, she became confused and frustrated. In desperation, she withdrew from him, both physically and emotionally. For this she started feeling guilty.

At this time she started seeing me again. After bringing me up to date on everything that had happened since our last session, she began sharing her determination to change the circumstances of her marriage. "I've tried running away from things but I now realize that it won't work. When I come home the problem is still there. My threat to divorce Harvey was not the answer, either. I'm old-fashioned, I guess, but my marriage and my family are important to me. I understand Harvey's devotion to the company; he's a good CEO and his work has brought him a lot of recognition and praise--even from our competitors. His hard work also has helped the company to grow, and I'm thankful for that, but something has to change. I'm married to Harvey and he's married to the company. How's that for a marriage?"

We continued monthly sessions during which she dwelt upon the changed circumstances of her marriage and her seeming inability to help Harvey to understand what was so plain to her. Throughout these sessions she resisted my suggestion to bring Harvey into our discussions. Sensing her anguish and frustration, and the futility of continuing as we were, I said to her, "I remember Harvey saying in one of our earlier, joint sessions that he was serving in the CEO position at your pleasure. Does that mean what I think it means?"

"What it does mean is that I nominated him to be CEO; he also is our chairman. With the shares daddy left me and my mother's proxy, I easily can outvote the rest of the board. It sounds tacky to say it but, yes, I gave him the job."

"Why don't you take it back and give it to someone else?" I blurted out, almost disbelieving that I had said those words.

"You mean fire him, don't you? I have secretly considered that possibility but rejected it because I want Harvey to come back on his own. I don't guess he's going to do that though. What do you think? I could really get his attention that way, but I wouldn't do it if I thought he would hang it over my head."

I asked her to think about it and suggested that we discuss it some more during our next session. Two days prior to our meeting, Joanna called to cancel it. She was excited about what she referred to as an unexpected turn of events. "I bit the bullet and confronted Harvey with my feelings. I told him that I would not sit idly by and let the business ruin our marriage. Well, after the initial shock--after he saw that I meant what I was saying--he showed more understanding than I ever would have imagined. Agreeable, too. He then raised a possibility that I had not considered. He told me that he had been approached a few months back by some people who wanted to buy the business. Their offer was very generous. We discussed the idea with Mother and she gave her blessing to it. She and I are talking to our lawyers now about some of the financial arrangements and the tax consequences. Isn't this exciting? I'll keep you posted."

The business was sold and now, months later, it seems that everyone is living happily ever after. Harvey has begun studying for a master's degree in history so he can teach in a local high school. The last time we talked I congratulated them. "It was Joanna," Harvey answered. "I lost sight of what was important. I was tiring of the pace but didn't know how to end it. Fortunately, Joanna gave me a wake-up call. The credit is hers."

Commitment Means Giving Something More

When we join or affiliate with a group or organization we assume, as a condition of membership, an obligation to conform and support its values and goals. Groups impose these requirements as a means of securing predictable, dependable behavior from its members. People who join but fail to conform to a group's expectations not only frustrate the work and purposes of the group but also discredit themselves in the eyes of the other group members. New members can comply at a minimal level, doing just enough to maintain their membership, or they can perform above the minimum expectations and become valued members of the group.

I easily can recall the oath that I took when I entered the Air Force. I swore "...to obey the lawful orders of my superiors...to defend the Constitution...etc. Every new member of the Air Force must take that oath. People who violate their oath become a liability because they cannot be depended upon, and they are not permitted to remain in the Air Force. Other people play by the rules but do no more than is necessary to retain their membership. Their maximum effort is equal to the minimum expectations of the Air Force; they languish in the lower ranks. It is obvious that the Air Force could not perform its mission if all its members performed at this low level. Fortunately, there are people who always give something more in terms of commitment, dedication, and loyalty. This something more is rewarded by challenging assignments and rapid promotions.

These qualities were missing in those few people who, although they had served in military organizations for long periods of time, enjoying all the opportunities and benefits of membership, refused to go to Saudi Arabia during the 1991 Desert Storm Operation. Their refusal to honor their oath and other concomitant obligations in this instance raises questions about whether they would honor their obligations in other social situations, e.g., work, church, and marriage. Would they, for example, renounce their marital commitments with the excuse, "Marriage is more trouble than it's worth?"

Getting married is in many ways comparable to the process of joining a group or an organization. Through the exchange of vows commitments are made, expectations are established. Although the words in the vows are subject to interpretation, mere compliance with the vows will not make a great marriage. Compliance at this level can prevent a marriage from coming apart but it cannot, alone, make a marriage great. We can comply in a grudging, what's-in-it-for-me manner, as though it were something we had to do, or we can give something more--we can go beyond our vows with expressions of unconditional love and commitment. Giving something more expresses our belief that what goes around comes around. The more love we share, the more love we receive; the more love we receive, the more love we have to share. These things we do, not because we have to, but because we want to. It's a choice we make.

Marriage is a Human Enterprise

The institution and practice of marriage has existed in some form in all known societies, from the ancient world to the present. Although today we are witnessing a lot of experimentation in the forms and purposes of marriage, traditional marriage remains the most ideal and pervasive form. Open marriage, trial marriage, closed marriage, two-step marriage, and serial marriage are some trendy forms that have surfaced in recent years. Throughout this period of marital experimentation, however, traditional marriage has remained the standard from which all the deviations were made. These alternative forms of marriage emerged not because traditional marriage was tried and found lacking, but, rather, because it was not really tried. They failed for the same reason that communism failed in eastern

Europe and Russia: they are antithetical to human nature. Fads come and go in marriage as they do in styles of clothing and sounds in music, but there is only one genuine form of marriage. People who have predicted or called for the end of traditional marriage are very careful not to burn their bridges behind themselves. They know that historically the process of dialectical change revolves around and returns to the thesis (status quo) of traditional marriage. Within the institution of marriage, as in other arenas of human activity, the more something changes, the more it tends to remain the same. Traditional marriage has not only survived this experimentation, it has prevailed.

Society values and seeks to preserve traditional marriage simply because no other form of heterosexual union provides the advantages to society that it does. For this reason, society protects marriage through enactment of laws designed to bestow sanctity and legitimacy upon it. Many religions also sanctify marriage by recognizing it as a sacrament.

Unfortunately, in all these concerns about marriage there is a nearly universal tendency to take an instrumental view toward it; marriage is spoken of as though it had a separate existence apart from the partners who created it. Partners in a marriage reinforce this practice, unknowingly perhaps, when they use expressions such as "My marriage...." In my work with couples in therapy I often am confronted with complaints like "My marriage is failing" or "My marriage no longer satisfies my needs." All these expressions imply that marriage is something that is owned or possessed. It is something that was acquired as a result of a wedding.

Now, you might be questioning my reasoning at this point. You might be thinking "Come on, it's just a convention we use. We don't mean that we really own our marriage. You're creating a semantic problem where there is none."

Maybe you're right, but hear me out. Your argument is valid up to the point where we fall into the trap of detaching marriage from its creators. Unfortunately, this is just what people often do. "My marriage has gone bad, can you fix it?" is a question frequently asked of me in therapy. People who ask this question don't see their problem as one of their own creation. They want their marriage fixed without having to change themselves.

A marriage is created by two people in a relationship--at their best, hopefully--but it is still a human creation. As such, it is no better or worse and no more or less, than the two people who comprise it. No matter how much we may revere or value our marriage, it has no supernatural powers. It does not work by itself, with its own brain and motor. Its strength is the combined strength of the partners who are united in and committed to it; its survival depends upon this strength and this commitment. Through our commitment our marriage is nurtured and sustained. We may praise or attack it, whatever judgment we make about it is a judgment about ourselves. We cannot expect marriage to give us what we previously have not given to it.

Partners in a marriage have rights, but they also have responsibilities. People who think only in terms of their rights fail to comprehend the grander purpose and possibilities of marriage. Those who do comprehend the opportunities and benefits of marriage are attracted to it; they desire the rights; they freely accept the responsibilities. They approach marriage without any mental reservations, realizing that their marriage will be what they make it. They choose to make it growthful, enriching, and enduring. These are the rewards of a helping relationship.

A Final Word

In my office where I meet with clients, I have an unusual paperweight. It is a horseshoe mounted on a mahogany-colored plaque. It was given to me by the owner of a stable where I was taking riding lessons. I attached a drawer-pull handle inside the "U" of the horseshoe and now use the plaque as a paperweight.

Over the years I have had numerous clients ask about the horseshoe. They will ask, for example, "You don't really believe in horseshoes do you?"

I assume that anyone who would ask that question must be thinking, "If that horseshoe is all he has going for him, maybe we should see someone else."

In an effort to counter their possible suspicions and to project a scientific, non-superstitious image, I typically respond, "Of course not."

For most of the people who ask about the horseshoe my response is adequate and they are ready to proceed with the therapy session. For a few, however, it is not enough. They will follow up by asking, "Well, if you don't believe in it, why do you have it on your desk?"

"Because it works whether you believe it or not," I always reply.

And I feel the same way about a helping relationship in marriage: it works whether you believe in it or not. It can transform a lukewarm, devitalized marriage into one that is growthful and richly rewarding. If your marriage is already filled with mountain-top experiences, a helping relationship can propel it even higher--into orbit.

Nourish a vision of the marriage you want to have. Commit yourself to that vision. Give all you can and then give some more.

The message of the horseshoe is that you will see it when you believe it.

References

Berne, E. (1961). <u>Transactional Analysis in Psychotherapy</u>. New York: Grove Press.

Buber, M. (1970). <u>I and Thou</u>. (W. Kaufman, Trans.). New York: Schribner. (Original work published 1937.)

Buechner, F. (1980). <u>Whistling in the Dark</u>. New York: Harper and Row.

Egan, G. (1975). <u>The Skilled Helper: A Model for Systematic Helping and Interpersonal Relating</u>. Monterey, CA.: Brooks/Cole Publishing Co.

Funk, W. and Lewis, N. (1971). <u>Thirty Days to a More Powerful Vocabulary</u>. New York: Pocket Books.

Harris, T. A. (1969). <u>I'm OK - You're OK</u>. New York: Avon

Horney, K. (1950). <u>Neurosis and Human Growth</u>. New York: W. W. Norton & Co.

Jourard, S. M. (1963). <u>Personal Adjustment: An Approach Through the Study of Healthy Personality</u>. New York: Macmillan.

Lewis, C. S. (1960). <u>The Four Loves</u>. New York: Harcourt Brace Jovanovich.

Luft, J. (1969). <u>Of Human Interaction</u>. Palo Alto, CA: National Press Books.

Maslow, A. H. (1954). <u>Motivation and Personality</u>. New York: Harper.

Peck, M. S. (1978). <u>The Road Less Traveled</u>. New York: Simon and Schuster.

Rifkin, J. (1981). <u>Entropy</u>. New York: Bantam Books.

Rogers, C. R. (1961). <u>On Becoming a Person</u>. Boston: Houghton Mifflin Company.

Rubin, T. T. (1983). <u>One to One: Understanding Personal Relationships</u>. New York: Viking Press.

Thibaut, J. W. and Kelley, H. H. (1959). <u>The Social Psychology of Groups</u>. New York: Wiley.